998
PAID96

D1286141

SAS® System: A Programmer's Guide

Other McGraw-Hill Books of Interest

0-07-006551-9	Bosler	*CLIST Programming*
0-07-044129-4	Murphy	*Assembler for COBOL Programmers: MVS, VM*
0-07-006533-0	Bookman	*COBOL II for Programmers*
0-07-046271-2	McGrew, McDaniel	*In-House Publishing in a Mainframe Environment*
0-07-051265-5	Ranade et al.	*DB2: Concepts, Programming, and Design*
0-07-054594-4	Sanchez, Canton	*IBM Microcomputers: A Programmer's Handbook*
0-07-002467-7	Aronson, Aronson	*SAS® System: A Programmer's Guide*
0-07-002673-4	Azevedo	*ISPF: The Strategic Dialog Manager*
0-07-007248-5	Brathwaite	*Analysis, Design, and Implementation of Data Dictionaries*
0-07-009816-6	Carathanassis	*Expert MVS/XA JCL: A Guide to Advanced Techniques*
0-07-015231-4	D'Alleyrand	*Image Storage and Retrieval Systems*
0-07-016188-7	Dayton	*Integrating Digital Services*
0-07-017606-X	Donofrio	*CICS: Debugging, Dump Reading, and Problem Determination*
0-07-018966-8	Eddolls	*VM Performance Management*
0-07-033571-0	Kavanagh	*VS COBOL II for COBOL Programmers*
0-07-040666-9	Martyn, Hartley	*DB2/SQL: A Professional Programmer's Guide*
0-07-050054-1	Piggott	*CICS: A Practical Guide to System Fine Tuning*
0-07-050686-8	Prasad	*IBM Mainframes: Architecture and Design*
0-07-051144-6	Ranade, Sackett	*Introduction to SNA Networking: Using VTAM/NCP*
0-07-051143-8	Ranade, Sackett	*Advanced SNA: A Professional's Guide to VTAM/NCP*

Database Experts Series

0-07-020631-7	Hoechst et al.	*Guide to Oracle®*
0-07-033637-7	Kageyama	*CICS Handbook*
0-07-016604-8	DeVita	*The Database Experts' Guide to FOCUS*
0-07-055170-7	IMI Systems, Inc.	*DB2/SQL/DS: A User's Reference*
0-07-023267-9	Larson	*The Database Experts' Guide to DATABASE 2*
0-07-039002-9	Lusardi	*Database Experts' Guide to SQL*
0-07-048550-X	Parsons	*The Database Experts' Guide to IDEAL*

Communications Series

0-07-055327-0	Schlar	*Inside X.25: A Manager's Guide*
0-07-005075-9	Berson	*APPC: Introduction to LU6.2*
0-07-034242-3	Kessler	*ISDN: Concepts, Facilities, and Services*
0-07-071136-4	Wipfler	*Distributed Processing in CICS*
0-07-002394-8	Arnell, Davis	*Handbook of Effective Disaster/Recovery Planning*
0-07-009783-6	Cap Gemini America	*DB2 Applications Development Handbook*
0-07-009792-5	Cap Gemini America	*Computer Systems Conversion*

SAS® System: A Programmer's Guide

Monte Aronson
Automated Concepts, Inc.

Alvera L. Aronson
Reader's Digest Association, Inc.

McGraw-Hill, Inc.

New York   St. Louis   San Francisco   Auckland   Bogotá
Caracas   Hamburg   Lisbon   London   Madrid   Mexico
Milan   Montreal   New Delhi   Paris
San Juan   São Paulo   Singapore
Sydney   Tokyo   Toronto

Library of Congress Cataloging-in-Publication Data

Aronson, Monte.
  SAS systems : a programmer's guide.

  1. SAS (Computer program)   I. Aronson, Alvera L.
II. Title.
QA276.4.A76   1990   005.2'22   90-6313
ISBN   0-07-002467-7

SAS, SAS/Graph, and SAS/STAT are registered trademarks of SAS
Institute Inc.; dBASE II and dBASE III are registered trademarks of
Ashton-Tate, Inc.; Lotus 1-2-3 is a registered trademark of Lotus
Development Corporation; IBM, TSO, and ISPF are registered
trademarks of International Business Machines Corporation. Trademarks
not known as such that may have been used inadvertently in this book
are the property of their respective owners.

SAS software, Version 6.03, copyright © 1988 by SAS Institute Inc.,
Cary, NC, was used by permission to produce the screens in this book.

    3 4 5 6 7 8 9 0   DOC/DOC   9 6 5 4 3 2

ISBN 0-07-002467-7

The sponsoring editor for this book was Theron Shreve, and the
production supervisor was Suzanne W. Babeuf. It was set in Century
Schoolbook by Archetype, Inc.

Printed and bound by R.R. Donnelley & Sons Company.

Contents

Preface   xi
Acknowledgments   xiv

Chapter 1. Overview of the SAS System   1

   1.1   What is it?   1
   1.2   Who uses it?   3
   1.3   When to use it   3
   1.4   How to use it   4

Chapter 2. Introduction to the SAS Language   5

   2.1   The SAS System Concept   5
      2.1.1   SAS Programs are Made up of Steps   5
      2.1.2   SAS Steps are Made up of Statements   7
      2.1.3   Where's the Read Statement?   10
      2.1.4   Passing Information: the SAS Dataset   11
      2.1.5   Constructing SAS Datasets   12
   2.2   The SAS System Environment   16
      2.2.1   What Keeps It Together: The SAS Session   16
      2.2.2   How the Session Works   17
   2.3   The SAS Language   18
      2.3.1   Structure of the Language   18
      2.3.2   Writing SAS Code   19
      2.3.3   Three-step Plan of a SAS Program   19

Chapter 3. Converting Raw Data into SAS Datasets   21

   3.1   Overview of the Data Step   21
      3.1.1   Identifying Your Output: the DATA Statement   22
      3.1.2   General Naming Conventions   22
      3.1.3   Identifying Your Input: INFILE Statement   24
      3.1.4   Defining Variables and Their Attributes: The INPUT Statement   25
      3.1.5   Associating Values with the Variables: More on the INPUT Statement
         27

3.2 **The SAS Log: A Runtime Journal   29**
   3.2.1 SAS Log Description   29
   3.2.2 Error Processing   31
3.3 **More Processing Control   34**
   3.3.1 Preventing Unwanted Input Line Wrapping   36
   3.3.2 End-of-file Processing   40
   3.3.3 Holding the Input Line   42
   3.3.4 Reading Files with a Variable Length Header   46
3.4 **Processing Instream Data   47**
   3.4.1 The Instream Conversion DATA Step   47
   3.4.2 List Input   47
   3.4.3 List Input Format Modifiers   49
   3.4.4 Listing the Variables in a SAS Dataset   50

Chapter 4. Simple Report Preparation

53

4.1 **Whole-file Operations: The PROC Step   53**
4.2 **Instant Report #1: PROC PRINT   54**
   4.2.1 Detail Lists: An Extended Example   55
   4.2.2 Selecting and Ordering the Printed Variables   56
   4.2.3 Accumulating Totals Automatically   58
   4.2.4 Using Dataset Options to Limit the Number of Observations   59
4.3 **Working with Sorted Data: PROC SORT   60**
   4.3.1 Sorting the Data   60
   4.3.2 Control Breaks   62
   4.3.3 Summary of PROC PRINT Features   64
4.4 **Instant Report #2: PROC FREQ   65**
   4.4.1 Sample Frequency Distribution   66
   4.4.2 Missing Values and PROC FREQ   68
4.5 **Reformatting Your Data   69**
   4.5.1 Preloaded Character Formats   70
   4.5.2 Numeric Formats   70
   4.5.3 Permanent vs Temporary Formats   74
   4.5.4 Custom Formats   76
4.6 **Redesigning Your Report   86**
   4.6.1 Titles and Footnotes   87
   4.6.2 Adding Descriptive Column Titles: LABEL Statement   90
   4.6.3 Printing Labels: LABEL and SPLIT Options   90

Chapter 5. More Data Handling Techniques

93

5.1 **More DATA Step Uses   93**
   5.1.1 Creating a Dataset from an Existing Dataset   94
5.2 **Changing the Sample Size   97**
   5.2.1 Controlling I/O   98
   5.2.2 Removing Duplicates and Summarizing   100
   5.2.3 Limiting Sequential Processing: FIRSTOBS and OBS   103
   5.2.4 Using Conditionals to Bypass Processing   103
   5.2.5 How to Output Multiple Datasets   107
5.3 **Adding and Deleting Variables and Values   111**
   5.3.1 Selecting the Variables You Need: DROP, KEEP, and RENAME   111
   5.3.2 Creating New Variables   114

5.3.3   Creating New Variables from Old Variables: SUBSTR and
        Concatenation   115
5.3.4   Accumulating Values across Iterations: the Sum Variable   117
5.3.5   Retaining Values Across Iterations: RETAIN   119

Chapter 6. External File Output   **121**

6.1   **Creating a File**   121
      6.1.1   Defining the External Output File   122
      6.1.2   Formatting Output Records   124
      6.1.3   Specifying Output Positions   125
      6.1.4   Specifying Output Formats   127
6.2   **Creating a Custom Format with PROC FORMAT**   129
      6.2.1   PRINT Files as External Files   130
      6.2.2   A Simple Report with Headings   131
      6.2.3   Forcing Page Breaks and Using Page Footings   133
      6.2.4   Full-page Formatting   136
      6.2.5   Redirecting Print Files   138
6.3   **Additional Control Statements**   140
      6.3.1   The SELECT Statement   140
      6.3.2   The LINK Statement   143
      6.3.3   The GOTO Statement   146

Chapter 7. Loops and Table Handling   **149**

7.1   **The Loop/Table Relationship**   149
      7.1.1   Delimiting a Block of Code   149
      7.1.2   Nonlooping DO   150
      7.1.3   Iterative DO (Pattern Type)   151
      7.1.4   Iterative DO (List Type)   152
      7.1.5   Deliberate Exit from the Loop   153
      7.1.6   Conditional Loops   155
      7.1.7   Compound Conditional Loops   156
7.2   **Tables**   156
      7.2.1   Explicit Subscript Array   157
      7.2.2   Implicit Subscript Arrays   160
      7.2.3   Multidimensional Arrays   163
      7.2.4   Operating Systems Constraints   164

Chapter 8. Time/Space Savers   **167**

8.1   **Automatic Variables and Automatic Dataset Names**   167
      8.1.1   Keeping Track of Iterations   168
      8.1.2   Processing Checks (__ERROR__)   172
      8.1.3   Automatic Dataset Names (__LAST__ and __DATA__)   175
      8.1.4   The Null Dataset (__NULL__)   177
      8.1.5   How to Output a Line of Raw Data (__INFILE__)   178
      8.1.6   How to Output a Line of SAS Data (__ALL__)   181
      8.1.7   A Few PROC Step Automatic Variables   181
8.2   **SAS Functions**   182
      8.2.1   Arithmetic and Math Functions   183
      8.2.2   Character Functions   184

8.2.3   Two Functions that Let You Pass and Retrieve Data from Other DATA
        Steps (SYMPUT and SYMGET)   186
8.2.4   Other Functions   187

Chapter 9. Joining Datasets   189

9.1   **Adding Observations**   189
      9.1.1   Adding Observations from One Dataset to Another   189
      9.1.2   PROC APPEND   194
      9.1.3   Interleaving Observations from Other Datasets   197
9.2   **Combining Observations**   199
      9.2.1   The Merge Operator   200
      9.2.2   Positional Merge   200
      9.2.3   Match Merge   203
      9.2.4   Match Merge with No Duplicates   203
      9.2.5   Match Merge of Input Datasets with Duplicates   209
9.3   **Updating a Database**   215

Chapter 10. Basic Statistical and Reporting Procedures   219

10.1   **Graphic Reporting Procedures: PROC CHART and PROC PLOT**   220
       10.1.1   Summary Graphics Using PROC CHART   220
       10.1.2   Controlling the Number of Sections in a Chart   223
       10.1.3   Controlling the Meaning of Sections in a Chart   224
       10.1.4   Grouping Sections in a Chart   227
       10.1.5   Detail Graphics Using PROC PLOT   229
10.2   **Summarizing a Dataset in Table Form: PROC FREQ**   231
       10.2.1   One-way Frequency Tables Using PROC FREQ   232
       10.2.2   Cross-tabulations Using PROC FREQ   237
       10.2.3   Statistical Analysis in PROC FREQ   239
       10.2.4   Using PROC FORMAT with PROC FREQ   243
10.3   **Creating a Summary Dataset: PROC SUMMARY**   244
       10.3.1   Contents of the PROC SUMMARY Output Dataset   244
       10.3.2   Using PROC SUMMARY   248
10.4   **Other Statistical and Reporting Procedures**   251

Chapter 11. Constructing Reusable SAS Code   253

11.1   **What is Reusable Code and Why Use it?**   253
       11.1.1   SAS Tools that Allow You to Create Reusable Code   254
       11.1.2   Including SAS Statements from Other Programs   254
11.2   **Introduction to the SAS Macro Subsystem**   256
       11.2.1   Macro Definition and Invocation   257
       11.2.2   Macros with Parameters and Defaults   258
       11.2.3   Simple Macro Debugging Tools   261
11.3   **Processing the Macro**   264
       11.3.1   MACRO Compilation and Execution   264
       11.3.2   The Current Environment   264
       11.3.3   Permanent Storage of Macros   265
11.4   **Macro Elements**   266
       11.4.1   Creating and Assigning Macro Variables   266
       11.4.2   Macro Variable Usage and the Double Quote   269

11.4.3 Automatic Macro Variables   272
11.4.4 Creating Macro Variables from DATA Step Variables   272
11.4.5 Overview of Macro Functions   275
11.4.6 Macro Control Statements   276

Chapter 12. Special Features for PC Users   **281**

12.1 **Starting the SAS Session**   281
    12.1.1 Display Manager Mode   282
    12.1.2 Batch Mode   282
    12.1.3 Creating Your Own Startup Procedure   283
12.2 **Using the Display Manager**   284
    12.2.1 The Windowing Environment   285
    12.2.2 The Primary Windows: PGM, LOG, and OUTPUT   285
    12.2.3 Other Windows   286
    12.2.4 Defining Your Own Windows   290
    12.2.5 Changing Window Configuration   290
    12.2.6 Saving Display Manager Commands   298
    12.2.7 Using Function Keys   299
12.3 **The Procedure Menu System**   300
    12.3.1 Invoking a Procedure Menu   300
    12.3.2 Example: The PROC SORT Menu   300
12.4 **Interfacing with Other Software**   302
12.5 **The Micro-to-Host Link**   303
    12.5.1 Using the Micro-to-Host Link   304
    12.5.2 Submitting SAS Programs to Run on the Host   305
    12.5.3 Transferring Files Between the PC and Host   305

Chapter 13. Optimizing SAS Applications   **307**

13.1 **System Options**   307
13.2 **Optimizing Through Program Design**   308
    13.2.1 Optimizing Storage of SAS Datasets   308
    13.2.2 Reducing the Number of Variables   308
    13.2.3 Reducing Variable Lengths   309
    13.2.4 Reducing the Number of Observations   310
    13.2.5 Handling Sorts   312
    13.2.6 Error Exits   314
    13.2.7 When to Create Permanent Datasets   315
    13.2.8 Storing Compiled Formats   316
13.3 **Database Design**   316

Index   318

Preface

Scope of this book

This book is a programmer's guide to basic SAS® software. It provides an introduction to the most common and useful features of the SAS System and indicates directions for those who want to learn more. We have stressed the features we find most helpful and have deemphasized or omitted those topics which are not essential for the beginning SAS user. It is not intended to be a reference book, but it will get you started and provide quick help for everyday or occasional SAS users.

Who should read this book

This book was specifically written for professional programmers and analysts. We have found that many data-processing professionals do not take full advantage of SAS software. Possibly because of its origins as a statistical package, the SAS System is sometimes perceived as a specialty product. And unfortunately, some DP veterans dismiss it as a user's language, unsuitable for real programmers.

We hope to demonstrate that the SAS System is a full-featured general purpose tool that happens to be remarkably easy to use. SAS software was written to provide full support for all levels of expertise, from information-center user to the most experienced systems professional.

Up to now there has not been a guide for programmers who are beginners to SAS programming, but not beginners to programming. This is a programmer's guide to the SAS System. It is for you if you are comfortable with COBOL or another production language, but find it no longer adequate; if you need to produce reports that users change constantly; if you need to know if a file has bad data in it;

®SAS is a registered trademark of SAS Institute Inc., Cary, NC, USA.

if you need to throw graphs together and produce ad hoc reports; if you need to do it *fast*. . . before the "crisis du jour" gets out of hand. SAS software is probably already installed at your site and you've probably seen some intriguing uses of it, but you are not sure how to go about using it yourself. What you need to know is how to get started. This book covers the most basic and useful elements of base SAS software.

We believe SAS software belongs in the programmer's working tool kit, and we emphasize the features that are most valuable for everyday use. This is not an exhaustive treatment by any means! (If you want to find out more about the SAS System, SAS Institute, Inc. publishes an excellent set of reference manuals and guides.) We show you how to use SAS software effectively for reporting, file manipulation, basic graphics and statistics.

How to use this book

The book is organized into three parts. In Chapters 1 and 2, we introduce you to SAS software, tell you how to understand it and how to begin working with it. Chapters 3 through 7 cover the real essentials of writing SAS programs: the nuts and bolts information you'll need to construct most applications. Chapters 8 through 13 introduce some topics of special interest, such as graphics and statistics, and provide guidelines for writing better SAS programs.

If you're just becoming acquainted with SAS software, or if you're more experienced in other programming languages, we strongly recommend that you read Chapter 2 before you begin writing SAS programs. It is in Chapter 2 that the basic concepts of SAS programs and the SAS environment are described. SAS software can be quite perplexing at first to systems professionals trained in the nuances of conventional languages because it hides or automates many routine chores and program structures.

You probably have some specific use in mind for SAS software, even if it is only a single program. Chapters 3 through 7 will tell you how to write your program. The chapters cover the most common SAS statements and procedures and they build on each other. However, as the system is easy to understand, you can skim through the chapters to find examples that look "close" to your applications or needs. For the simplest types of reporting, Chapters 3 and 4 will be all you need. Chapter 5 goes into more detail about handling input, and Chapter 6 does the same for output. Chapter 7 introduces the common looping and control structures you'll need to construct more complicated programs.

Chapters 8 through 13 are all independent, and can be read as your needs and interests dictate. Chapter 8 describes additional features of the SAS language that may make your life easier and/or your programs more effective; it is the chapter to read if you want to continue learning more about SAS programming. Chapter 9 describes, in detail, the methods of combining information from multiple datasets; with emphasis on the powerful MERGE statement.

Chapter 10 is an introduction to reporting and statistical analysis using SAS software. It is aimed at the nonstatistician, but professional statisticians should find it a useful guide to the general SAS statistics syntax. Chapter 11 covers the basics of SAS program libraries and macro handling. Chapter 12 describes some features of the SAS System for personal computers. Finally, Chapter 13 points out some ways to optimize your SAS programs, a topic of interest if you will be developing production applications using the SAS System.

We have tried to present this material in a sequence which will be helpful for an experienced programmer trying to pick up SAS concepts quickly. For example, some "basic" programming structures (such as DO loops) are deferred until Chapters 5 and 7 in favor of an early presentation of external file applications and the PRINT, SORT, FORMAT and FREQ procedures. This emphasizes the features which are most novel and attractive to the beginning SAS user, rather than those which are similar to other languages.

Acknowledgments

We would like to acknowledge our debt to our colleagues at SEI Information Technology and Guideposts Associates, Inc., all of whom have contributed greatly to our understanding. We are especially grateful to Monika Krueger and Aliki Karampelas for their confidence in us, to Michael Harward and James Trefren for introducing us to SAS programming, and to Connie Roan for helping inspire this book.

We are grateful to Automated Concepts, Inc. for their financial and professional support in the preparation of this book. We would also like to thank the many people who contributed advice and support. We'd particularly like to thank Tom Brostek and Kevin Galway of Automated Concepts, Inc. for their encouragement, Carol Lehn for many invaluable suggestions, and Jay Ranade for giving generously of his time. Maureen Cook guided the manuscript (and the authors) skillfully and patiently through its final stages. Finally, we'd like to thank our families for their love and support.

Overview of the SAS® System

This chapter presents a general overview of the SAS System. It discusses what the SAS System is, and who uses it. It also provides some general guidelines for when and how to use it. The focus is on how SAS software can be most useful to programming professionals.

1.1 WHAT IS IT?

SAS software is many things to many people. SAS users run the gamut from scientists and business users to seasoned systems professionals. Whatever their background, they are attracted by the unusual combination of power, flexibility, and ease-of-use that the SAS System provides. They tend to enjoy working with SAS software, and constantly find new uses for it. At the same time, the SAS System remains somewhat mysterious to nonusers. They are not quite sure what "SAS" is, or does, or just what went into the impressive reports and graphs produced by their SAS-using colleagues.

Both groups are reacting to the flexible nature of the SAS System. SAS software is not designed to handle a particular application or class of applications. Instead, it provides an approach for dealing

®SAS is a registered trademark of SAS Institute Inc., Cary, NC, USA with data in general. It is an open-ended system that can satisfy diverse needs, while providing individual users with powerful and precisely defined procedures.

The SAS System is a data analysis and programming system published by SAS Institute, Inc. ("SAS" is not an acronym, and it should not be represented as "S.A.S.") The system actually incorporates a variety of products. Each product, in turn, provides many procedures and programming tools. For example, SAS/GRAPH software is used for generating graphic output, and contains specialized procedures for different types of charts and maps; SAS/STAT software contains numerous advanced statistical procedures. In this book, we will look primarily at the "base SAS software", which includes general analysis, programming, and report-generating features. Base SAS software is available to all SAS users; other products may or may not be available, depending on your installation.

The SAS System bridges an important gap between conventional, do-it-yourself languages (such as COBOL) and more highly-developed database management and applications packages. It recognizes, on one hand, that much of the data encountered by programmers and other users arises outside the well-defined structures of the corporate database. Professional programmers spend much of their time writing one-shot or emergency programs to handle such situations. SAS software provides a full-fledged programming language which is well suited to managing raw or poorly understood data.

On the other hand, the SAS System is specifically designed to organize and analyze this data. To this end, it provides a wide-ranging and powerful set of prewritten procedures that can be invoked in one or two commands. These procedures can handle virtually any summary reporting or data analysis task. The SAS System also provides a simple, generic data model that can be used to build a temporary or permanent database.

From a programmer's point of view, however, it is all simply SAS software. The language and procedure syntax is consistent across the diverse SAS product line. This means that with a basic understanding of SAS software, you are well equipped to use any tool in the SAS System.

SAS software also provides a complete programming environment. Online users, as well as users of the SAS System for PCs, work within a session controlled by the SAS supervisor. This encourages an interactive, experimental approach. The same SAS programs will run in batch mode, without any change to source code.

The SAS System is highly modular and is constantly being extended to provide new features, many of which originate with user requests or user-written programs. Because of the consistent syntax, any SAS System user can easily take advantage of new system features.

1.2 WHO USES IT?

There are over one million users of the SAS System worldwide, representing over 12,000 site licenses. The system supports most of the hardware and software configurations in common use, including IBM mainframes (under OS, DOS/VSE, and VM/CMS), IBM PCs, DEC, Hewlett-Packard, Prime, Data General, and Sun Microsystems computers.

SAS software is used by individuals at all skill levels. Many SAS users are not data processing professionals at all, but scientific or business users who take advantage of the powerful prewritten PROC programs to analyze data. To them, the SAS System is a boon, a simple programming language that requires no programmers.

More complex SAS applications are written by SAS programmers. The SAS DATA step provides a full programming language that can be used like COBOL or PL/1 to code sophisticated programs similar to how you would use COBOL or PL/1. SAS datasets can be saved to form a permanent database which can be used as the nucleus of an entire application system.

SAS software is also used by systems programmers who rely on special features. For example, there are formats to analyze SMF data and provide library management functions.

Finally, the SAS System is used with increasing frequency by programmers whose main interest is not SAS software at all, but who find it a convenient tool for many everyday data processing tasks. These programmers typically use SAS software to provide ad hoc reports, or to analyze or reformat an unusual dataset.

1.3 WHEN TO USE IT

Many SAS users are first attracted by a particularly revealing report or graph. Their first question is usually "how hard is that to do?" More often than not, it is surprisingly easy. This is because the SAS System was specifically developed to assist researchers who had large amounts of unorganized data and needed to develop meaningful summary information quickly.

The SAS System was designed for data analysis. It handles all of the tasks associated with getting raw data into the system, storing and managing the database, manipulating the data, and analyzing the data so that results can be communicated clearly and easily. This design goal explains much about SAS software. For example, unlike most data processing languages, the SAS language gracefully handles "missing" data. At a more fundamental level, the importance placed on standard PROC steps for reports, graphs, and statistical analysis reflects the importance of organizing and interpreting data.

SAS software is an excellent tool for those situations where "something is happening but you don't know what it is". A complex or poorly defined situation can be analyzed with very little programming effort. Experienced SAS users learn to stop thinking "how am I going to program this?" Instead, they ask "what do I have, and what do I need to know?"

1.4 HOW TO USE IT

The SAS System is ideally suited for an experimental approach. It assumes that you will want to get at your data in many different ways. The SAS approach permits you to develop many variations on the "theme" of your database, with virtually no programming effort. Perhaps a different breakdown would be more revealing, so you add a PROC SORT and PROC PRINT. Still can't picture what's going on? Maybe a PROC CHART will help. And so on. Each of these experiments requires only two or three lines of code.

Just as important, the "experiments" can be performed without disturbing your existing code. Programs are highly modular, so each step acts independently, and you can always rerun your program from the beginning.

Finally, SAS programs are difficult to break. You'll have to work hard to get an infinite loop in a SAS program. It is practically impossible to get SAS to terminate abnormally. If something does go wrong, the SAS log provides helpful diagnostic information without your having to ask for it. As a result, you can sit down and start using SAS software with very little preparation. About all you need is the format of your input file and some idea of what you want to do. You can draft the SAS program in a few minutes and run it. If something is wrong, you can make the appropriate changes and rerun it immediately. If everything is right, and you want to add more, the modular approach of the SAS System allows you to do so without upsetting your existing program.

2

Introduction to the SAS Language

In this chapter, we begin to explore programming in the SAS System. You will learn the basic concepts of DATA and PROC steps, and how they are used to construct SAS programs. You will also be introduced to some features of the SAS environment, and the basic language structure.

2.1 THE SAS SYSTEM CONCEPT

A typical program in any language reads in data, processes it, then produces a file or report. When this typical program is coded in a third generation language, there are no input conventions and no output defaults. You must build what you need when you need it, and frequently reinvent the wheel.

Now contrast this with the SAS System. The SAS System has hundreds of procedures already written, tested, and well documented. Once your data is imported to a SAS dataset, it can be used as input to these easily modified routines.

2.1.1 SAS programs are made up of steps

A SAS program is really a series of one or more "steps". There are two types of steps: DATA steps and PROC steps. Each step reads in data, processes it according to your instructions or system defaults, and generates output. The output may be passed to a later step. Steps really are miniprograms because the SAS System software compiles and executes them separately, each step in turn as it is encountered in the program.

DATA steps are the most like "ordinary" programs. You'll recognize familiar constructs like IF..THEN..ELSE and DO WHILE. DATA steps will be used for the parts of your SAS application which read and write external files. They will also be used whenever you have to do any application-dependent processing which is not provided by a PROC. Here is an example of a DATA step which reads a customer file, selects customers 65 years old or older, and creates a SAS dataset including their names, addresses, and account numbers. (We'll discuss the individual statements later on.)

```
DATA CUST65;
    INFILE CUSTMAST;
    INPUT  @653 AGE    PD2.
           @1    ACCT   7.
           @8    NAME   $CHAR30.
           @38   ADDR   $CHAR30.
           @68   CITY   $CHAR20.
           @88   STATE  $CHAR2.
           @90   ZIP    $CHAR5.;
    IF AGE < 65 THEN DELETE;
```

PROC steps, on the other hand, are used solely to call the prewritten procedures included in the SAS software itself. Each one of these procedures has a one-word name, such as SORT or PRINT, so SAS users talk about PROC SORT or PROC PRINT. PROC steps, unlike DATA steps, do not look much like ordinary programs. The PROC step simply names the procedure and specifies parameters; the procedure itself is a "black box". Here is a PROC step that sorts the SAS dataset we just created by ZIP code. (We'll cover PROC SORT in detail in Chapter 4.)

```
PROC SORT DATA=CUST65 OUT=CUST65;
    BY ZIP;
```

In general, DATA steps create special files called "SAS datasets", and PROC steps use the SAS datasets as a source for reports or specialized output datasets. A simple SAS program, therefore, might consist of a DATA step that organizes your data into a SAS dataset and then a PROC step that generates statistics from it. However, it is unwise to get too carried away with the differences between DATA and PROC steps. As far as your SAS program is concerned, one is not more important than the other. PROC steps are not subroutines of DATA steps, or vice versa. They are on an equal footing, and simply execute in the order they occur in the program. The only difference is that the inner workings of a PROC step have already been written for you, while DATA steps are strictly do-it-yourself affairs.

Fig. 2.1 shows a top-level view of a SAS program. This SAS program consists of two steps.

Step 1. DATA step reads raw data input and creates a SAS dataset as output.

Step 2. PROC step reads in the SAS dataset and produces a report.

Any combination of DATA and PROC steps can be used to form your SAS program. Fig. 2.2 shows some other possibilities.

2.1.2   SAS steps are made up of statements

Although we've talked about a SAS program consisting of steps, if you're looking at a SAS program for the first time, you won't see any steps at all (especially if each step is not documented individually). Instead, the code may appear to be an unorganized series of statements one after the other, as you can see from this example:

```
DATA CUST65;
INFILE CUSTMAST;
INPUT   @653 AGE    PD2.
        @1   ACCT   7.
        @8   NAME   $CHAR30.
        @38  ADDR   $CHAR30.
        @68  CITY   $CHAR20.
        @88  STATE  $CHAR2.
        @90  ZIP    $CHAR5.;
IF AGE < 65 THEN DELETE;
PROC SORT DATA=CUST65 OUT=CUST65;
BY ZIP;
PROC PRINT;
```

Of course, this is the DATA and PROC steps we've already seen, plus an additional PROC step (PROC PRINT) which prints the final SAS dataset in a usable format. Thus, there are three steps in this SAS program. However, this is not apparent at first glance.

A good rule to follow, when you are looking at an unfamiliar SAS program, is to look immediately for the DATA and PROC step head-

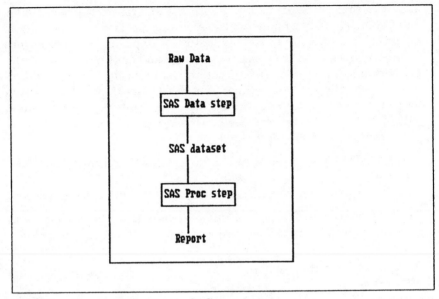

Figure 2.1   Overview of a simple SAS program

ers. They will show you the organization of the program. Of course, when you are writing a program, you will want to use indentation, spacing, and comments to highlight the steps and make things easier for the next person.

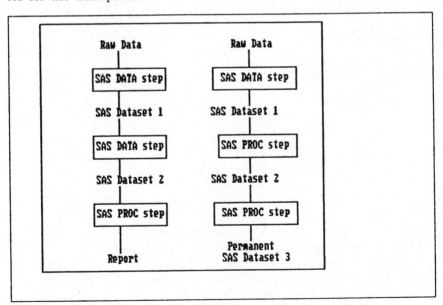

Figure 2.2   More complex SAS programs

```
* READ THE CUSTOMER FILE, KEEPING THOSE 65 OR OLDER;
  DATA CUST65;
      INFILE CUSTMAST;
      INPUT  @653 AGE   PD2.
             @1   ACCT  7.
             @8   NAME  $CHAR30.
             @38  ADDR  $CHAR30.
             @68  CITY  $CHAR20.
             @88  STATE $CHAR2.
             @90  ZIP   $CHAR5.;
      IF AGE < 65 THEN DELETE;
* SORT THE 65-OR-OLDERS INTO ZIP CODE SEQUENCE;
  PROC SORT DATA=CUST65 OUT=SORT65;
      BY ZIP;
* PRINT THE 65-OR-OLDERS IN ZIP CODE SEQUENCE;
  PROC PRINT;
  RUN;
```

Statements immediately following a PROC or DATA statement are assumed to belong to that step. The step includes all statements until one of two things occurs: either a new step is encountered (a new DATA or PROC statement), or a RUN statement is encountered. Either of these conditions signals the end of the step. Note that we added a RUN statement after the the last step in our program to make sure the step was executed; this is generally a good idea.

Let's take a closer look at our example. Each statement contains at least one keyword that identifies the function of the statement: DATA steps always start with a statement that includes the keyword DATA; PROC steps always start with the keyword PROC, while other statements contain keywords that are directly related to their function.

The DATA statement tells the SAS supervisor to create a SAS dataset called CUST65 which will receive the output from this DATA step. (An indepth discussion of SAS datasets will be presented in the following sections. For the moment, however, just think of a SAS dataset as a temporary file used to pass information between steps.)

The INFILE statement identifies the input file CUSTMAST and reads in a record. The INPUT statement tells the supervisor what fields to include in the dataset that is being created. Each field is represented by its position in the input record (in our example, AGE is at byte 653), its format (AGE is a two-byte packed decimal value), and the name it will have in the SAS dataset. This name is used only within the SAS program and does not have to correspond to the field name used by the program that created the file. However, within the SAS program you must use this name consistently.

The IF statement deserves some explanation. This statement says: if the value of AGE for a particular input record is less than 65, do not create an output observation for that record. Notice that DELETE does not mean that the record is physically eliminated from the input dataset. It means that the record is not included in the output SAS dataset.

Next, the PROC keyword signals that this is the start of a new step. The first thing to happen is that the previous DATA step is executed. (Up to now, we have simply been collecting statements for the DATA step, without actually executing any of them.) Once that is done, statement collection begins for the PROC step. The SORT keyword identifies the particular procedure. The DATA= and OUT= keywords identify the input and output SAS datasets; in this case, we will sort CUST65 and create a new SAS dataset called SORT65 containing the sorted observations. Finally, the BY statement identifies the sort key. Note that the field name ZIP matches the name used when the SAS dataset was created.

When we encounter another PROC keyword, we recognize the end of the prior step; the PROC SORT is executed. Statement collection begins for the PROC PRINT step. In this case, there is only one statement invoking the procedure. When the RUN statement is encountered, PROC PRINT is executed. By default, this procedure will print a formatted list of the output SAS dataset from the preceding step.

In analyzing this program, comment lines are encountered. There are two ways to include comments in a SAS program. In our example, each comment begins with an asterisk and continues until a semicolon is encountered. The other way is to begin a comment with "/*" and end it with "*/".

Let's summarize our example. The first step reads an external file called CUSTMAST and creates a SAS dataset called CUST65, containing only those customers age 65 or older. The second step, PROC SORT, sorts these customers into ZIP code sequence. The third and final step in this example, PROC PRINT, prints a formatted list of the selected customers.

2.1.3   Where's the read statement?

You'll notice that there are no explicit "read" statements in either of the steps. This is because each step is an implied loop, designed to process all input records. The step is executed repeatedly, once for each input record. Only when all input records have been processed does the program go on to the next PROC or DATA step. In programming terms, there is an unwritten "DO WHILE NOT END-OF-FILE" surrounding the step.

Fig. 2.3 shows how a SAS program breaks down to a series of loops. If there are 100 records in the input file, the DATA step is executed 100 times. The output of the DATA step is passed to PROC PRINT, which reads and prints the 100 records. Note that the DATA step will always process all records before control is passed to the next step.

2.1.4 Passing information: the SAS dataset

The principal way that data is passed from one program step to another is through a "SAS dataset". A SAS dataset is a file that contains the actual data as well as control information needed for the system to work "transparently" from step to step. It is very much like a table, with columns representing the variables and rows representing the records (known as observations). Each observation contains values for each variable.

Fig. 2.4 is a schematic diagram of a small SAS dataset. This dataset has four observations and three variables. Observation #1 contains the values "Smith", "Payroll", and "300.00"; observation #2 contains the values "Janek", "Payroll", and "355.00". As you can

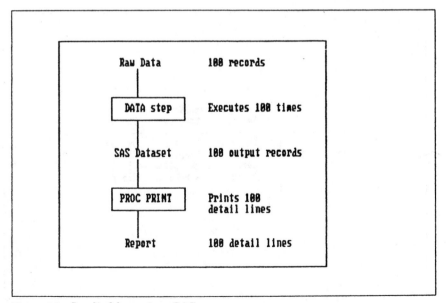

Figure 2.3 Implied loops in a SAS program

see, each observation corresponds to a row; and therefore, also can be thought of as a record.

There is a header on the dataset, which contains information about the names of the variables and each variable's format and length. In this case, the header contains the variable names "Emp_Id", "Emp_Dept", and "Emp_pay". It also contains a format and length for each of these; for example, "Emp_Id" may be defined as a 12-byte character field. Each variable may also have a "label", a long form of the name which will appear on printed procedure output. For example, "Emp_Id" may have a label containing "Employee ID". All this information is stored on the header only, and is not repeated in the individual observations. Fig. 2.5 shows the information saved for each variable. Except for the variable value, which is different for each observation, this descriptive information is saved only once in the SAS dataset header.

Although we have discussed the header and descriptive information for the sake of completeness, you can work as if the dataset contained only the data values. That is, you can assume a SAS dataset is a table, containing one row for each observation (record), and one column for each variable.

2.1.5   Constructing SAS datasets

SAS datasets are managed by the SAS system itself. The individual datasets do not have to be identified externally (i.e., they do not have

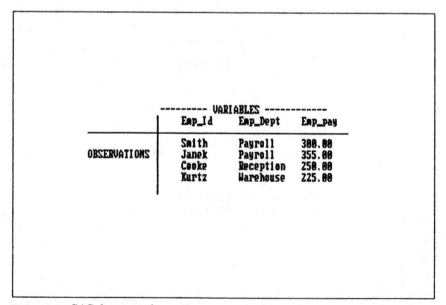

Figure 2.4   SAS dataset schematic

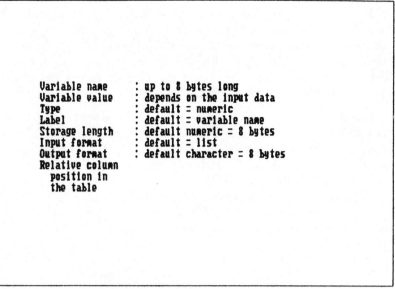

```
Variable name        : up to 8 bytes long
Variable value       : depends on the input data
Type                 : default = numeric
Label                : default = variable name
Storage length       : default numeric = 8 bytes
Input format         : default = list
Output format        : default character = 8 bytes
Relative column
  position in
  the table
```

Figure 2.5 SAS dataset descriptive information

to be named in JCL (Job Control Language) or other allocation statements). However, a workfile must be allocated to hold all the SAS datasets created in your session (see Chapter 3).

Creation of SAS datasets is handled by SAS software using the information you provide in your DATA step. For convenience, we will differentiate between two main functions of the DATA step: converting raw data to a SAS dataset and creating a new dataset from a previously created SAS dataset. The only difference is in how you identify your input dataset.

Conversion DATA Step This is the step that imports non-SAS data into a SAS dataset. You only need to specify a few details, then the SAS System's internal processing handles construction of the table and storage of the descriptive data needed to retrieve it in later steps. You will generally specify the variable name, length, and format for each variable. This information is specified in the INPUT statement. We'll discuss this type of DATA step in detail in Chapter 3.

Regular DATA Step This step allows you to create a new SAS dataset from one that already exists. You would use this DATA step if you needed to make changes, such as adding new variables, limiting the view of the table (observations or variables), or merging or splitting several files, to your original table or to copy that table.

Because the seed table is already built, you do not have to re-specify the descriptive information for each variable. You name the dataset (in a SET statement), and all the header information is automatically available. Thus, the regular DATA step does not have any INPUT statement and can concentrate on its functional processing. In all other ways, it is the same as a conversion DATA step.

Example 2.1 Sample program (inventory list). This example illustrates the two types of DATA steps. We'll first use a conversion DATA step to create a SAS dataset from data in a non-SAS (external) file. Then we'll use a regular DATA step to create a second SAS dataset from selected information in the first SAS dataset.

Suppose you have an inventory list of shelf items. You'd like a list of those that have fewer than three left on the shelf. Your inventory interface provides this data (your store is small and only carries these five items):

Item	Quantity	Code
Pliers	12	A012
Wrench	2	A012
Hammer	1	B012
Scissors	10	C011
Files	3	C009

We'll assume this data is available in card-image form, with one record per item. We'll assume further that each card contains the three values for ITEM, QUANTITY, and CODE separated by spaces. This allows us to dispense with specifying lengths and formats; they will be determined automatically. (We'll see in Chapter 3 how the external file is attached to the SAS program; for the moment, we'll assume that it is available in a file called RAWDATA.)

Let's first create a SAS dataset containing all the information. We'll call this dataset ALLOFIT.

```
* CREATE SAS DATASET CONTAINING ALL DATA;
  DATA ALLOFIT;
      INFILE RAWDATA;
      INPUT ITEM QUANTITY CODE;
```

ALLOFIT is created using a conversion DATA step. The DATA statement names the output SAS dataset, and the INFILE statement names the input external file. The INPUT statement sets up a table with columns ITEM, QUANTITY, and CODE. These three values are stored for each item in a new row (observation); since our store sells five items, there will be five observations in dataset

ALLOFIT. Remember that there is a read loop implied by the DATA step, so the INPUT statement is executed once for each input record.

Now, let's get back to our original question. Which items have a quantity less than three? We do not have to go back to the original external file, since we have already done the work of reading our data into a SAS dataset. We can read ALLOFIT and create a second dataset called LESS3, containing only the desired information. For efficiency's sake, we'll leave the variable CODE out of the new dataset.

```
* CREATE SAS DATASET OF ITEMS WITH QUANTITY < 3;
  DATA LESS3 (DROP=CODE);
     SET ALLOFIT;
     IF QUANTITY < 3 THEN OUTPUT;
```

LESS3 was created from the ALLOFIT dataset. As before, the DATA statement names the output SAS dataset. Note, however, that there are no INFILE or INPUT statements. Instead, the SET statement indicates that an existing SAS dataset is to be used for input. (We know that the dataset ALLOFIT exists, because we just created it.) This means that the DATA step will retrieve each observation in dataset ALLOFIT automatically including the values for ITEM, QUANTITY, and CODE. Because the DATA statement says to drop the variable called CODE, our new dataset LESS3 will only include ITEM and QUANTITY. The IF statement limits the output to only those observations with QUANTITY less than 3. In effect, LESS3 is a subset of ALLOFIT having only the variables ITEM and QUAN-TITY, and having only two observations (for Hammer and Wrench) rather than the five in the original dataset.

After running both steps, we have created two SAS datasets. Dataset ALLOFIT contains five observations and three variables, with the following values:

Item	Quantity	Code
Pliers	12	A012
Wrench	2	A012
Hammer	1	B012
Scissors	10	C011
Files	3	C009

Dataset LESS3 contains two observations and two variables, with this information:

Item	Quantity
Wrench	2
Hammer	1

Once created, both datasets remain accessible throughout the session. Permanent datasets which remain accessible across SAS sessions also can be created. You'll learn how to do this in Chapter 3.

2.2   THE SAS SYSTEM ENVIRONMENT

The SAS System provides a minioperating system subordinate to your actual operating system. The SAS supervisor handles your program requests for file access and storage as well as performing program management and error handling.

2.2.1   What keeps it together: the SAS session

Whether you execute your SAS program as a batch program, as an interactive online job, or as a PC exec, one SAS session is created. We can consider that the SAS session consists of:

1. the SAS supervisor
2. a temporary workfile
3. the SAS log
4. attached files

plus the SAS steps you've written for this particular job run.

The SAS Supervisor   The SAS supervisor manages memory, access to SAS datasets and external files, log messages, global options and macros. The supervisor handles SAS step processing from instruction validation and compilation to inclusion of external data, to step execution.

Temporary Workfile   The temporary workfile is a SAS library dynamically allocated to your session. It is used to store all temporary files plus any macros created in the session. It is similar in function to the partitioned dataset familiar to OS users, although it is not actually a PDS. (SAS maintains the directory internally.)

The workfile size default (as well as the size of sortwork areas) is determined on installation, but you can override it in your JCL. For all but interactive sessions, the temporary workfile is deleted when the session ends.

The SAS Log   The SAS log is a runtime journal of your SAS program processing. It allows the supervisor to record messages, report on successful or unsuccessful processing, or provide other descriptive information about the SAS session.

Fig. 2.6 shows part of a typical SAS log. This run, from a PC session, shows the last log line from a PROC PRINT execution ("The PROCEDURE PRINT used 9.00 seconds"). Next, a DATA step is read; each statement is listed on the log. Remember that this step will not actually be executed until a RUN statement or a new step is encountered, so one additional statement will be listed before the DATA step execution begins. In fact, what we find is PROC PRINT. This line is listed, followed by the log output from the DATA step execution. Information is listed about the input file, then the output SAS dataset. Finally, we are told that "the DATA statement used 16.00 seconds".

Meanwhile, our PROC PRINT is still hanging and will not be executed until we find either a RUN statement or a new step. So, we read a new card, which is listed on the log; it is a RUN statement, so the PROC PRINT is executed. The last line shown shows that "the PROCEDURE PRINT used 12.00 seconds".

Attached Files Files or other types of data can be attached as needed. This will be addressed in more detail in Chapter 3.

2.2.2 How the session works

When an SAS program is executed, the SAS supervisor interacts with the operating system to attach all required files and storage to

```
┌LOG══════════════════════════════════════════════════════════════════════════
│Command ===>
│
│NOTE: The PROCEDURE PRINT used 9.00 seconds.
│   11    DATA Test; /* Output data set will be called 'TEST' */
│   12    INFILE 'c:\Examples\Chapt2\test.dat'; /* Input file */
│   13    Input Alpha $        /* Input character var. ALPHA  */
│   14          Beta           /* .. then numeric var. BETA   */
│   15          Gamma $        /* .. then char.  var. GAMMA   */
│   16          Delta          /* .. then numeric var. DELTA  */
│   17        ;                /* Semicolon ends INPUT stmt.  */
│   18    PROC PRINT;          /* Print the output dataset    */
│NOTE: The infile 'c:\Examples\Chapt2\test.dat' is file
│      C:\EXAMPLES\CHAPT2\TEST.DAT.
│NOTE: 9 records were read from the infile C:\EXAMPLES\CHAPT2\TEST.DAT.
│      The minimum record length was 20.
│      The maximum record length was 20.
│NOTE: The dataset WORK.TEST has 9 observations and 4 variables.
│NOTE: The DATA statement used 16.00 seconds.
│   19    RUN;
│NOTE: The PROCEDURE PRINT used 12.00 seconds.
```

Figure 2.6 Sample DATA step log messages

your SAS session. Then the SAS supervisor scans your code and breaks it up into manageable pieces. The program statements are validated and compiled into object code.

The step is executed immediately after compilation. If there are syntax or runtime errors in the step, the remaining steps in the program will not be executed; only the remaining code will be validated. Error messages and notes about processing are written to the SAS log. Output is routed to the file you (or your installation) have indicated. This file can be the terminal, the print file, or another attached file.

2.3 THE SAS LANGUAGE

SAS software provides a fourth generation language. Like all 4GLs, it allows you to concentrate most of your energies on analytical rather than procedural problem solving. However, you do have to learn a few rules of grammar to get started.

2.3.1 Structure of the language

SAS steps are constructed from SAS statements. Each statement is either instructive or informational. A statement can consist of one or more keywords, plus operators, variables, constants, special characters, and statement options. All statements must end with a semicolon, as these following examples illustrate:

```
DATA First;
%LET Initial = '001';
X = SUBSTR(Keyline,1,1);
LENGTH DEFAULT = 4;
RUN;
```

Keywords are used in SAS programs to identify certain operations and are easy to understand because they are written in English. Included in the language are the keywords KEEP, DROP, LENGTH, IF, THEN, DO, END, INPUT, FORMAT, RENAME, MERGE, TITLE, as well as several more. These keywords will be covered in detail in later chapters.

Operators and special characters also perform specific functions in the SAS language. The character $, for example, when placed after the name of a variable being added to the dataset, indicates that the variable is character rather than numeric. % before a name indicates that it is a macro reference. Other operators include, but are not limited to, the familiar +, −, *, /, and =.

2.3.2 Writing SAS code

There are few, if any, formal restrictions on SAS code. You can:

- start in any column you want
- skip lines arbitrarily
- spread statements over several lines
- code in upper and/or lower case

But each complete statement *must* end in a semicolon.

Example 2.2 SAS code has few restrictions.

```
datA Eazy; SET SASdata
(drop=
      first SECOND third)
      ;
If Weekday = 'Monday' then output;
```

In referencing SAS dataset variables you can:

- refer to sequentially numbered variables in range form (Month1–Month12)
- change the character or numeric classification by treating it in a "converted" manner. For example, a character variable ABC is converted to numeric by testing: If ABC > 1 then do......;

There are several varieties of comments:

Example 2.3 SAS comments illustrated.

```
/* This is a comment */ /*...*/
```

This type of comment can appear anywhere. It does not require a semicolon to delimit it, since the */ serves the same purpose. (Don't start it in column 1 of JCL instream data or it will be treated as an end-of-file marker!)

```
* This, too, is a comment ; *....;
```

This type of comment requires a semicolon to delimit it.

2.3.3 Three-step plan of a SAS program

SAS procedures are powerful, and can create many commonly required reports, but they may require their input to be in a particular format. The best way to prepare to write a SAS program is to turn it upside down.

1. *Plan your output.* Identify what type of output you want to produce. Is it a report based on user specs, an ad hoc report, a graph or chart, or is it just for your own information?

2. *Identify the SAS procedure.* Once you know what you want to produce, find the SAS PROC that accomplishes it (the basic descriptive procedures are covered in this book, and SAS software provides many more). For example, a simple listing of fields can be accomplished with PROC PRINT. A count of different values for a given variable can be produced with PROC FREQ.

If you want to examine, reformat, or create your own data, the DATA step is your best bet. It is the most flexible process in the SAS repertoire. Although our examples so far have been overly simple, don't be misled: one DATA step can perform a variety of operations on your file or files.

3. *Define your raw data conversion.* You should identify all fields you'll need from your input file. This saves you the overhead of reading your file a second time to pick up values you missed.

When you've identified the fields to be used, you can begin to code your raw data conversion SAS datasets. Let's look at how to do this in detail.

Converting Raw Data into SAS Datasets

This chapter describes the programming statements required to read an external data file and convert it to the internal format used by SAS procedures. You will learn how to use the DATA, INFILE, and INPUT statements to define inputs and outputs, including some special techniques for unusual situations. You will also see how to use the SAS log to interpret the results of your program.

3.1 OVERVIEW OF THE DATA STEP

The SAS System offers a wide range of analytical tools. But in order for you to use them, you must have the data you wish to analyze available in a SAS dataset. If your data is not available in this form, your first step is to convert it into a SAS dataset. Raw data conversion is one of the most useful, and often necessary, SAS steps to know.

Conversion of raw data is always performed in a DATA step. The DATA step is actually a template for a read loop. Input is retrieved one record at a time from an external dataset. The SAS variables are defined and their data values are stored in a SAS dataset.

The simplest conversion DATA step requires only three statements. The DATA statement marks the beginning of the step and names the output SAS dataset. The INFILE statement names the input external file. And the INPUT statement identifies the individual fields to be read, converted, and stored in the SAS dataset. Figure 3.1 illustrates the statements used in a simple conversion DATA step.

3.1.1 Identifying your output: the DATA statement

Don't confuse the DATA step with the DATA statement. The DATA step contains several different statements associated with creating a SAS dataset. The first statement in the DATA step is the DATA statement.

The DATA statement indicates that you will be creating a SAS dataset, and provides a name for the output SAS dataset. It has only two required components: the word DATA, followed by the name of the output SAS dataset.

The output dataset can be permanent or temporary. If it is temporary, the dataset is available on a workfile throughout the job, but will not be available after the job is ended. Permanent datasets are saved, so they are available to you or another SAS user in a later SAS session.

3.1.2 General naming conventions

In general, SAS enforces the following naming conventions:

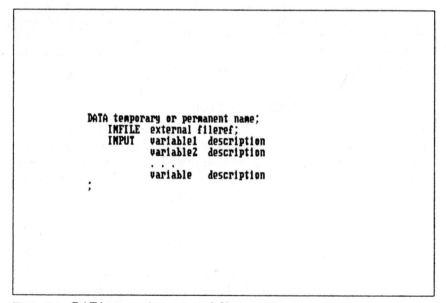

```
DATA temporary or permanent name;
   INFILE  external fileref;
   INPUT   variable1  description
           variable2  description
           . . .
           variable   description
   ;
```

Figure 3.1   DATA step using external file input

1. Names must be one to eight characters long.

2. Names must start with a letter or underscore.

3. Names can have numbers, letters, or underscores in characters 2 through 8.

4. The underscore is the only special character allowed.

These rules apply to all SAS names. In particular, they apply to the naming of SAS datasets. Temporary datasets are identified by a single level name. Permanent datasets are identified by a double level name: two valid SAS names separated by a period. In this case, the first level is actually the DDname of the output file. For example, the statement

```
DATA FOREVER.STATS;
```

will create a permanent dataset called STATS within the file whose DDname is FOREVER. Your JCL will have to include a definition of FOREVER, but does not refer to STATS. For example:

```
//SAS      EXEC SAS
//FOREVER    DD DSN=MY.SAS.DATA,DISP=OLD
```

Temporary datasets are created and stored just like permanent datasets; however, their names do not include the DDname. In this case, the DDname defaults to "WORK". It so happens that "WORK" is allocated by default in the SAS procedure, and deleted at the end of the SAS step. So, the SAS dataset is temporary. For example, the statement

```
DATA TEMP;
```

will create a temporary dataset called TEMP.

SAS datasets are stored as members within a larger data library (FOREVER or WORK in our examples). This is analogous to the "partitioned datasets" familiar to MVS users. However, an actual PDS is not used. Instead, SAS software manages the data and maintains the directory.

Because standards may vary from installation to installation, we will not give any rules for allocating SAS data libraries. See the technical-support person responsible for SAS software at your shop. You can get a quick idea of the allocation parameters by looking at the DD statement for file WORK in your SAS procedure.

General naming conventions apply to all identifiers.

The rules are:
1) names must be no more than eight bytes long
2) names can start with a letter or underscore
3) names can have numbers in bytes 2 thru 8 only
4) no special characters other than the underscore

Figure 3.2 Naming conventions

Example 3.1 Input and output file associations in OS. In this example, we read an external file called AR.MASTER to create a temporary SAS dataset called TEMP1. This temporary dataset is then input to a second step which creates a permanent SAS dataset called PERM1 in a library called PERM.SAS.LIBRARY. We've omitted some statements for clarity.

```
//SAS      EXEC SAS
//ARFILE   DD DSN=AR.MASTER,DISP=SHR
//PERMSAS  DD DSN=PERM.SAS.LIBRARY,DISP=SHR
//SYSIN    DD *
  DATA TEMP1;          /* NAMES SAS DATASET #1   */
      INFILE ARFILE;   /* IDENTIFIES INPUT DDNAME */
      . . .
  DATA PERMSAS.PERM1; /* NAMES SAS DATASET #2   */
      SET TEMP1;       /* DATASET #1 IS INPUT     */
```

3.1.3 Identifying your input: INFILE statement

The second statement in the DATA step, the INFILE statement, provides the DDname of the external file from which the raw data will be retrieved. The statement has two components: the word INFILE, and the DDname of the external file. An external input file is defined as any file that is not a SAS file. That is, the data is not yet stored in the table form of rows (observations) and columns (variables) recognized by SAS procedures.

The DDname must be associated with your external file prior to execution of the DATA step. On OS systems, the association is made in a DD statement or TSO ALLOCATE. The file can be a sequential file, a member of a partitioned dataset, or a VSAM file. For example, the following JCL shows how to attach a file called SOME.RAW.DATA to your SAS DATA step:

```
//SAS      EXEC SAS
//MYDATA   DD DSN=SOME.RAW.DATA,DISP=SHR
//SYSIN    DD *
   DATA TEMP;
      INFILE MYDATA;
```

Note: There is an alternative to the INFILE statement. The CARDS statement can be used when data is to be included "instream". Following the CARDS statement, all subsequent input lines are assumed to contain data (not SAS program statements), until a line is reached containing only a semicolon. The following example shows instream data with three records, each containing values for A and B:

```
DATA TESTIT;
   INPUT A B;
   CARDS;
   73 24
   10 56
   92 03
   ;
```

3.1.4 Defining variables and their attributes: the INPUT statement

The third statement in the DATA step is the INPUT statement. This statement actually performs two functions: defining the variables, and loading the actual data values. We will look at variable definition now; assigning values to variables will be discussed in Sec. 3.1.5.

Approximately 4000 variables may be defined in a SAS dataset. The INPUT statement will include a definition of each variable. The variable definition provides information needed by the SAS supervisor to set up the dataset. You must define the variable name, type, position (within the input record), and input format.

Figure 3.3 describes the rules for variable name, type, and position. Figure 3.4 shows how to specify an input format. In Sec. 3.1.5, we discuss how external data values are assigned to the SAS dataset variables.

Variable name: You are allowed to define an
approximate maximum of 4000 variables per
observation. Each must have a unique name based
on SAS naming conventions (see Figure 3.2).

Type: Types are character ($) or numeric.
The default is numeric.
Define a variable as character by placing a
'$' immediately after its name.

Position: Position is relative to other variables
in the same observation. You control position by
listing variable names in the order you want
to keep them in the output dataset.

Input format: This tells SAS the exact
specifications (format and length) for associating
raw data with its SAS variable. Additionally, it
serves as the default output format.

Figure 3.3   Variable attributes

All SAS formats follow this general structure:

[$] [format name] total_length . decimal_places
1   2   3   4   5

1 : $ indicates a character variable
2 : descriptive format name
3 : total length (required)
4 : the period is required in all formats
5 : the number of bytes of total length reserved
    for decimal places (optional)

Formats are generally classed into two groups:
character formats and numeric formats

Figure 3.4   Input format schematic

Example 3.2 Commonly used formats. The following chart gives examples of what happens to raw data when different formats are used. In each case, the raw data is shown in hex format. The SAS input format is shown, along with a brief description of its interpretation. Finally, we see the value which will be stored in the SAS dataset.

Remember that the formats are used in an INPUT statement. The first format shown ($5.) would appear in a statement similar to this:

```
INPUT ITEMCODE $5.;
```

Effects of Different SAS INPUT Formats

Raw data	Format	Description	Value
40 40 F1 F2 F3	$5.	5 byte CHAR (drop lead blanks)	123
40 40 F1 F2 F3	$CHAR5.	5 byte CHAR (keep lead blanks)	bb123
F0 F0 F1 F2 F3	5.	5 byte NUM	123
F0 F0 F1 F2 F3	5.2	5 byte DECIMAL NUM	1.23
F0 F0 F1 F2 3C	ZD5.	5 byte ZONED	123
00 00 01 23 4C	PD5.	5 byte PACKED	1234
00 00 00 00 7B	IB5.	5 byte BINARY	123

A special note on dates: There are special SAS formats for dates. If you read a date as an ordinary numeric variable, SAS software will not be able to do date calculations or output date formatting. Always use the date input formats; the two most common are MMDDYY. and YYMMDD. That is, if the date field contained a value such as 123190 (representing December 31, 1990) you would code:

```
INPUT END_DATE MMDDYY.;
```

If the date was stored externally as 901231, you would code:

```
INPUT END_DATE YYMMDD.;
```

3.1.5 Associating values with the variables: more on the INPUT statement

The other function of the INPUT statement is to tell the DATA step where to find the raw data to associate with your variable definition. There are several ways to do this depending on the file layout, the input format, and other requirements.

For fixed format files, column input style is most useful. This style directs the SAS internal pointer to the starting position of the field. In your program, you code an "@" sign to indicate that you are using column input, followed by a number representing the relative byte in the input record. When a number immediately follows the @, the internal pointer is moved to that position in the input record. For example:

```
INPUT @1 EMP_CODE $CHAR1.;
```

directs the DATA step to associate the first byte of the record (@1) with the 1-byte SAS character variable ($CHAR1.) named EMP_CODE.

```
INPUT @12 CITY_CODE   2.
      @1  STATE_CODE $CHAR2.
      @12 CITY_PFX    1.;
```

says to associate the two bytes starting at byte 12 (@12) with the two-byte numeric variable (2.) named CITY_CODE. Bytes 1 through 2 (@1,$CHAR2.) are assigned to a character variable ($CHAR2.) called STATE_CODE. Finally, byte 12 (@12) is assigned to a one-byte numeric variable (1.) called CITY_PFX. Note that CITY_PFX is also the first byte of CITY_CODE (they both begin in relative byte 12); you don't have to do anything special to indicate that a field is being redefined.

As this example shows, the variables need not be listed in the order they appear on the input record and they may overlap. Also, you do not have to code anything about columns that you will not be using.

Let's consider one last example. The data to be analyzed is an external file containing six fields on each record, with the following layout:

Field	Position	Format
Account number	1–5	Character
Full ZIP code	6–14	Character
Includes:		
Five-digit ZIP	6–10	Numeric
"ZIP+4"	11–14	Character
Amount paid	15–18	Packed decimal, two decimal place
Codes not needed by this application	19–28	Character
Demographic code	29–30	Zoned decimal

A DATA step to read this data and create a permanent SAS dataset called INITIAL.READ would look like this:

```
DATA INITIAL.READ;
     INFILE RAWDATA;
     INPUT @1  ACCT    $5.   /* POS.1,  5-BYTE CHAR   */
```

```
@6  FULLZIP 9.     /* POS.6,  9-BYTE NUMERIC */
@6  ZIP     5.     /* POS.6,  5-BYTE NUMERIC */
@11 ZIP_4   4.     /* POS.11, 4-BYTE NUMERIC */
@15 PAID    PD4.2  /* POS.15, 4-BYTE PACKED, */
                   /*     2 DECIMAL PLACES    */
@29 CODE    ZD2.;  /* POS.29, 2-BYTE ZONED    */
                   /*     DECIMAL             */
RUN;
```

3.2 THE SAS LOG: A RUNTIME JOURNAL

When you have completed coding your module and you submit it (batch or interactive), the SAS supervisor begins the two-step process of translation and execution. Messages from the supervisor are displayed as a runtime journal on the SAS log. These messages include dataset creation statistics, CPU resource usage, processing notes, and error messages.

3.2.1 SAS log description

The SAS Log is a record of processing for one job or terminal session. The log gives you:

- a numbered list of the statements executed
- information about datasets that were created (including the name, number of observations, number of variables)
- the time and memory used in each step
- printed output page references (batch only)
- the number of records of raw data read in
- error messages and other processing notes

The SAS log is displayed on the terminal for all interactive and non-interactive sessions. Batch jobs route SAS log output based on installation defaults (normally to a printer or disk file).

Example 3.3 Sample SAS log. Take a look at Fig. 3.5. This shows the log output from a successful DATA step, followed by an unsuccessful PROC PRINT. The first thing we see listed on the log are SAS program statements for the DATA step. Notice that each statement is numbered as it is listed on the log. We see the three statements we've been discussing: DATA, INFILE, and INPUT. This step was written to create a temporary SAS dataset called TEST, containing the variables ALPHA, BETA, GAMMA, and DELTA. ALPHA and

GAMMA are character variables (notice the "$"), while BETA and DELTA are numeric. Since no column positions are specified, the data values were assumed to be separated by spaces.

If you are a mainframe programmer, you may be puzzled by the INFILE statement. Didn't we say that INFILE names the DDname? What is "c:\Examples\Chapt2\test.dat"? The answer is that this example was run on a PC, and on PCs you can provide the fully qualified external file name on the INFILE statement.

When the PROC PRINT statement was encountered, this signaled the end of the preceding DATA step. So the next thing we see is a series of messages produced by the supervisor as it executed the DATA step. Each message is preceded by the word "NOTE:".

The first message is one which appears for every INFILE statement. It tells us what the actual dataset name was. In this case, the message doesn't tell us anything we didn't already know (since we specified the fully qualified file name), but when the INFILE statement only names a DDname, it is helpful to know the actual dataset name.

Next, we see another message, telling us that nine records were read from the input file, and that both the minimum and maximum record lengths were twenty. Since the input file had nine records, we would expect the output SAS dataset to have nine observations; and in fact, the next message tells us that "the dataset WORK.TEST has 9 observations and 4 variables". The four variables are, of course, ALPHA, BETA, GAMMA, and DELTA. Notice that because we only specified a single level name (TEST) on the DATA statement, the default library name WORK was used; this is why the dataset is called WORK.TEST.

The last log message associated with the DATA step tells us that its execution used 15.00 seconds. With this step complete, we are free to resume reading additional program statements. Recall that we have already read the PROC PRINT statement. The VARS statement directs the PROC PRINT to print values of a variable EPSILON. We never created anything called EPSILON, only ALPHA, BETA, DELTA, and GAMMA. Sure enough, the next message we see says "ERROR:" rather than "NOTE:", and tells us that the variable EPSILON was not found.

Although a RUN statement is found which would normally start processing of the PROC PRINT step, we see a message which says "The SAS System stopped processing this step because of errors". The expected PROC PRINT output will not be created.

Finally, we see a note that the PROC PRINT step used 9.00 seconds. (Even though it did not complete normally, it did do some processing.)

From this example, we can get a flavor of the SAS log. It contains a simple listing of the program statements as they are read, interspersed with informational and error messages produced as the statements are processed. You need to remember that the program listing is sometimes one statement ahead of the execution (because a step is not executed until the next step is encountered).

Apart from error messages, possibly the most useful message is the one that says "the dataset...has x observations and y variables". This can give you a quick idea that the DATA step is at least generally correct. (If you see, "the dataset...has 0 observations", you probably have a problem!)

3.2.2   Error processing

The SAS supervisor accesses parsing modules which contain validation data for the different SAS steps. Although the supervisor can be forgiving in some instances, it cannot correct spelling or change punctuation. Error messages are printed on the SAS log. When a severe error is encountered, the supervisor will prevent execution of that step as well as all remaining steps in the program, but it will translate all remaining statements, detecting syntax errors that may be present in the later statements.

Certain severe, raw data input errors can cause the supervisor to

```
┌LOG
│Command ===)
│
│    1    DATA Test;
│    2    INFILE 'c:\Examples\Chapt2\test.dat';
│    3    Input Alpha $
│    4          Beta
│    5          Gamma $
│    6          Delta
│    7       ;
│    8    PROC PRINT;
│NOTE: The infile 'c:\Examples\Chapt2\test.dat' is file
│      C:\EXAMPLES\CHAPT2\TEST.DAT.
│NOTE: 9 records were read from the infile C:\EXAMPLES\CHAPT2\TEST.DAT.
│      The minimum record length was 28.
│      The maximum record length was 28.
│NOTE: The dataset WORK.TEST has 9 observations and 4 variables.
│NOTE: The DATA statement used 15.88 seconds.
│    9    VAR EPSILON;
│ERROR: Variable EPSILON not found.
│   18    RUN;
│NOTE: The SAS System stopped processing this step because of errors.
│NOTE: The PROCEDURE PRINT used 9.88 seconds.
```

Figure 3.5 Sample SAS log

print the data-record contents and all individual values. These errors include:

Lost Card End-of-file was reached on input before all INPUT variables could be read. (Note that input records are still referred to as "cards".)

Non-numeric Value for a Numeric Variable The system expects to find numeric values for numeric variables. It expects a period to indicate a missing numeric value (a blank will not do).

Example 3.4 Sample error diagnostics. Consider the following SAS program. It expects to read in five character values (A$, B$, C$, D$, and E$) and a numeric value (F) on each line of input. The input data is presented instream, preceded by a CARDS statement (see Sec. 3.1.3). Notice that only the first card contains all six of the expected values. What will happen when we try to read the rest?

```
DATA Errors;
INPUT A$ B$ C$ D$ E$ F;
CARDS;
a  b  c  d  e  1
a  b  c  d  e
a  b  c  d
a  b  c
a  b
a
;
```

Figure 3.6 is a snapshot of the log when we attempted to run this program. Notice that there are several messages about "invalid data for F", and another that says "SAS went to a new line when INPUT statement reached past the end of a line." Also notice that the output dataset (WORK.ERRORS) had only three observations, even though there were six input lines.

What happened was that the program "wrapped" the input lines in order to fill in as much as possible for each INPUT statement. When processing an INPUT statement, it will read as many cards as necessary to provide values for all the variables. When the INPUT statement is complete, any additional values on the current card are thrown away.

The first line ("a b c d e 1") was complete; all variables were filled, and an observation was created. However, when the second line ("a b c d e") was read, only five values were found; there was no value for F. So the supervisor went right on and read the next card ("a b c d"), and took the first value it found ("a") as the value of F. Unfortunately, this was the wrong value. But it completed the second input, and a second observation was created. Because the input is complete, the remainder of this card is discarded.

The third input finds an even stranger line ("a b c"), and it has to read two additional lines (first "a b", then "a") before it is complete. Now variables D, E, and F all have the wrong values! Still, a third observation is created. Since there is no more data, the DATA step ends here.

The remaining lines show execution of a PROC FREQ step. The output of the PROC FREQ will show us what values have actually been assigned to our six variables. We suspect that they will show some peculiar information.

The results for variables A and B are shown in Fig. 3.7. There's nothing very strange here. Variable A contains the value "a" three times, and variable B contains the value "b" three times.

Now look at Fig. 3.8. It says that variable C contains the value "c" three times, which is fine. But variable D contains "a" once, and "d" twice. The "a" snuck in when the program had to read extra cards for the third observation. Similarly, Fig. 3.9 shows that variable E has one incorrect value ("b").

Figure 3.9 also shows that even though variable F apparently does not have any incorrect values, there are two values "missing"

```
┌LOG══════════════════════════════════════════════════════════════════════
│Command ===)
│
│   65    DATA Errors;
│   66    INPUT A$ B$ C$ D$ E$ F;
│   67    CARDS;
│NOTE: Invalid data for F in line 70 1-1.
│RULE:----+----1----+----2----+----3----+----4----+----5----+----6----+----7---
│   70 a b c d
│A=a B=b C=c D=d E=e F=.  _ERROR_=1 _N_=2
│NOTE: Invalid data for F in line 73 1-1.
│   73 a
│A=a B=b C=c D=a E=b F=.  _ERROR_=1 _N_=3
│   74    ;
│NOTE: SAS went to a new line when INPUT statement reached past the end of a
│      line.
│NOTE: The dataset WORK.ERRORS has 3 observations and 6 variables.
│NOTE: The DATA statement used 17.88 seconds.
│   75
│   76    PROC FREQ;
│   77    TABLES  A B C D E F;
│   78    RUN;
│NOTE: The PROCEDURE FREQ used 22.88 seconds.
```

Figure 3.6 Wrapping of input lines

(because the total frequency is only one instead of three). Because F is a numeric variable, and the incorrect values were not numeric, they were never actually filled in. This is the source of the two error messages about "invalid data for F". (__N__=2 and __N__=3 refer to the fact that these errors occurred on the second and third observations.) This message will not always appear when incorrect values are assigned, only when there is a numeric vs character mismatch; notice that no messages were printed for D and E.

What have we learned from this rather exhaustive analysis? First, that SAS does not necessarily preserve the physical input lines; we saw that several input lines were combined into one observation. Second, that you should be very careful to ensure that the list on your INPUT statement corresponds to the actual data; the only reliable warning is a somewhat weak "SAS went to a new line when INPUT statement reached past the end of a line." Third, that SAS does print the complete input record when it recognizes a problem. And fourth, that some problems are not enough to stop SAS from going ahead and processing the rest of the program.

3.3 MORE PROCESSING CONTROL

The SAS System provides many options for standard as well as non-standard external file INFILE conversions. Additionally, there are

```
┌OUTPUT══════════════════════════════════
│Command ===>

                        SAS

                              Cumulative  Cumulative
  A        Frequency  Percent  Frequency    Percent
  ---------------------------------------------------
  a            3      100.0         3        100.0


                              Cumulative  Cumulative
  B        Frequency  Percent  Frequency    Percent
  ---------------------------------------------------
  b            3      100.0         3        100.0



```

Figure 3.7 PROC FREQ with wrapped input lines

```
┌OUTPUT════════════════════════════════════════════
│Command ===>
│                              SAS
│
│                                   Cumulative  Cumulative
│         C      Frequency   Percent  Frequency    Percent
│         ---------------------------------------------------
│         c          3       100.0        3        100.0
│
│
│                                   Cumulative  Cumulative
│         D      Frequency   Percent  Frequency    Percent
│         ---------------------------------------------------
│         a          1        33.3        1         33.3
│         d          2        66.7        3        100.0
│
│
```

Figure 3.8   Continuation of Figure 3.7

```
┌OUTPUT════════════════════════════════════════════
│Command ===>
│                              SAS
│
│                                   Cumulative  Cumulative
│         E      Frequency   Percent  Frequency    Percent
│         ---------------------------------------------------
│         b          1        33.3        1         33.3
│         e          2        66.7        3        100.0
│
│
│                                   Cumulative  Cumulative
│       F    Frequency   Percent  Frequency    Percent
│       ---------------------------------------------------
│       1        1       100.0        1         100.0
│
│              Frequency Missing = 2
│
```

Figure 3.9   Continuation of Figure 3.8

various INPUT methods for reading a variety of formatted raw data. This section covers some of the most frequently used raw data input options.

3.3.1 Preventing unwanted input line wrapping

Normally, one record is translated variable by variable into one observation. This means the program expects to find values for each variable listed in your code. If there are not enough values, the program will proceed to the next line to acquire data values for the remaining variables. We saw the effects of this in the previous section 3.2.2. You can override this default of line "wrapping" by using the MISSOVER or STOPOVER options. Both MISSOVER and STOPOVER are specified on the INFILE statement.

MISSOVER tells the supervisor to assign a value of "missing" to variables that have been defined but for which no values were found prior to the end of an input record. Note that "missing" has a definite meaning in a SAS dataset. It explicitly indicates that there is no data value for the variable in this observation. In output from SAS report procedures, the variable will print as a period ("."). MISSOVER (and the "missing" value in general) is useful in research, where some data fields may have been impossible to collect.

STOPOVER says to stop processing immediately, rather than assign missing values, thereby constituting an error. STOPOVER is preferable when it would be illogical for any data value to be missing.

Example 3.5 MISSOVER and STOPOVER. In this example, we'll see the effect of the MISSOVER and STOPOVER options. We'll use an input file which does not match the INPUT statement. We'll run our program three times: first, with neither MISSOVER nor STOPOVER; second, with MISSOVER; and third, with STOPOVER.

Here is the input file, a PC file called c:MISSTOP.DAT:

```
1 2 3 4 5 6 7 8 9
1 2 3 4 5 6
1 2 3 4 5
1 2 3 4
1
1 2 3 4 5 6 7 8 9
```

Each of the following programs reads it into a SAS dataset. The first program does not specify MISSOVER or STOPOVER.

Program 1

```
DATA _data_;
INFILE 'c:misstop.dat';
INPUT one two three four five six seven eight nine;
PROC PRINT;
RUN;
```

Figures 3.10 and 3.11 show the log and output of this program. As you can see, the DATA step has assigned the values to the variables in a "first come, first served" fashion. As a result, the output shows only three observations from a six-records input.

Notice our telltale error message ("SAS went to a new line . . ."), and the "wrapped" values in variables FIVE, SIX, SEVEN, EIGHT, and NINE. (ONE, TWO, THREE, and FOUR are all right, since there are always enough values to fill them.)

Now, let's try the same program, but with the MISSOVER option. Note that it's specified on the INFILE statement.

Program 2

```
DATA _data_;
INFILE 'c:\examples\chapt3\misstop.dat' MISSOVER;
INPUT one two three four five six seven eight nine;
```

```
┌─LOG───────────────────────────────────────────────────────────┐
│ Command ===>                                                    │
│                                                                 │
│     11          DATA _data_;                                    │
│     12          INFILE 'c:\examples\chapt3\misstop.dat';        │
│     13          INPUT one two three four five six seven eight nine; │
│     14          PROC PRINT;                                     │
│ NOTE: The infile 'c:\examples\chapt3\misstop.dat' is file       │
│       C:\EXAMPLES\CHAPT3\MISSTOP.DAT.                           │
│ NOTE: 6 records were read from the infile C:\EXAMPLES\CHAPT3\MISSTOP.DAT. │
│       The minimum record length was 1.                          │
│       The maximum record length was 17.                         │
│ NOTE: SAS went to a new line when INPUT statement reached past the end of a │
│       line.                                                     │
│ NOTE: The dataset WORK.DATA3 has 3 observations and 9 variables. │
│ NOTE: The DATA statement used 15.00 seconds.                   │
│     15          RUN;                                            │
│ NOTE: The PROCEDURE PRINT used 11.00 seconds.                  │
│                                                                 │
│                                                                 │
│                                                                 │
│                                                                 │
└─────────────────────────────────────────────────────────────┘
```

Figure 3.10   Default line wrap processing

```
┌OUTPUT═══════════════════════════════════════════════════════════════
│Command ===)
│                                SAS
│OBS    ONE    TWO    THREE    FOUR    FIVE    SIX    SEVEN    EIGHT    NINE
│ 1      1      2       3       4       5       6       7        8        9
│ 2      1      2       3       4       5       6       1        2        3
│ 3      1      2       3       4       1       1       2        3        4
│
│
│
│
│
│
│                         ⌁
│
│
│
│
│
│
│
└──────────────────────────────────────────────────────────────────────
```

Figure 3.11   Output from Figure 3.10

```
PROC PRINT;
RUN;
```

Figures 3.12 and 3.13 show the log and output of this program. The
DATA step has assigned values to the variables as they are found
on the current input record. If there are not enough values on the
current input record, the remaining variables on that input record
are set to "missing". With MISSOVER (in this instance), the number of records read in equals the number of records output.

Now, let's see how STOPOVER affects our processing.

Program 3

```
DATA _data_;
INFILE 'c:\examples\chapt3\misstop.dat' STOPOVER;
INPUT one two three four five six seven eight nine;
PROC PRINT;
RUN;
```

Figures 3.14 and 3.15 show the log and output of this program.
Note that STOPOVER immediately halted the processing when it
found an input record which did not have a value for each variable

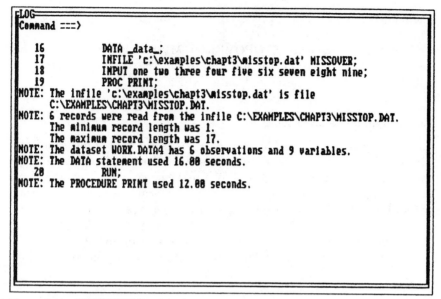

```
┌LOG══════════════════════════════════════════════════════════════════
│Command ===>
│
│   16              DATA _data_;
│   17              INFILE 'c:\examples\chapt3\misstop.dat' MISSOVER;
│   18              INPUT one two three four five six seven eight nine;
│   19              PROC PRINT;
│NOTE: The infile 'c:\examples\chapt3\misstop.dat' is file
│      C:\EXAMPLES\CHAPT3\MISSTOP.DAT.
│NOTE: 6 records were read from the infile C:\EXAMPLES\CHAPT3\MISSTOP.DAT.
│      The minimum record length was 1.
│      The maximum record length was 17.
│NOTE: The dataset WORK.DATA4 has 6 observations and 9 variables.
│NOTE: The DATA statement used 16.00 seconds.
│   20              RUN;
│NOTE: The PROCEDURE PRINT used 12.00 seconds.
│
│
```

Figure 3.12   MISSOVER processing

```
┌OUTPUT════════════════════════════════════════════════════════════════
│Command ===>
│
│                                    SAS
│
│   OBS    ONE    TWO    THREE    FOUR    FIVE    SIX    SEVEN    EIGHT    NINE
│
│    1      1      2       3       4       5       6      7        8        9
│    2      1      2       3       4       5       6      .        .        .
│    3      1      2       3       4       5       .      .        .        .
│    4      1      2       3       4       .       .      .        .        .
│    5      1      .       .       .       .       .      .        .        .
│    6      1      2       3       4       5       6      7        8        9
│
│
│
```

Figure 3.13   Output from Figure 3.12

defined (so the output dataset only has the first, complete observation).

If you do not specify STOPOVER or MISSOVER, you will probably get a LOSTCARD error message when the INPUT statement is "out of sync" with the actual data values.

3.3.2 End-of-file processing

You can specify a variable that represents the end-of-file condition. It is a Boolean variable in that it is initialized to 0 and is set to 1 when the current input record is the last record in the file. This option is most useful when you want to perform a statement or group of statements after all input lines have been read.

You specify the end-of-file variable by using the END= option on the INFILE statement. For example, to create an end-of-file variable called DONE for an input file called CUSTMAST, you would code

```
INFILE CUSTMAST END=DONE;
```

Note that the END=boolean has a value of 1 while the last record is being processed. This is different from some other languages (notably COBOL), where you must wait until after the last record to realize the end-of-file condition. Because the SAS supervisor acts as

```
┌LOG
│Command ===>
│
│    21          DATA _data_;
│    22          INFILE 'c:\examples\chapt3\misstop.dat' STOPOVER;
│    23          INPUT one two three four five six seven eight nine;
│    24          PROC PRINT;
│ERROR: INPUT statement exceeded record length.
│       INFILE 'c:\examples\chapt3\misstop.dat' OPTION STOPOVER specified.
│RULE:----+----1----+----2----+----3----+----4----+----5----+----6----+----7---
│    2 1 2 3 4 5 6
│ONE=1 TWO=2 THREE=3 FOUR=4 FIVE=5 SIX=6 SEVEN=. EIGHT=. NINE=. _ERROR_=1 _N_=2
│NOTE: The infile 'c:\examples\chapt3\misstop.dat' is file
│      C:\EXAMPLES\CHAPT3\MISSTOP.DAT.
│NOTE: 2 records were read from the infile C:\EXAMPLES\CHAPT3\MISSTOP.DAT.
│      The minimum record length was 11.
│      The maximum record length was 17.
│NOTE: The dataset WORK.DATA5 has 1 observations and 9 variables.
│NOTE: The DATA statement used 16.00 seconds.
│    25          RUN;
│NOTE: The PROCEDURE PRINT used 11.00 seconds.
```

Figure 3.14 STOPOVER processing

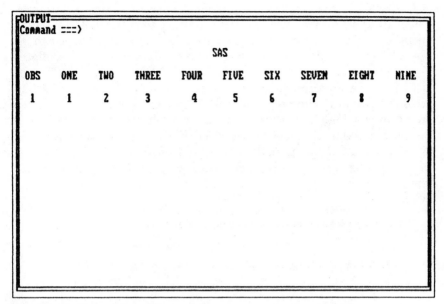

Figure 3.15 Output from Figure 3.14

a layer between your program and the actual I/O, it can "look ahead" and "tell" the program this additional information.

Example 3.6 INFILE with END = boolean option. In this example, we will read through an input file called RESPONSE, setting an end-of-file variable called FINISHED when the last record is being processed. For each record, we accumulate a field called RESP into a total called TOTRESP. When FINISHED is set, we print the final value of TOTRESP. (Note: We have not previously seen this "spontaneous creation" of a variable that is not on the input dataset. TOTRESP is created as a numeric variable simply because it is to be used in an arithmetic statement.)

```
DATA;
INFILE RESPONSE END=FINISHED;
INPUT @1 ACCT 9.
      @10 SCORE ZD5.4
      @15 RESP 3.;
TOTRESP + RESP;
IF FINISHED PUT 'TOTAL RESPONSE: 'TOTRESP;
```

Note: "IF FINISHED" means the same as "IF FINISHED = 1". There are some cases in which the END= option will not work. In particular, when you use instream data (using the CARDS statement), the SAS program cannot do the "look ahead" required to set the END= variable properly. For instream data or other unbuffered files, you can use the EOF= option. With EOF=, you do not name a Boolean variable; instead, you name a statement label; i.e. a particular location in the program. (SAS statement labels are names followed by a colon.) This creates an implicit GOTO when end-of-file is reached, similar to the COBOL "AT END" clause. As with "AT END", the EOF= option does not take effect until after the last record has been processed. EOF= always works; that is, it works for the cases when END= works and also those where END= does not work.

Example 3.7 INFILE with EOF= statement label option.

```
DATA;
INFILE RESPONSE EOF=FINISHED;
INPUT @1 ACCT 9.
      @10 SCORE ZD5.4
      @15 RESP 3.;
TOTRESP + RESP;
RETURN;
FINISHED: PUT 'TOTAL RESPONSE: 'TOTRESP;
RETURN;
```

Note: The RETURN statement acts as the read loop delimiter. Its function is to "get" another record and return to the statements at the top of the implied read loop. Most of the time a RETURN statement is not necessary, since there is an implied RETURN at the end of the DATA step. However, here we must avoid falling through to the FINISHED routine; hence, the RETURN statement. For a more detailed explanation of RETURN and how to use it, see Chapter 6.

3.3.3 Holding the input line

If you look closely at the INPUT statement format, you'll see that although it allows you to read in many variables, it is actually just one statement. When the supervisor encounters the semicolon that indicates the end of the INPUT statement, it automatically releases the input line (although not the output observation, which is held until the end of all statements in this iteration of the DATA step loop.) But suppose that you want to stop input temporarily, to check a data value, for example. You will have to tell the DATA step to hold the input line if you intend to stop and then resume input of other values.

Example 3.8 When and how to hold the input line. Suppose you want to read in a file that may have bad data in columns 5–6. These columns are supposed to contain a 2-byte number, but the raw data may contain spaces in that position. Your job is to read the data into a SAS dataset and at the same time, correct the missing codes by changing them to zero.

To accomplish this, we must examine more closely the "@" sign we've been using in our INPUT statements. Up to now, we've been using it solely to point to a particular column on the input record. For example, we've been coding

```
INPUT @72 AGE 2.;
```

The "@" sign has a more general use, however. It represents the SAS internal pointer. If you use it without a column number, it holds the line until any of these statements is executed: a RETURN (implied or explicit), a DELETE, or another INPUT statement that does not end with @. When the @ sign is used to hold an input line, it is called a "trailing @" sign.

This means we can input selected variables from a record, then stop and check them. If appropriate, we can then input some more variables (and so on). As always, the variables do not have to be in order; the first INPUT statement can name a variable at the end of the record, and the second INPUT statement can take fields from the beginning.

Here's a program that checks and fixes our problem values in columns 5–6. Note the "trailing @" in the first INPUT statement. This ensures that the input record will be held for the second INPUT statement (which might otherwise wrap to the next line).

```
DATA FIX;
   INFILE MIXEDATA;
   INPUT @5 CODE        $CHAR2.
        @;  /* holds the line */
   IF CODE = '  ' then CODE = '00';
   INPUT @1  SUBSCRIP  IB4.;
   RUN;       /* implicit RETURN releases the line */
```

This technique is also useful in cases where there are several different types of records intermixed on the input file. For example, an "H" in column 80 may denote a header record, which has a different input layout from detail records, which have "D" in column 80. In the following code, we first read this record type, holding the input line with a trailing @. Then we select the appropriate processing (including additional INPUT) depending on its value.

```
DATA PAYFILE;
    INFILE RAWDATA;
    INPUT @80 RECTYPE $CHAR1.
        @;
    IF RECTYPE = 'D'
        THEN INPUT @1 EMP_ID $CHAR5.
                   @10 SALARY PD7.2;
    IF RECTYPE = 'H'
        THEN INPUT @12 CTRL_TOT PD9.2;
```

Remember that input records are always released at the bottom of the DATA step read loop. That is, each time we return to the top of the loop, the current record is discarded and a new record will be read. The trailing @ does not change this; it only holds the input line until the end of the current iteration of the read loop.

There are times when you may need to hold the input line even after a RETURN is issued, such as when your input spans several input lines or your input record contains several observations. You will need something stronger than a single trailing @ sign. It may come as no surprise that this stronger hold is accomplished with a "trailing @@" sign! The @@ at the end of a fixed format or formatted input will hold the position in the line until another INPUT statement is executed that *does not* end in a "@@" or until end-of-file is reached.

Example 3.9 Multiple observations from a single input line.   In this example, our input contains several logical observations on each input record. We want to separate them and create several observations in the SAS dataset. By default, the DATA step will release the entire record after creating the first observation, causing us to lose the rest of the information. However, by using a trailing @@, we can hold the input line across repetitions of the DATA step loop and achieve correct results.

```
DATA MULTI;
INPUT TEST @@;
CARDS;
111 222 333 444 555 666 777
;
```

The results are shown in Fig. 3.16. Notice that the dataset WORK.MULTI has seven observations and one variable. The seven observations correspond to the seven values on the input record. By using the trailing @@, we were able to hold that record until all data was exhausted. Without the trailing @@, we would have created one observation and then discarded the record.

Example 3.10 A single observation from multiple input lines. This example is the converse of the preceding one. Here, we want to combine seven input lines into a single observation. The observation will contain an array of seven values.

```
DATA Single;
Array nums {*} $3 n1-n7;
DO i = 1 to 7;
    Input nums {i} @@;
END;
CARDS;
111
222
333
444
555
666
777
;
```

```
┌LOG──────────────────────────────────────────────────────────
│Command ===>
│
│   45      DATA Multi;
│   46      Input test @@;
│   47      CARDS;
│   49        ;
│NOTE: SAS went to a new line when INPUT statement reached past the end of a
│      line.
│NOTE: The dataset WORK.MULTI has 7 observations and 1 variables.
│NOTE: The DATA statement used 13.00 seconds.
```

Figure 3.16   Multiple observations from a single input line

Note the results in Fig. 3.17. As desired, we created one observation. The eight variables are the seven elements of our array, plus one.

3.3.4 Reading files with a variable length header

Sometimes, production programs attach a leading header identifying the date and/or job description to output files. This effectively changes the absolute positions of the data values, but not their position relative to the start of the actual record.

In order to create a conversion DATA step that can be used regardless of the length of the leading header, you can use relative position input. This simply means replacing the literal numbers in the "@" clauses with variables and expressions. Instead of coding

```
INPUT @72      AGE    2.
      @74      WEIGHT 3.;
```

we can code

```
INPUT @COL     AGE    2.
      @COL + 2 WEIGHT 3.;
```

This makes the INPUT statement instantly "relocatable", just by

```
┌LOG────────────────────────────────────────────────────────┐
│Command ===)                                                │
│                                                            │
│  64    DATA Single;            /* Output data set is 'SINGLE'       */
│  65    Array nums {*} $3 n1-n7; /* Define array: 7 occurs, 3 byte char */
│  66    DO i = 1 to 7;          /* Read the 7 values ...             */
│  67       Input nums {i} @@;   /* .. using @@ to keep same input line */
│  68    END;                                                │
│  69    CARDS;                  /* CARDS means data follows ...       */
│  77    ;                       /* .. end of data (data is not shown)  */
│NOTE: SAS went to a new line when INPUT statement reached past the end of a │
│      line.                                                  │
│NOTE: The dataset WORK.SINGLE has 1 observations and 8 variables. │
│NOTE: The DATA statement used 17.00 seconds.                │
│                                                            │
└────────────────────────────────────────────────────────────┘
```

Figure 3.17 Single observation from multiple input lines

changing the value of COL. (COL is not a keyword; you can use any valid SAS name.)

Example 3.11 Relative position input. In this example, the input file PROD001 may start with a 16-byte header identified by the word "PROD" in position 1 through 4. If this is the case, then the value for ACCOUNT is actually in bytes 17 through 25 and LST_TRAN's value is found in position 26 through 29. If PROD001 does not have the 16-byte header, the program will begin accepting the values from an offset of 0.

```
DATA OUTPUT.DATA;
    INFILE PROD001;
    INPUT @1  HEADER $CHAR4. @;
    IF HEADER =  'PROD' THEN COLUM = 16;
                       ELSE COLUM = 0;
    INPUT   @COLUM + 1   ACCOUNT   9.
            @COLUM + 10  LST_TRAN  $CHAR4.
            @COLUM + 14  REVENUE   IB4.
            @COLUM + 18  RETURNS   IB4.
            ;
```

3.4 PROCESSING INSTREAM DATA

There are times when you want to process a few records and don't really want to bother with setting up an external file. You may have summary statistics or point coordinates to graph; you may just have test data. At any rate, you'd like to include your data directly in the SAS program. The CARDS statement is used to accomplish this.

3.4.1 The instream conversion DATA step

Instream data, because it is not yet in SAS table form, is considered external data and must be converted prior to use. Figure 3.18 shows the DATA step using instream data. (The description can include the same attributes described in external file input or you may want to take advantage of list INPUT, as we've done in several preceding examples.)

The instream conversion DATA step is identical to the external file conversion DATA step with one exception: the INFILE statement is replaced by a CARDS statement.

3.4.2 List input

List input was designed to let you define input variables quickly and easily. It can be used with external files, but is most frequently used

```
DATA temporary or permanent name;
   INPUT variable1 description
         variable2 description
         . . .
         variable  description
   ;
   CARDS;
   data values
   ;
```

Figure 3.18 DATA step for instream input

for instream input. Instead of coding start position, variable name, and format, all you have to do is code the variable name (putting a "$" after the name if the variable is character). For example,

```
INPUT ACCT_NUM NAME $ ADDR $ CITY $ BALANCE;
```

In order to use $, your raw data must comply with certain rules.

1. Data values must be separated by at least one space.

2. Each input record must have a data value (or a missing value '.') for every variable named in the INPUT statement.

3. Character variables may not contain blanks, and may be no more than 8 bytes long (unless format modifiers "&" or ":" are used, as described in the next section).

Example 3.12 List input. This program reads an instream card file. Each record is expected to contain three values, representing the color, ID number, and price of an item. Color is a character variable (notice the "$"); ID number and price are numeric. Notice that in list input, the supervisor takes all responsibility for understanding the length and format of each item, including proper handling of decimal places.

Note: If you do not include the "." missing value place saver in the last card, the value 1.26 would be wrongly associated with ID_NUM instead of PRICE. The supervisor would attempt to get another input card for PRICE, and then print a LOSTCARD message on the SAS log because it can't find the final data value.

```
DATA LIST;
   INPUT COLOR $ ID_NUM PRICE;
   CARDS;
   RED 12345 3.95
   YELLOW 10006 2.97
   GREEN . 1.26
   ;
```

3.4.3 List input format modifiers

The format modifiers ":" and "&" can be used to help read in character variable data values that do not conform to the list input rules (i.e., only eight characters and no blanks).

The length modifier ":" instructs the DATA step to assign a specific number of bytes of data to the variable. These bytes can contain embedded spaces. Place : before the $ if you want the variable to include only bytes up to the first embedded blank found. This overrides the 8-byte restriction, but not the "no blanks" restriction.

The format modifier "&" allows you to read in values that contain blanks. The only requirement is that data values be separated by at least two spaces, rather than one. This overrides both the 8-byte and "no blanks" restrictions, but requires additional care to make sure that the values are separated by two spaces.

Example 3.13 List input with format modifiers. This example shows how you would read in variable position data or data with embedded blanks. Our data includes CITY, which does not include any blanks (none of our customers lives in Los Angeles or Des Moines). We also have a single field called STATEZIP, which includes both the state and ZIP code, separated by a blank, and a NAME, which may also include blanks.

The format : $ indicates that the value for the character variable CITY includes all characters up to the first blank (thus, it does not spill over to the state information).

The format & $ indicates that STATEZIP can contain blanks, but not two blanks in a row. "&" before a character format lets you read in character data that is longer than 8 bytes and also contains embedded blanks.

Refer to Fig. 3.19 for the output of this program. Notice that the values were grouped correctly and assigned to the proper variables.

```
DATA SPECIALS;
INPUT CITY : $   STATEZIP & $ NAME & $20.;
CARDS;
Chicago IL  60611    Lotta Nerve
Brooklyn NY 11235    Will N. Testament
;
PROC PRINT;
RUN;
```

3.4.4   Listing the variables in a SAS dataset

After you have created a SAS dataset, you can check to see that it includes all the correct variables by running PROC CONTENTS.

PROC CONTENTS shows information about the SAS dataset as a whole and lists each variable in the dataset, along with its type, length, position, and label. Actual values of the variables are not shown (You would use PROC PRINT for that.) Two examples are:

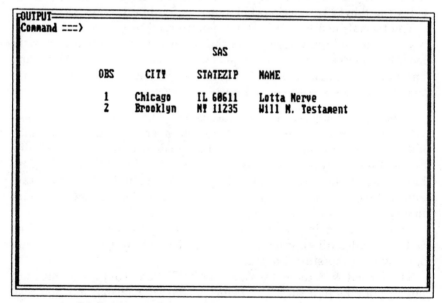

Figure 3.19   Dataset created with list input

```
PROC CONTENTS DATA=REVENUE;
PROC CONTENTS DATA=SASLIB1.PAYROLL;
```

We have now seen how to create SAS datasets from all forms of external raw data. This has required a fair amount of programming. In the next chapter, you will see how this pays off, as you learn to generate some useful reports that require very little programming at all.

Simple Report Preparation

The SAS System has a number of procedures designed to create informal as well as formal reports. In this chapter you will be introduced to several of the more common report procedures: PROC PRINT and PROC FREQ. You'll also learn two other procedures (PROC SORT and PROC FORMAT) that are used to get your data in shape for more descriptive reporting.

PROC PRINT and PROC FREQ allow you to create quick, attractively arranged reports with a minimum of coding (sometimes one line is enough!). For more control over the output of your report, see Chapter 6, which describes the use of the DATA step as a reporting tool.

4.1 WHOLE-FILE OPERATIONS: THE PROC STEP

In Chapter 3 you became familiar with using the DATA step. The DATA step allows you to control processing at the detail level of variables and observations. PROC steps, on the other hand, are designed primarily for "whole-file" operations; the procedure seems to act on the file as a whole. For example, PROC SORT takes in a SAS dataset, and produces a new SAS dataset in sort sequence. Other procedures may calculate the mean or other statistics on the entire dataset. The inner workings of the procedure are transparent.

Example 4.1 Scope of DATA vs PROC steps. Here's a DATA step which reads through a SAS dataset and outputs selected records.

```
DATA PICKEM;
   SET BUDGET;
   IF ACCT = 755 THEN OUTPUT;
```

We can see exactly what is going on, because the DATA step is programmed at a detail level. Remember that the DATA step is actually a read loop, so the whole group of statements is executed once for each input observation.

Now here's a PROC step which sorts a SAS dataset.

```
PROC SORT DATA=BUDGET;
   BY CYCLE;
```

PROC steps may look more inscrutable, because you cannot see the inner workings. The statements which follow them don't specify any procedure or action; instead, they are basically parameters to the "whole-file" operation. It doesn't make sense to think of PROC SORT as a loop, doing something called "BY CYCLE" for each observation. You have to think of it as a whole: it will sort the entire BUDGET file on a key called CYCLE.

4.2   INSTANT REPORT #1: PROC PRINT

We refer to PROC PRINT as an instant report. It is perhaps the most frequently used PROC for quick ad hoc reporting, and it is breathtakingly easy to specify. To execute PROC PRINT, you code:

```
PROC PRINT;
```

That's all! Of course, there are variations on this, but just the simple PROC PRINT will provide a neatly formatted list of all the values in a dataset. Each observation is listed on a new line, and there is a column for each variable. The variable names are shown as column headings, and proper page breaks are taken.

PROC PRINT can act only on SAS datasets, not external files. This is true of all PROCs. Now you know why information on converting raw data into a SAS dataset presented in Chapter 3 is so important.

By default, PROC PRINT acts on the SAS dataset you created in the most recent step. To print another dataset, you can use the DATA= option. For example, to print a dataset called BUDGET, you would code:

```
PROC PRINT DATA=BUDGET;
```

4.2.1 Detail lists: an extended example

Suppose that your installation creates sales performance reports from data electronically transmitted to your mainframe. Although you have a batch COBOL program that updates the Sales master file with this information (including a 10 percent commission and a 22-cent-per-mile allowance for miles traveled), you want to check a sample before authorizing the job to update.

The following program converts the raw data and creates a SAS dataset. Then, it runs PROC PRINT. This is the easiest way to check the data.

The results are shown in Fig. 4.1. Notice that each observation is listed on a new line. The observations are numbered in a column labeled "OBS". The remaining columns represent the variables in the SAS dataset, which are the variables created in the DATA step. Any missing values are indicated by the usual "."; there was no SALES_ID found for observations 5, 8, and 16.

```
/* READ THE RAW DATA FILE    */
DATA SLSPRF;
     INFILE   SALESIN;
     /* INPUT VARIABLES:     */
     INPUT
     @ 1    SALES_ID    4.
     @ 5    MONTH       $CHAR2.
     @ 7    MEALS       5.2
     @ 17   MILEAGE     5.
     @ 22   SALES       7.
     ;
     /* THE FOLLOWING STATEMENTS CREATE NEW */
     /* VARIABLES                           */
     M_ALLOW        = .22 * MILEAGE;
     COMMISS        = .10 * SALES;
RUN;
/* PRINT THE ENTIRE SAS DATASET, ONE LINE PER */
/* OBSERVATION:                               */
PROC PRINT;
/* WE COULD ALSO SAY "PROC PRINT DATA=SLSPRF;" */
RUN;
```

The output in Fig. 4.1 illustrates "full default" processing. It makes the following assumptions. (The following sections in this

```
┌OUTPUT══════════════════════════════════════════════════════
│Command ═══>
│                              SAS
│ OBS   SALES_ID   MONTH   MEALS   MILEAGE   SALES   M_ALLOW   COMMISS
│  1       5        82     22.25     115     18755    25.38    1875.5
│  2       1        85     27.83      14     74357     3.88    7435.7
│  3       1        84     38.94      99     38787    21.78    3878.7
│  4       1        82     43.38      67     98755    14.74    9875.5
│  5       .        83     45.78     117     44674    25.74    4467.4
│  6      11        84     63.36      51     34677    11.22    3467.7
│  7       1        83     62.44     221     44673    48.62    4467.3
│  8       .        85     63.53      18     87832     2.28    8783.2
│  9       1        81     75.53     123     45755    27.86    4575.5
│ 10       5        84     74.36     189      8787    23.98     878.7
│ 11      11        85     74.98     201     87832    44.22    8783.2
│ 12       5        85     77.98     214     87832    47.88    8783.2
│ 13      11        82     88.25     111     98475    24.42    9847.5
│ 14      11        81     88.25      15     58657     3.38    5865.7
│ 15       5        83    117.88      73     34673    16.86    3467.3
│ 16       .        81    118.25      34     58657     7.48    5865.7
│ 17      11        83    142.88      33     44674     7.26    4467.4
└─────────────────────────────────────────────────────────────
```

Figure 4.1   Simple PROC PRINT output

chapter will show you how to make modifications to most of the defaults.)

1. Input dataset is the last SAS dataset created.

2. Output is directed to the default output device indicated for your installation.

3. Values will be printed for every variable and observation in the input dataset in the order they were named in the step which created the original dataset.

4. Observations are numbered on the report.

5. Report layout is determined by the system to produce what it considers a good fit for each line, centered on the page.

6. Column labels are simply the variable names.

7. Report title defaults to "SAS".

8. Print formats for each variable are chosen by the system; they will accurately represent all values, but may not be the most "reasonable" format. (Note: only one decimal place for COMMISS in Fig. 4.1.)

4.2.2 Selecting and ordering the printed variables

By default, PROC PRINT displays all of the values for all of the variables in all of the observations in the dataset. They are listed in the order they were read and/or created by the converting DATA step. If you want to include only some variables, you can add a VAR statement. The VAR statement consists of the keyword VAR, followed by names of all the variables you want to display, separated by spaces. Any other variables will not be displayed. Figure 4.2 is a listing of our SLSPRF dataset using the following PROC PRINT:

```
PROC PRINT;
    VAR SALES_ID MONTH MEALS M_ALLOW COMMISS;
```

You can also use the VAR statement to list the variables in a different order, for clarity or emphasis. The output in Fig. 4.3 was produced with this PROC PRINT:

```
PROC PRINT:
VAR MONTH SALES_ID COMMISS MEALS M_ALLOW;
```

In our examples so far, PROC PRINT has identified the observations by automatically numbering them in an OBS column. Suppose you thought a different variable would provide a more useful ID than the sequential numbers. The numbering sequence can be replaced by using the ID statement. This statement consists of the ID keyword, plus the name of the identification variable. When you use ID, the

```
┌OUTPUT═══════════════════════════════════════════════════
│Command ═══>
│                              SAS
│
│    OBS     SALES_ID    MONTH    MEALS    M_ALLOW    COMMISS
│
│     1         .          81     110.25      7.48     5865.7
│     2         .          83      45.78     25.74     4467.4
│     3         .          85      63.53      2.20     8783.2
│     4         1          81      75.53     27.86     4575.5
│     5         1          82      43.30     14.74     9875.5
│     6         1          83      62.44     48.62     4467.3
│     7         1          84      38.94     21.78     3870.7
│     8         1          85      27.03      3.08     7435.7
│     9         5          82      22.25     25.30     1875.5
│    10         5          83     117.88     16.86     3467.3
│    11         5          84      74.36     23.98      870.7
│    12         5          85      77.90     47.08     8783.2
│    13        11          81      80.25      3.30     5865.7
│    14        11          82      80.25     24.42     9847.5
│    15        11          83     142.88      7.26     4467.4
│    16        11          84      63.36     11.22     3467.7
│    17        11          85      74.90     44.22     8783.2
```

Figure 4.2   PROC PRINT using VAR

```
┌OUTPUT════════════════════════════════════════════════════════╗
│Command ===)                                                   ║
║                            SAS                                ║
║                                                               ║
║   OBS   MONTH   SALES_ID   COMMISS   MEALS   M_ALLOW          ║
║    1     81        .        5865.7   110.25    7.48           ║
║    2     83        .        4467.4    45.78   25.74           ║
║    3     85        .        8783.2    63.53    2.20           ║
║    4     81        1        4575.5    75.53   27.06           ║
║    5     82        1        9875.5    43.30   14.74           ║
║    6     83        1        4467.3    62.44   48.62           ║
║    7     84        1        3870.7    38.94   21.78           ║
║    8     85        1        7435.7    27.03    3.08           ║
║    9     82        5        1875.5    22.25   25.30           ║
║   10     83        5        3467.3   117.88   16.06           ║
║   11     84        5         870.7    74.36   23.98           ║
║   12     85        5        8783.2    77.90   47.88           ║
║   13     81       11        5865.7    80.25    3.30           ║
║   14     82       11        9847.5    80.25   24.42           ║
║   15     83       11        4467.4   142.88    7.26           ║
║   16     84       11        3467.7    63.36   11.22           ║
║   17     85       11        8783.2    74.90   44.22           ║
╚═══════════════════════════════════════════════════════════════╝
```

Figure 4.3   PROC PRINT using VAR to reorder variables

column of observation numbers is replaced by a column for the specified variable. For example, we can print our SLSPRF dataset using SALES_ID as identification on each line, using the following PROC PRINT. The result is shown in Fig. 4.4.

```
PROC PRINT:
    VAR MONTH COMMISS MEALS M_ALLOW;
    ID SALES_ID;


    /* IT DOESN'T MATTER WHICH COMES FIRST: */
    /* THE VAR STATEMENT OR THE ID STATEMENT */
```

If you want to suppress the observation numbers without substituting an ID variable, you can use the NOOBS option on the PROC PRINT statement:

```
PROC PRINT NOOBS;
```

4.2.3   Accumulating totals automatically

The SUM statement allows you to include totals in your PROC PRINT output. Like VAR, the SUM statement consists of the keyword (SUM) followed by a list of variables, separated by spaces. (Are you seeing a pattern here? This is the basic format of most PROC

```
┌OUTPUT
│Command ===)

                            SAS

        SALES_ID   MONTH   COMMISS    MEALS    M_ALLOW
           .        81      5865.7    110.25      7.48
           .        83      4467.4     45.78     25.74
           .        85      8783.2     63.53      2.20
           1        81      4575.5     75.53     27.86
           1        82      9875.5     43.30     14.74
           1        83      4467.3     62.44     48.62
           1        84      3870.7     38.94     21.78
           1        85      7435.7     27.03      3.08
           5        82      1875.5     22.25     25.30
           5        83      3467.3    117.88     16.86
           5        84       870.7     74.36     23.98
           5        85      8783.2     77.90     47.08
          11        81      5865.7     80.25      3.30
          11        82      9847.5     80.25     24.42
          11        83      4467.4    142.88      7.26
          11        84      3467.7     63.36     11.22
          11        85      8783.2     74.90     44.22
```

Figure 4.4   PROC PRINT using ID

step statements.) In this case, the variables must be numeric. The effect is to print totals for each listed variable at the end of the report. The following PROC PRINT contains a SUM statement, which extends our report with the total lines shown in Fig. 4.5. You can use VAR, ID, and SUM in any order.

```
PROC PRINT;
    VAR MONTH COMMISS MEALS M_ALLOW;
    ID SALES_ID;
    SUM COMMISS MEALS M_ALLOW;
```

4.2.4 Using dataset options to limit the number of observations

A dataset option is an option that allows SAS to use a different view of the dataset for a particular step. Dataset options are always enclosed in parentheses immediately after the name of the dataset they modify. Remember that PROC PRINT (like most PROCs) uses the DATA= keyword to specify the input dataset. Up to now, we've only shown the dataset name after DATA=. Actually, the full syntax is:

```
PROC PRINT DATA=name (options);
```

Suppose your extract file contained many records and you really only want to check a few of them. The OBS= dataset option is one

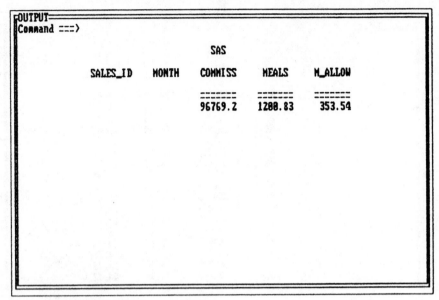

Figure 4.5   PROC PRINT using SUM

that lets you limit the number of observations input. It specifies the last observation to be included. In the following example, OBS=5 tells PROC PRINT not to go past observation 5. The output is shown in Fig. 4.6. You can see that the report includes only five observations and that SUM totals only those that appear on the report.

```
PROC PRINT DATA = SLSPRF (OBS=5);
    VAR  MONTH COMMISS MEALS M_ALLOW ;
    ID  SALES_ID;
    SUM COMMISS MEALS M_ALLOW;
```

4.3 WORKING WITH SORTED DATA: PROC SORT

Reports are usually easier to interpret if the data is meaningfully sorted. We've seen how the ID statement can be used to identify observations within PROC PRINT. But ID leaves the original dataset in unsorted sequence. To sort a dataset, we need to employ another procedure, PROC SORT.

4.3.1 Sorting the data

To sort the data before printing, use PROC SORT. This procedure takes a SAS dataset as input and creates a new SAS dataset con-

```
┌OUTPUT════════════════════════════════════════
│Command ===>
│                        SAS
│
│   SALES_ID   MONTH   COMMISS   MEALS   M_ALLOW
│        .       81    5865.7   118.25     7.48
│        .       83    4467.4    45.78    25.74
│        .       85    8783.2    63.53     2.28
│        1       81    4575.5    75.53    27.86
│        1       82    9875.5    43.38    14.74
│                     =======   ======   =======
│                     33567.3   338.39    77.22
│
│
│
│
│
│
│
└──────────────────────────────────────────────
```

Figure 4.6   PROC PRINT using OBS=

taining the original data in sorted order. The basic syntax of PROC SORT is shown in Fig. 4.7. Like PROC PRINT, PROC SORT specifies the input dataset using the DATA= option. Unlike PROC PRINT, PROC SORT produces an output dataset, which is named in the OUT= option. Remember, DATA= means input, and OUT= means output.

Both the input and output dataset names are optional. If you do not specify the input dataset, the default is the last created dataset. If you do not specify the output dataset, you will overwrite the input dataset with its sorted version.

There is only one additional statement in PROC SORT, and it is required. It is the BY statement. This statement is used to identify the variable(s) that will be used to order the dataset. Variables are sorted in ascending order, unless you specify DESCENDING. If you specify more than one variable on the BY statement, the SAS System will sort the variables in the order you give.

For example, the following PROC SORT will sort SLSPRF in order of SALES__ID, then MONTH. It will replace the original SLSPRF with a new SLSPRF in sorted order (because we omitted the OUT= option).

```
PROC SORT DATA=SLSPRF;
    BY SALES_ID MONTH;
```

```
PROC SORT [DATA =  Input SAS dataset
           OUT  =  Output SAS dataset];
   BY [descending] var1 [descending] var2...;
```

Figure 4.7   PROC SORT simplified syntax

4.3.2   Control breaks

Now let's return to PROC PRINT. PROC PRINT can also use a BY statement. But here, the BY statement does not mean that you want to sort the dataset; that's strictly the job of PROC SORT. Instead, BY indicates that the data is already sorted in order of the variables listed.

Why would you use this? PROC PRINT will work just as well on sorted data as on unsorted data, so why bother telling it that the data is sorted? The answer is simple: by using the BY statement, you can include subtotals and headings in your report. The program is alerted to monitor the change in values of the variables listed. Each time one of these "BY variables" changes its value, subtotals are generated for the previous value, and a heading line is created to group the next set of observations. This is referred to as a "control break".

To generate control breaks, simply use the same BY statement in PROC PRINT as you used in PROC SORT. For instance, the output in Figs. 4.8 and 4.9 was generated with the program statements below. As you can see, when a variable is named as a BY variable in PROC PRINT, the report includes a dashed line separating the BY value groups. The value of the BY variable listed on the line is the same for all of the observations listed below it. (Remember that "SALES_ID=." means that the SALES_ID was missing in this

group). Compare this with Fig. 4.4, and observe how the BY statement provides clearer groupings than the ID statement.

If several BY variables are used in PROC PRINT, the separator
line is printed each time any one of them changes. For ease of reference, all the BY variables are listed on each separator line.

If you also use a SUM statement, you will get subtotals each time
any one of the BY variables changes in value. At the lowest level
break, you will get one set of subtotals. At higher level breaks, you
will get subtotals for each BY variable, in order from lowest to highest.

```
PROC SORT;
    BY SALES_ID;
    /* THE BY STATEMENT HERE SAYS TO SORT THE */
    /* DATASET INTO SALES_ID SEQUENCE         */
PROC PRINT;
    BY SALES_ID;
    /* THE BY STATEMENT HERE SAYS THAT THE    */
    /* DATASET HAS BEEN SORTED BY SALES_ID    */
```

You can use both BY and ID in the same PROC PRINT. For
example, if you wanted breaks by SALES_ID, but you also wanted
months listed in order within each value of SALES_ID, you could

```
┌─OUTPUT═════════════════════════════════════════════════════════════════╗
│Command ===>                                                             │
│                                                                         │
│                                 SAS                                     │
│------------------------------ SALES_ID=. ------------------------------ │
│                                                                         │
│    OBS    MONTH    MEALS    MILEAGE    SALES    M_ALLOW    COMMISS       │
│                                                                         │
│     1      83      45.78      117      44674     25.74     4467.4        │
│     2      85      63.53       10      87832      2.28     8783.2        │
│     3      81     110.25       34      58657      7.48     5865.7        │
│                                                                         │
│------------------------------ SALES_ID=1 ------------------------------ │
│                                                                         │
│    OBS    MONTH    MEALS    MILEAGE    SALES    M_ALLOW    COMMISS       │
│                                                                         │
│     4      85      27.83       14      74357      3.88     7435.7        │
│     5      84      38.94       99      38787     21.78     3878.7        │
│     6      82      43.38       67      98755     14.74     9875.5        │
│     7      83      62.44      221      44673     48.62     4467.3        │
│     8      81      75.53      123      45755     27.86     4575.5        │
│                                                                         │
└─────────────────────────────────────────────────────────────────────────┘
```

Figure 4.8   SORT using one BY variable

```
┌─OUTPUT════════════════════════════════════════════════════
│Command ===)
│
│--------------------------- SALES_ID=5 ---------------------------
│
│  OBS    MONTH    MEALS    MILEAGE    SALES    M_ALLOW    COMMISS
│
│    9      02     22.25      115      18755     25.38     1875.5
│   10      04     74.36      109       8707     23.98      870.7
│   11      05     77.90      214      87832     47.08     8783.2
│   12      03    117.88       73      34673     16.86     3467.3
│
│--------------------------- SALES_ID=11 ---------------------------
│
│  OBS    MONTH    MEALS    MILEAGE    SALES    M_ALLOW    COMMISS
│
│   13      04     63.36       51      34677     11.22     3467.7
│   14      05     74.98      201      87832     44.22     8783.2
│   15      02     88.25      111      98475     24.42     9847.5
│   16      01     80.25       15      58657      3.30     5865.7
│   17      03    142.88       33      44674      7.26     4467.4
│
└────────────────────────────────────────────────────────────
```

Figure 4.9   Continuation of Figure 4.8

sort SLSPRF using SALES__ID as your primary key and MONTH as your secondary key:

```
PROC SORT DATA=SLSPRF;
   BY SALES_ID MONTH;
```

But since you don't want a control break every time MONTH changes values, don't include it in the BY statement of the PROC PRINT. The result is shown in Fig. 4.10.

```
PROC PRINT:
   VAR COMMISS MEALS M_ALLOW;
   ID MONTH;
   BY SALES_ID;
```

4.3.3 Summary of PROC PRINT features

Let's review what we've learned about PROC PRINT. We've seen that a simple PROC PRINT consists of the PROC statement itself, with optional VAR, ID, SUM, and BY statements following it in any order. Like all SAS statements, each one ends with a semicolon. Figure 4.11 summarizes all the PROC PRINT features we have covered.

The PROC statement names the procedure (PRINT), and may also specify the input dataset (DATA=) and the last observation to be printed (OBS=, in parentheses).

```
┌OUTPUT══════════════════════════════════════════
│Command ═══)
│
│                            SAS
│  ------------------------------ SALES_ID=.  -----------------------------
│
│              MONTH    COMMISS    MEALS    M_ALLOW
│
│               81      5865.7    110.25     7.48
│               83      4467.4     45.78    25.74
│               85      8783.2     63.53     2.20
│
│
│  ------------------------------ SALES_ID=1  ----------------------------
│
│              MONTH    COMMISS    MEALS    M_ALLOW
│
│               81      4575.5     75.53    27.86
│               82      9875.5     43.30    14.74
│               83      4467.3     62.44    48.62
│               84      3870.7     38.94    21.78
│               85      7435.7     27.03     3.08
└══════════════════════════════════════════════════
```

Figure 4.10   SORT using two BY variables

The VAR statement lists specific variables to be printed. They will print in the order listed on this statement.

The ID statement causes a particular variable to be listed in the first column of the report, taking the place of the observation numbers. When the data has already been sorted by the ID variable, the values will appear in ascending order.

The SUM statement names numeric variables which will be totaled and printed at the end of the report. If the BY statement is also used, subtotals will also be printed at each control break.

The BY statement tells PROC PRINT that the input data has already been sorted by certain variables. Control breaks (i.e., subtotals and headings) will be produced whenever any of the BY variables changes in value from one observation to the next.

Note: If you include the BY statement, your input SAS dataset *must* be sorted by the BY-variable names, but the sort does not have to be performed through PROC SORT. In other words, if you sort your data before reading it into a SAS dataset (for instance, using your system's sort utility), you can PROC PRINT it with those BY variables immediately after the initial conversion to a SAS dataset.

4.4   INSTANT REPORT #2: PROC FREQ

PROC FREQ lets you create a table of all of the values present in your dataset. This frequency distribution can be very useful when

```
PROC PRINT [ Data = Input dataset name
             (OBS = number of observations) ];
      VAR variable names and/or range;
      ID  variable names and/or range;
      SUM variable names and/or range;
      BY  sort key(s);
```

Figure 4.11   PROC PRINT simplified syntax

you need to validate data or want a quick list of the values present
in the sample.

PROC FREQ produces printed output as does PROC PRINT. However, PROC FREQ does not print one line per observation. Instead,
it analyzes the dataset before printing and prints only a summary
for each observed value of the specified variable or variables. Let's
look at some of the basic uses of PROC FREQ. (Additional applications will be covered in Chapter 10.)

4.4.1   Sample frequency distribution

A simple PROC FREQ step consists of just two lines: the PROC
statement itself, and a TABLES statement which names the variables to be analyzed.

The PROC statement names the procedure (FREQ), and may specify an input dataset by using the DATA= option. This is similar to
PROC PRINT.

The TABLES statement names the variables you are interested in.
Other variables will be ignored in the PROC FREQ execution. For
now, we'll say that this statement consists of the TABLES keyword,
followed by a list of variables separated by spaces. Each variable is
analyzed separately. Later, we'll see other forms of this statement
which make it more powerful.

Let's look again at the SLSPRF dataset. Suppose you wanted to

check the values of SALES_ID to make sure that only valid sales-
person's codes were present on the file. This is a classic job for PROC
FREQ. By using this procedure, we will get a list of every value of
SALES_ID that was found in the dataset, along with a count of how
many times each value occurred.

The following program produces the desired output, as shown in
Fig. 4.12. Notice that several columns are printed. The first lists the
observed values of SALES_ID, in order. Each value is listed only
once. The second column, labeled "Frequency", shows how many
times each value occurred. There were five observations with
SALES_ID = 1, four observations with SALES_ID = 5, and five
observations with SALES_ID = 11. Note that the observations with
"missing" SALES_IDs are not analyzed; instead, only a missing
count appears at the bottom of the report ("Frequency Missing = 3").

The remaining columns are derived from the frequency counts.
"Percent" is the percent of this value's frequency relative to all
observations in the dataset. We have $(5+4+5) = 14$ observations
total, so the percentage for SALES_ID 1 is $5/14$, or 35.7%. The percentage for SALES_ID 5 is $4/14$, or 28.6%, and the percentage for
SALES_ID 11 is 5.14, or 35.7%. Note that the "missing" observations were not counted in these calculations.

"Cumulative Frequency" simply provides a running total of the
"Frequency" values. Each cumulative frequency value is the total
number of observations with the current value of SALES_ID, plus
those with any lower value. The bottommost cumulative frequency
value is the total number of observations analyzed. Similarly,
"Cumulative Percent" is a running total of the "Percent" values,
and the bottommost value will always be 100%.

You can calculate frequencies on several variables in the same
PROC FREQ, by listing each one on the TABLES statement. Each
variable is analyzed separately. You can also include several
TABLES statements in the same PROC FREQ step. This allows you
to specify different options on each TABLES statement. (We'll see
some options later in this section.)

Either of the following PROC FREQ steps will produce two separate analyses, one for SALES_ID and one for MONTH:

```
PROC FREQ;
    TABLES SALES_ID MONTH;
    RUN;
PROC FREQ;
    TABLES SALES_ID;
    TABLES MONTH;
    RUN;
```

```
┌OUTPUT═══════════════════════════════════════════════════════════════
│Command ===>
│
│                                SAS
│
│                                      Cumulative  Cumulative
│            SALES_ID  Frequency   Percent  Frequency    Percent
│            -----------------------------------------------------
│               1          5       35.7        5         35.7
│               5          4       28.6        9         64.3
│              11          5       35.7       14        100.0
│
│                      Frequency Missing = 3
│
│
│
│
│
│
└──────────────────────────────────────────────────────────────────────
```

Figure 4.12   PROC FREQ output

Warning! If you try to create a table for a variable that has too many different values (dollar or decimal value variables, for example), PROC FREQ will not be able to store all the values it needs to set up the table. It will not process that table but will log an error. When you do need a summary of this sort of variable, you have two options: you can use PROC SUMMARY (instead of PROC FREQ) or you can reformat the values into only a few classes so that PROC FREQ can create a distribution of the classes. (See PROC SUMMARY and a more detailed version of PROC FREQ in Chapter 10.)

4.4.2   Missing values and PROC FREQ

As we saw when we looked closely at the output of PROC FREQ in Fig. 4.12, not all values were included in the analysis (even though the total percentage is 100). Specifically, the missing SALES_ID values were not included in the cumulative or individual percentages. This is the standard default processing in PROC FREQ.

Many SAS procedures allow you to specify whether or not you want to include missing values. PROC FREQ allows you to modify each TABLES statement to include or exclude missing values. You do this by adding the clause '/ MISSING' on the TABLES statement. The '/' alerts PROC FREQ that options will follow which will override the default processing. The MISSING keyword following this indicator says specifically that you want missing values treated as any other values.

Example 4.2 PROC FREQ with missing values. Suppose you wanted to see what percent of the SALES_ID values were missing. As we saw in Fig. 4.12, the default options only provide a simple count of missing values. To include these values in the detailed analysis, your TABLES statement must include the MISSING option. The PROC FREQ step would look like this, and the result would look like Fig. 4.13:

```
PROC FREQ;
TABLES SALES_ID / MISSING;
RUN;
```

4.5 REFORMATTING YOUR DATA

PROC FREQ (and PROC steps in general) can be relied on to use an appropriate default format for printing data values. You don't have to specify output formats. But reformatting can improve your report and result in the impact you want. You can:

- edit certain fields to include a dollar sign and/or commas
- translate codes into readable descriptions
- highlight or print special messages when certain values are encountered

```
┌OUTPUT══════════════════════════════════════════════════
│Command ===)
│
│                              SAS
│
│                                   Cumulative  Cumulative
│          SALES_ID   Frequency  Percent  Frequency   Percent
│          ----------------------------------------------------
│              .          3       17.6        3        17.6
│              1          5       29.4        8        47.1
│              5          4       23.5       12        70.6
│             11          5       29.4       17       100.0
```

Figure 4.13   PROC FREQ including missing values

- group a range of values and give the range a single descriptive name

These modifications are accomplished in one of two ways: with the FORMAT statement, or with a very sophisticated procedure known as PROC FORMAT. Let's look first at the FORMAT statement.

4.5.1 Preloaded character formats

The FORMAT statement consists of the FORMAT keyword, then the variable name, then the format (all separated by spaces), and ending with a semicolon. For character variables, there are basically two choices of formats:

$n.   specifies a length of n characters, and trims leading blanks

$CHARn.   specifies a length of n characters, but does not trim leading blanks

The dollar sign ($), CHAR, and period (.) all appear in the format. The only variation is in the length specifier n.

Since most character variables use the same input and output formats, you will probably not use a FORMAT statement for character variables unless you need to suppress or retain leading blanks. See the two examples below.

```
FORMAT STUDENT $CHAR35.; /* 35 CHARS, KEEPS BLANKS */
FORMAT COURSE  $4.;      /* 4 CHARS, TRIMS BLANKS  */
```

4.5.2 Numeric formats

The most common numeric formats are COMMAn.d, DOLLARn.d, BESTn.d, and just plain n.d. COMMA and DOLLAR formats provide the common print format that inserts commas between three-digit groups. DOLLAR formats also include a dollar sign. The BEST format permits the procedure to choose what it considers to be the best format for the space provided (this is the default).

As in the character formats, the period (.) is required. The literal COMMA, DOLLAR, or BEST is also required. The length specifier n tells the total width of the field. The optional decimal length specifier d tells how much of this field should be used for decimal places; if the values do not have decimal places, you can omit d. If the length you specify is not long enough, the procedure will attempt to output the most significant digits possible by omitting extraneous characters (commas, dollar sign), rounding off least significant digits,

```
FORMAT character variable(s) and or range
       $charformat.;

       (alignment is left)


Charformats include:
$n.    trims leading blanks and left aligns
       up to 200 characters (n = 1 to 200)
$CHARn. like $N., but does not trim leading blanks
```

Figure 4.14 PROC FORMAT character syntax

and/or using scientific notation. Example 4.3 illustrate the effect of three different formats.

Example 4.3 Format examples. Let's compare the different reports you can create using FORMAT statements. We'll use PROC PRINT below with our familiar SLSPRF dataset as input. The output is shown in Fig. 4.16.

```
PROC PRINT
DATA = SLSPRF (OBS = 5);        /* ONLY USE 5 OBS   */
    VAR   MONTH  SALES  COMMISS  /* PRINT THESE VARS */
          MILEAGE M_ALLOW;
    ID  SALES_ID;                /* 1ST COLUMN IS ID */
    SUM COMMISS SALES            /* NUM VARS TO SUM  */
        M_ALLOW MILEAGE;
RUN;
```

Now, let's try to add proper formats to our dollar values (COMMISS, M_ALLOW, and SALES). Note that we include two decimal places in COMMISS and M_ALLOW, but none in SALES; SALES are maintained in whole dollars. The output is shown in Fig. 4.17.

```
PROC PRINT
DATA = SLSPRF (OBS = 5);
    VAR   MONTH  SALES  COMMISS
```

```
FORMAT numeric variable(s) and/or range
       numericformat.;

(alignment is right)

Numericformats include:
n.[d]          Numeric with maximum length n.  If d is
               specified, one place is reserved for a
               decimal point, and two places are
               reserved for the decimal value
COMMAn.[d]     places are reserved for commas
DOLLARn.[d]    places are reserved for $ and commas
BESTn.[d]      SAS chooses the best notation
```

Figure 4.15   PROC FORMAT numeric syntax


```
┌OUTPUT══════════════════════════════════
│Command ===>

                         SAS

   SALES_ID   MONTH   SALES   COMMISS   MILEAGE   M_ALLOW

       5       82     18755    1875.5      115     25.38
       1       85     74357    7435.7       14      3.08
       1       84     38787    3878.7       99     21.78
       1       82     98755    9875.5       67     14.74
       .       83     44674    4467.4      117     25.74
                      ======   ======    ======   ======
                     275248   27524.8      412     90.64
```

Figure 4.16   PROC PRINT with default formats

```
      MILEAGE M_ALLOW;
ID  SALES_ID;
SUM COMMISS SALES
    M_ALLOW MILEAGE;
FORMAT COMMISS M_ALLOW DOLLAR7.2;
FORMAT SALES DOLLAR10.;
FORMAT MILEAGE COMMA5.;
RUN;
```

But wait! The values of COMMISS were not formatted even
though we said to use a dollar format. Why? Because the field width
we specified (7) was not big enough to hold the values of COMMISS
(5 digits plus 2 decimal digits), and the dollar sign, decimal point,
and commas. So PROC PRINT jettisoned what it considered to be
less important characters.

We can fix that COMMISS format by increasing the width to 10,
as in the following program. The corrected output is shown in Fig.
4.18.

```
PROC PRINT
DATA = SLSPRF (OBS = 5);
   VAR   MONTH  SALES COMMISS
         MILEAGE M_ALLOW;
```

```
┌OUTPUT════════════════════════════════════════════════╗
│Command ===>                                           │
│                           SAS                         │
│                                                       │
│ SALES_ID  MONTH    SALES   COMMISS  MILEAGE  M_ALLOW   │
│       5     02   $18,755   1875.5      115   $25.38    │
│       1     05   $74,357   7435.7       14    $3.88    │
│       1     04   $38,707   3870.7       99   $21.78    │
│       1     02   $98,755   9875.5       67   $14.74    │
│       .     03   $44,674   4467.4      117   $25.74    │
│                  ========  =======   =======  =======  │
│                  $275,248    27525      412   $98.64   │
└═══════════════════════════════════════════════════════╝
```

Figure 4.17 PROC PRINT with formats too small

```
ID SALES_ID;
SUM COMMISS SALES
    M_ALLOW MILEAGE;
FORMAT COMMISS M_ALLOW DOLLAR10.2;
FORMAT SALES DOLLAR10.;
FORMAT MILEAGE COMMA5.;
RUN;
```

4.5.3 Permanent vs temporary formats

The FORMAT statement lets you associate an output format with one or more variables. Up to now, we've used the FORMAT statement in PROC steps to improve the readability of the PROC step output. The action of the FORMAT statement in this case is temporary; any subsequent steps will pick up the default formats unless you repeat the FORMAT statement.

You can also use FORMAT statements in a DATA step. When you associate a variable and its format during the DATA step, that format becomes the permanent format for the variable. You do not have to repeat the FORMAT statement for each subsequent step, because the formats are saved in the dataset header.

Example 4.4 Temporary and permanent formats. Let's add formats to the DATA step that creates the SLSPRF dataset.

```
┌OUTPUT═══════════════════════════════════════
│Command ===>
│
│                          SAS
│
│  SALES_ID   MONTH    SALES      COMMISS    MILEAGE   M_ALLOW
│
│     5        82     $18,755    $1,875.50     115      $25.30
│     1        85     $74,357    $7,435.70      14       $3.88
│     1        84     $38,787    $3,878.70      99      $21.78
│     1        82     $98,755    $9,875.50      67      $14.74
│     .        83     $44,674    $4,467.40     117      $25.74
│                    ---------   ----------   ------    --------
│                    $275,248   $27,524.80     412      $98.64
```

Figure 4.18 PROC PRINT with corrected formats

```
DATA SLSPRF;
    INFILE    'a:salesin.dat';
    INPUT
    @  1    SALES_ID4.
    @  5    MONTH       $CHAR2.
    @  7    MEALS        5.2
    @  17   MILEAGE      5.
    @  22   SALES        7.
    ;
    M_ALLOW              =  .22 * MILEAGE;
    COMMISS              =  .10 * SALES;
    FORMAT MEALS M_ALLOW  DOLLAR7.2;
    FORMAT SALES          DOLLAR10.;
    FORMAT COMMISS        DOLLAR10.2;
RUN;
PROC PRINT DATA=SLSPRF (OBS=5);
VAR SALES_ID MONTH MEALS M_ALLOW SALES COMMISS;
RUN;
```

Because the FORMAT statements are inside the DATA step, we have now created permanent output formats for the variables MEALS, M_ALLOW, SALES, and COMMISS. Whenever these variables appear in procedure output, the associated permanent formats will be used automatically. We have not created permanent output formats for SALES_ID or MONTH. Therefore, the PROC PRINT should pick up the output formats for MEALS, M_ALLOW, SALES, COMMISS and use default formats for SALES_ID and MONTH. Take a look at the output in Fig. 4.19.

Now, suppose we wanted to change the formats just for this one report. Remember, the FORMAT statement used in a PROC step only produces temporary formats. So we can temporarily override the permanent formats for a particular PROC step. In the following PROC PRINT, the FORMAT statement overrides the formats we saved for MEALS, M_ALLOW, SALES, and COMMISS. But the override is effective only during this step. The permanent formats are still saved, and will be effective on any other step (assuming that they are not overridden again).

As you can see in Fig. 4.20, the formats for MEALS, M_ALLOW, SALES, and COMMISS are different from the permanent formats assigned during the DATA step. (SALES_ID and MONTH are the same because they're still using the default.) The COMMA5. format was used for MEALS, M_ALLOW, SALES, and COMMISS. The field width is narrowed and the dollar sign is gone. In SALES and COMMISS, even the comma was "squeezed out" because the field width is too narrow.

```
┌OUTPUT══════════════════════════════════════════════════
│Command ===>

                                 SAS

   OBS    SALES_ID    MONTH    MEALS    M_ALLOW      SALES      COMMISS

    1        5          02     $22.25    $25.38     $18,755    $1,875.58
    2        1          05     $27.83     $3.08     $74,357    $7,435.78
    3        1          04     $38.94    $21.78     $38,787    $3,878.78
    4        1          02     $43.38    $14.74     $98,755    $9,875.58
    5        .          03     $45.78    $25.74     $44,674    $4,467.48
```

Figure 4.19   PROC PRINT with permanent and temporary formats

```
PROC PRINT DATA=SLSPRF (OBS=5);
    VAR SALES_ID MONTH MEALS M_ALLOW SALES
        COMMISS;
    FORMAT MEALS M_ALLOW SALES COMMISS
        COMMA5.;
RUN;
```

Let's rerun the earlier PROC PRINT to see if the permanent formats are really permanent. The results, shown in Fig. 4.21, indicate that they are.

```
PROC PRINT DATA=SLSPRF (OBS=5);
    VAR SALES_ID MONTH MEALS M_ALLOW SALES
        COMMISS;
RUN;
```

If you want to remove the "permanent" format, code a FORMAT statement with a null format as follows. The variable is left with a default format.

```
FORMAT variable;
```

4.5.4   Custom formats

In addition to the standard formats, such as COMMA, DOLLAR, and $CHAR, you are permitted to define your own formats. Custom formats are useful for:

```
┌OUTPUT════════════════════════════════════════════════════════════════
│Command ===>
│                               SAS
│
│     OBS    SALES_ID    MONTH    MEALS    M_ALLOW    SALES    COMMISS
│
│      1        5         02      22.25     25.30     18755     1876
│      2        1         05      27.03      3.08     74357     7436
│      3        1         04      38.94     21.78     38707     3871
│      4        1         02      43.30     14.74     98755     9876
│      5        .         03      45.78     25.74     44674     4467
│
│
│
│
│
│
│
│
└═══════════════════════════════════════════════════════════════════════
```

Figure 4.20   Overriding permanent formats

```
┌OUTPUT════════════════════════════════════════════════════════════════
│Command ===>
│                                SAS
│
│   OBS    SALES_ID    MONTH     MEALS    M_ALLOW      SALES      COMMISS
│
│    1        5         02      $22.25    $25.30     $18,755    $1,875.50
│    2        1         05      $27.03     $3.08     $74,357    $7,435.70
│    3        1         04      $38.94    $21.78     $38,707    $3,870.70
│    4        1         02      $43.30    $14.74     $98,755    $9,875.50
│    5        .         03      $45.78    $25.74     $44,674    $4,467.40
│
│
│
│
│
│
└═══════════════════════════════════════════════════════════════════════
```

Figure 4.21   Checking permanent formats

- translation of codes
- grouping continuous values into ranges of values
- grouping values into classifications

You can create formats for both character and numeric variables. Most operating systems allow you to save the loaded formats in a permanent library for later reference. If you wish to save your formats, you must attach an established directory (on PCs) or a valid library. If you do not specify a library reference, the formats are temporary, and will be deleted at the end of your session.

Custom formats are created using PROC FORMAT. PROC FORMAT used with the VALUE clause can create either numeric or character formats. The PICTURE clause is used to create numeric edited formats. Figure 4.22 shows the syntax of PROC FORMAT.

Do not confuse PROC FORMAT with the FORMAT statement. PROC FORMAT does not, in itself, provide a format for any specific variables. Instead, it creates a formatting rule, just like $CHAR or DOLLAR, which can then be used on any variable. Once the format is created, you can name it in FORMAT statements to associate it with specific variables. For example, we have seen how the standard DOLLAR format is used to associate a particular output format with dollar variables:

```
FORMAT SALARY DOLLAR10.2;
```

But suppose our application had a particular need for a format that placed a dash ("−") after the first digit of a six-digit account number, and another dash before the last digit. With PROC FORMAT, we could predefine a format—in this case, DASHER—to use just as we do DOLLAR.

```
FORMAT ACCTNUM DASHER8.;
```

(Notice that we specified a length of 8 to allow for the two dashes!) By including a PROC FORMAT step early in your SAS program, or by maintaining a permanent format library, you can provide subsequent steps with a variety of formats tailored to the needs of your application.

You must specify a name (like DASHER) that you'll use to refer to the format. The name must be eight characters or less and cannot end in a number (because we need to be able to append a numeric length modifier—see the "8" in $CHAR8.). Note that the period (.) is not included in the PROC FORMAT definition, although it must be present in any FORMAT statements which use the new format. Character variable formats must have the character indicator ($) as the first character in the format name. (This depends on whether the actual variable is numeric or character, rather than the printed value. See the GRADES example following, which is a numeric format.)

The VALUE clause is used to convert internal values to display literals. After the keyword VALUE, it names the format, followed by a series of values or ranges. There's only one semicolon, after the last range. Each value (or range) is followed by an equal sign (=) and then the descriptive format that you would like to print. The descriptive format must be enclosed in single quotes. (If your description has a single quote in it, you must code two consecutive single quotes so it will be recognized correctly.) You can code descriptive of up to forty characters, but some of the SAS PROCs will truncate the description (PROC FREQ, for example).

Remember that the values to the left of the "=" are the actual values of the variable, and the values to the right of the "=" are what will be printed. The values to be printed are always enclosed in single quotes. The actual values are enclosed in single quotes for character variables; numeric variables do not require quotes.

For example, we can define a format called GRADES for a numeric variable as follows:

```
PROC FORMAT;
     VALUE GRADES
      0  - 65  = 'F'
     66 - 69  = 'D'
     70 - 79  = 'C'
     80 - 89  = 'B'
     90 - 100 = 'A';
```

If the values are not exact, you may have some ambiguities close to the range boundaries. (What is a grade of 89.4?) You can use an option called FUZZ= to determine into which range an ambiguous value will fall. For example, by coding

```
VALUE GRADES (FUZZ=.5)
```

we say to round down to the next formatted grade unless the actual grade is more than .5 away from its upper boundary. In other words, with FUZZ=.5, 89.4 is a B. 89.5 is still a B, but 89.6 is an A.

The value or range describes the values you want to format. These may be discrete character or numeric values, character or numeric

ranges, or combinations within the same type (character or numeric).
For example, suppose your installation had a two-byte code called
TTL for personal title codes, including the following:

```
'  ' = unknown
'01' = MRS.
'02' = MISS
'03' = MR.
'04' = DR.
'05' = JUDGE
'06' = SENATOR
'10' = MS.
```

To translate these codes for printing, you could include the following
PROC FORMAT in your program:

```
PROC FORMAT;
    VALUE $SALUTE
         '01' = 'Mrs.'
         '02' = 'Miss'
         '03' = 'Mr.'
         '04' = 'Dr.'
         '05' = 'Judge'
         '06' = 'Senator'
         '10' = 'Ms.'
         '  ' = 'Our Loyal Customer, '
    ;
```

Once this PROC FORMAT is executed, any subsequent DATA or
PROC step can automatically translate the TTL code to its meaningful display equivalent by including the statement

```
FORMAT TTL $SALUTE.;
```

This is a very powerful feature, much more powerful than it first
appears. It allows you to categorize data in many different ways
without changing any program statements other than the PROC
FORMAT. Suppose, for instance, you have a completely different use
for TTL—you want to group your customers by sex. You would simply code a different PROC FORMAT:

```
PROC FORMAT;
    VALUE $SEXCODE
       '01', '02', '10' = 'Female'
       '03'             = 'Male'
       '04'-'06', '  '  = 'Unknown'
    ;
```

Notice that the first label ('Female') describes a list of values separated by commas (they are the codes for Mrs., Miss, and Ms.); the second label ('Male') describes a single value (the code for Mr.); and the last label ('Unknown') includes both a range ('04'-'06', the professional titles) and a single value ('   ', for true unknowns) separated from the range by a comma.

Now you can automatically convert TTL to 'Female', 'Male', or 'Unknown' in procedure output by simply coding

```
FORMAT TTL $SEXCODE.;
```

The $SEXCODE format in no way interferes with the $SALUTE format we defined earlier. You can use them both freely, even within the same program. Of course, in a given step, TTL will use only one of the formats; but it would not be unusual to see something similar to the following program sequence, which counts our customers in two different ways.

```
PROC FREQ; /* COUNT CUSTOMERS BY SALUTATION */
    TABLES TTL;
    FORMAT TTL $SALUTE.;
PROC FREQ; /* COUNT CUSTOMERS BY SEX        */
    TABLES TTL;
    FORMAT TTL $SEXCODE.;
```

When you define a range, you can also make use of the range keywords HIGH, LOW, and OTHER. These keywords make it even easier to format numeric or alphanumeric ranges. Here's another possibility for the GRADES format.

```
PROC FORMAT;
    VALUE GRADES (FUZZ=.5)
    LOW - 70 = 'Fail'
    71 - 94 = 'Pass'
    95 - HIGH = 'Honors'
    OTHER = 'Incomplete'
    ;
```

Ranges can be defined using several operators. For example:

100 − 200 means 100 through 200 inclusive

100 < − 200 means more than 100 but less than or equal to 200

100 − < 200 means 100 or more but less than 200

So far, we have seen how the VALUE clause of PROC FORMAT can be used to convert numeric or character codes to display literals.

We emphasize "literals", because formats defined with the VALUE clause do not provide any way to include the actual value of the variable. The edit template in the PICTURE clause allows you to create dynamic formats.

For numeric variables, there is an alternative to the VALUE clause, which allows you to embed the actual value of the variable in a formatted description. This is the PICTURE clause. You code a PICTURE clause just as you do a VALUE clause for numeric variable, but now the right-hand side of the equation serves as an edit template rather than a simple literal.

Numeric characters in the template represent positions for numeric values: zeros in the template tell SAS print procedures to suppress leading zeros; nonzero integers tell the system to print leading zeros. At print time, these digits are replaced with the actual value of the variable.

The PICTURE clause in PROC FORMAT allows you to use different message formats depending on the value of your variables. For example, the following format will print temperatures from 32° to 89° "as is", but higher or lower temperatures will result in longer messages. A value of 101° will print as "A temperature of 101 is too hot'. A value of 10° will print as "A temperature of 10 is too cold". In all three cases, the program will fill in the actual value in place of the zeros (suppressing leading zeros).

```
PROC FORMAT;
   PICTURE F_Temp
      LOW -< 32 = 'A temperature of 000 is too
                  cold'
      32 -< 90 = '00'
      90 - HIGH = 'A temperature of 000 is too
                  hot'
   ;
```

Example 4.5 Sample custom formats. Let's format the print output of our trusty SLSPRF dataset. We'll also demonstrate how to create a "permanent" format. In the sample coding that follows, the LIBRARY= option on the PROC statement specifies that we want to save the formats in a dataset which we will call FMTLIB. Once the formats are saved, you can allocate the FMTLIB library in any SAS job or session, and the formats will be made available. You don't have to include the PROC FORMAT statements again in each program.

The LIBNAME statement shows how to specify the actual name of FMTLIB in a PC environment. In an MVS environment, FMTLIB

```
PROC FORMAT [LIBRARY = permanent library ref];
    VALUE  format name [options]
            single value            = 'label'
            value1, value2, value3 = 'label'
            range                   = 'label'
            range, value            = 'label'
                    ,
        PICTURE format name
            value/range             = 'edit template'
            . . .
            ;
```

Figure 4.22   PROC FORMAT syntax

is a DDname which you can allocate using a DD statement or TSO ALLOCATE.

If you omit the LIBRARY= option, the formats will only be available during the current job or session. This may be perfectly all right for your situation. In fact, it may be preferable if you're the only person using the format or it's for a one-time application.

```
LIBNAME FMTLIB  'c:\sas\fmts';
PROC FORMAT LIBRARY = FMTLIB;
/* THIS FORMAT CONVERTS MONTHS TO DISPLAY LITERALS: */
    VALUE $MONFMT
    '01' ='January'
    '02' ='February'
    '03' ='March'
    '04' ='April'
    '05' ='May'
    '06' ='June'
    '07' ='July'
    '08' ='August'
    '09' ='September'
    '10' ='October'
    '11' ='November'
    '12' ='December'
```

```
;
/* THIS FORMAT CONVERTS DOLLARS TO DISPLAY LITERALS */
   VALUE SALESRNG
   LOW     -<25000 = 'under $25,000'
   25000   -<50000 = '$25,000 to under $50,000'
   50000   -<75000 = '$50,000 to under $75,000'
   75000   - HIGH  = '$75,000 +'
;
/* THIS FORMAT EDITS NUMERIC CODES.                 */
/* VALUES 01-10 PRINT "AS IS";                      */
/* ALL OTHERS PRINT THE VALUE WITH                  */
/* ''- NEW SALES CODE'' APPENDED TO THE VALUE.      */
/* REMEMBER THAT 99 IS REPLACED WITH THE VALUE.     */
   PICTURE SALECODA
   01 - 10 = '99'
   OTHER = '99 - NEW SALES CODE'
;
/* THIS FORMAT IS THE SAME AS SALECODA,             */
/* EXCEPT THAT MISSING VALUES ARE BROKEN OUT        */
/* SEPARATELY AS "MISSING".                         */
/* (RECALL THAT . INDICATES A MISSING VALUE).       */
   PICTURE SALECODB
   01 - 10 = '99'
   .        = 'MISSING'
   OTHER    = '99 - NEW SALES CODE'
;
RUN;
```

Upon successful completion of this PROC FORMAT, the formats are available on the permanent catalog, which is 'c:\sas\fmts'. Let's look at how to use them.

The first thing we want to do is stop printing numbers for the months and print their formatted values. In the following sample code, pay particular attention to the FORMAT statement. It associates the $MONFMT format we just defined with the variable MONTH. It also associates the standard DOLLAR format with variable SALES. Note that the custom format $MONFMT is invoked in exactly the same way as DOLLAR, illustrating that once formats are defined, they are all equal. The PROC PRINT output in Fig. 4.23 shows the effect of this FORMAT statement.

```
PROC PRINT DATA = SLSPRF (OBS=5);
   VAR MONTH SALES;
   ID SALES_ID;
```

```
FORMAT MONTH $MONFMT.
        SALES DOLLAR10.;
RUN;
```

Because we did not associate these custom formats at the time SLSPRF was created, they are not permanently associated with the variables they format. Remember, PROC steps don't associate formats permanently. You have to repeat the FORMAT statement in each PROC. Therefore, if a variable will always be associated with a particular format, it's wise to make the association permanent by including the FORMAT statement in the DATA step that creates the variable.

In the previous example, we only used our custom formats for one of the variables in SLSPRF. Let's go further. Instead of a plain DOLLAR format, we'll now associate the SALESRNG format with variable SALES; observe the descriptive formats printed in Fig. 4.24.

We'll also associate the format SALECODA with the SALES_ID variable. Remember that SALESCODA was defined with the PIC-TURE clause, which allows the actual value to be included in a printed format. Notice in Fig. 4.24 that all the SALES_ID values from 01 to 10 are printed without modification, because the PIC-TURE clause specified only a plain "99" for these values. But when SALES_ID is 11, a more elaborate edit template is invoked: "99 −

```
┌OUTPUT═══════════════════════════════════════════════════════════
│Command ===)


                              SAS

             SALES_ID    MONTH          SALES

                 5      February       $18,755
                 1      May            $74,357
                 1      April          $38,787
                 1      February       $98,755
                 .      March          $44,674
```

Figure 4.23 Using custom VALUE formats

NEW SALES CODE". When the actual value is substituted for the "99", we see "11 — NEW SALES CODE".
There was one slightly unpleasant feature to the output in Fig. 4.24. Our three "missing" SALES_IDs were not formatted. We got the same old period (.). To correct this, we can use a slight variation on SALECODA called SALECODB (B instead of a number because format names can't end in numbers). SALECODB explicitly converts missing values to display "MISSING". Compare Fig. 4.25 with Fig. 4.24.

```
PROC PRINT DATA = SLSPRF;
    VAR MONTH SALES;
    ID SALES_ID;
    FORMAT MONTH $MONFMT.
           SALES SALESRNG.;
    FORMAT SALES_ID SALECODA.;
RUN;
```

4.6 REDESIGNING YOUR REPORT

A report isn't complete unless it also provides meaningful description with its data. You've probably noticed from the samples that

```
┌OUTPUT═══════════════════════════════════════════════════════════
│Command ===>

                              SAS

                SALES_ID    MONTH       SALES

                      85    February    under $25,000
                      81    May         $50,000 to under $75,000
                      81    April       $25,000 to under $50,000
                      81    February    $75,000 +
                       .    March       $25,000 to under $50,000
        11 - NEW SALES CODE April       $25,000 to under $50,000
                      81    March       $25,000 to under $50,000
                       .    May         $75,000 +
                      81    January     $25,000 to under $50,000
                      85    April       under $25,000
        11 - NEW SALES CODE May         $75,000 +
                      85    May         $75,000 +
        11 - NEW SALES CODE February    $75,000 +
        11 - NEW SALES CODE January     $50,000 to under $75,000
                      85    March       $25,000 to under $50,000
                       .    January     $50,000 to under $75,000
        11 - NEW SALES CODE March       $25,000 to under $50,000
```

Figure 4.24 Using custom PICTURE formats

```
┌OUTPUT═══════════════════════════════════════════════════════════
│Command ===>
│                            SAS
│
│        SALES_ID         MONTH      SALES
│
│                   05   February   under $25,000
│                   01   May        $50,000 to under $75,000
│                   01   April      $25,000 to under $50,000
│                   01   February   $75,000 +
│        MISSING         March      $25,000 to under $50,000
│        11 - NEW SALES CODE  April $25,000 to under $50,000
│                   01   March      $25,000 to under $50,000
│        MISSING         May        $75,000 +
│                   01   January    $25,000 to under $50,000
│                   05   April      under $25,000
│        11 - NEW SALES CODE  May   $75,000 +
│                   05   May        $75,000 +
│        11 - NEW SALES CODE  February  $75,000 +
│        11 - NEW SALES CODE  January   $50,000 to under $75,000
│                   05   March      $25,000 to under $50,000
│        MISSING         January    $50,000 to under $75,000
│        11 - NEW SALES CODE  March $25,000 to under $50,000
└═══════════════════════════════════════════════════════════════════
```

Figure 4.25 Formatting missing values

PROC PRINT and PROC FREQ have global defaults such as a report title (SAS), column description (the variable's name), and where to put page breaks (the default maximum page length defined by your installation). In this section, you will learn some of the ways to manipulate these elements more descriptively.

4.6.1 Titles and footnotes

TITLE statements allow you to give a descriptive heading of up to ten lines on your report. FOOTNOTE statements allow you to add up to ten lines of notes at the bottom of your report. The text is centered automatically. Figure 4.26 shows the syntax of TITLE and FOOTNOTE statements. There are two main forms of the TITLE statement. You can specify a simple one-line title with the TITLE keyword:

```
TITLE 'PAYROLL SUMMARY FOR AUGUST 1995';
```

Or, you can specify a multiline page header by using TITLE1, TITLE2, and so on, up to TITLE10:

```
TITLE1 'PAYROLL SUMMARY REPORT';
TITLE2 'TOTAL SALARY BY DEPARTMENT';
TITLE3 '--AUGUST 1995--';
```

FOOTNOTES are similar. You can specify either FOOTNOTE or
FOOTNOTE1 through FOOTNOTE10:

```
FOOTNOTE1 'S = SALARY';
FOOTNOTE2 'H = HOURLY WAGES';
```

Both titles and footnotes are displayed the same: the lowest-num-
bered item is at the top. With three titles and three footnotes, a page
will appear as follows:

```
TITLE1
TITLE2
TITLE3
```

. . . Body of the Report Page . . .

```
FOOTNOTE1
FOOTNOTE2
FOOTNOTE3
```

Once TITLEs and FOOTNOTEs are assigned, they remain in effect
until they're replaced, cleared, or the job ends. To replace a title,
code a TITLE or TITLEn statement with the new description in it
(and similarly for footnotes). To clear a TITLE or FOOTNOTE, code
a null statement for the correct line:

```
TITLE3 'Subdivision 467'; /* sets title line 3 */
...
TITLE3 'Dept. 46';        /* replaces line 3   */
...
TITLE3;   /* this statement clears line 3      */
```

Special note: You must be careful where you put these statements
in your program. As you know from previous chapters, the SAS
supervisor executes compiled steps when it encounters either of two
statements:

- a new PROC or DATA step
- a RUN statement

If you want to title your report correctly, you'll have to make sure
the TITLE statement is coded within the statements that make up
the PROC or DATA step that uses them, or immediately after the

```
TITLEn    ['description'];
FOOTNOTEn ['description'];

n is a number from 1 to 10.  It designates
the position of the particular line relative
from the top (TITLE) or bottom (FOOTNOTE)
If you do not specify n, the default is 1.
```

Figure 4.26 TITLE and FOOTNOTE syntax

previous step has run. Otherwise you may be assigning the wrong titles to your reports.

Example 4.6 Correct positioning of the TITLE statement. Assuming the "Final Report" numbers match the dataset numbers, titles will be incorrect in the following report. This is because execution of the first PROC PRINT is really not performed until the next PROC PRINT is encountered. By that time, TITLE 'Final Report #1' has already been overwritten with TITLE 'Final Report #2'.

```
TITLE 'Final Report #1';
PROC PRINT DATA=REPORT1;
TITLE 'Final Report #2';
PROC PRINT DATA=REPORT2; /* REPORT1 PRINTED NOW */
TITLE 'Final Report #3;
RUN;                     /* REPORT2 PRINTED NOW */
```

To match the correct title with the correct report, you can code it in either of two ways. You can put the TITLE statements after the procedures they are to modify:

```
PROC PRINT DATA=REPORT1;
TITLE 'Final Report #1';
PROC PRINT DATA=REPORT2; /* REPORT1 PRINTED NOW */
```

```
TITLE 'Final Report #2;
RUN;                       /* REPORT2 PRINTED NOW */
```

Or you can make sure to include RUN statements following each grouping of TITLE statements and program steps:

```
RUN;                       /* CLEAR OUT LAST STEP */
TITLE 'FinalReport #1';
PROC PRINT DATA=REPORT1;
RUN; /* FORCES EXECUTION OF REPORT1 STEP      */
TITLE 'Final Report #2';
PROC PRINT DATA=REPORT2;
RUN;   /* FORCES EXECUTION OF REPORT2 STEP       */
```

4.6.2 Adding descriptive column titles: LABEL statement

As we have seen in the previous examples, the default column description is the variable name. Since the SAS System variable names are only eight characters long at most, you may want to use a LABEL statement to attach a descriptive phrase of up to forty characters to each variable. (Some PROCs may truncate labels after the first eight or sixteen characters.)

The LABEL statement can be used in both PROC and DATA steps. When used in a PROC step, the effect is temporary; but when used in a DATA step, the label is permanently attached to the variable.

Fig. 4.27 shows the syntax of the LABEL statement. The LABEL keyword is followed by the variable name, an equal sign (=), and then the descriptive label itself enclosed in single quotes. For example, we could have arranged to replace our somewhat cryptic headings in the SLSPRF reports by coding:

```
LABEL SALES_ID = 'SALESPERSON ID';
LABEL COMMISS  = 'COMMISSION';
LABEL MEALS    = 'MEAL EXPENSES';
LABEL M_ALLOW  = 'MILEAGE ALLOWANCE';
```

4.6.3 Printing labels: LABEL and SPLIT options

On PROC PRINT, you must make one additional modification to get the descriptive labels as column headings, instead of the variable

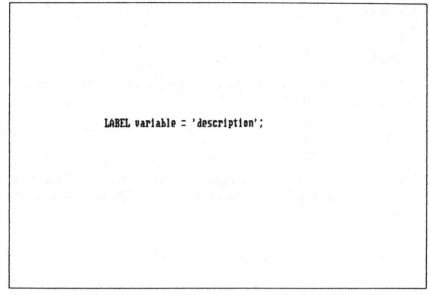

```
LABEL variable = 'description';
```

Figure 4.27 LABEL syntax

names. You must include the LABEL option on the PROC statement. The LABEL options tells PROC PRINT to look for a LABEL
statement. If it does not find a label there, it is to use a default
(either a permanent label or the variable name). For example,

```
PROC PRINT LABEL DATA=SLSPRF;
```

If the label is too long, PROC PRINT will split it across several lines.
This splitting may occur at any point in the label. Another option
called SPLIT lets you control exactly where the break occurs. The
SPLIT option identifies a special character which you can include in
your labels to specify where the label is to be split. The following
program sample says that all labels should be split wherever they
include the character '*'. The split character itself is not printed.

```
PROC PRINT SPLIT = '*';
   LABEL PCTORD = 'TOTAL*PERCENT*ORDERED';
```

The resulting column heading will look like this:

TOTAL

PERCENT

ORDERED

It's time to introduce you to more options on the **PROC PRINT**: the **LABEL** and **SPLIT** options:

```
PROC PRINT LABEL;
PROC PRINT SPLIT = 'character';
```

These step options can be combined with the **DATA=** step option and all the other **PROC PRINT** statements previously presented in this chapter.

More Data Handling Techniques

As you've seen, a simple SAS job stream consists of a DATA step that converts raw data into a SAS dataset and a PROC step which analyzes or prints the dataset. In many cases this is all the coding needed. But there are times when you might want to:

- add variables that were not present on the original raw data file
- summarize observations
- remove duplicates
- split the dataset into several different ones
- use a smaller sample size or only a few variables at a time
- change variable names

For situations such as these, you need more SAS tools.

5.1 MORE DATA STEP USES

The DATA step is used not only to import raw data into SAS datasets, but also to create new datasets or modify existing ones. Figure 5.1 shows the general syntax of a DATA step whose input is an existing SAS dataset.

5.1.1 Creating a dataset from an existing dataset

To create a SAS dataset from an existing one, you use the SET statement in your DATA step to name the input SAS dataset. This takes the place of the INFILE statement, which is used for external file input only. The SET statement consists of the SET keyword, plus the name of a temporary or permanent SAS dataset. Recall that temporary datasets have a one-level name, while permanent datasets have a two-level name in which the first level specifies the DDname.

The output dataset can also be permanent or temporary. As you saw in Chapter 3, the name of the output dataset is specified by indicating a one-level or two-level name on the DATA statement itself. It is not necessary for the output and input datasets to be of the same type; that is, you can create a permanent dataset from a temporary one, or vice versa. To retain a copy of your original dataset and to prevent it from being overlayed with the new one, make sure you use a different dataset name in the DATA statement.

In summary, DATA statements name output, and SET statements name input. The DATA statements always come first, because they also mark the beginning of the step.

Now that we've used a SET statement in place of INFILE, what do we do about the INPUT statement? When your input is a SAS dataset rather than an external file, you will not need an INPUT statement at all. This is because all the variables have already been defined, read, and stored in a form palatable to SAS programs. All the descriptive information (such as format, length, and label) has been stored in the dataset header. Simply by using the SET statement, you automatically have access to every variable in the dataset.

By default, all variables and observations in the input dataset are available to the DATA step. If you prefer, you can define a view of the dataset by specifying dataset options on the SET statement. We mentioned dataset options briefly in Chapter 4, where we used the OBS= option to limit the number of observations. When used on input datasets, they can limit the number of variables or observations available to the current DATA step.

Dataset options are listed in parentheses following the dataset name. For input datasets, they follow the dataset name on the SET statement. They can be used in any order. Some common options used on input datasets are:

DROP=   Blocks specified variables from being read in the current DATA step. They are not actually deleted in the dataset; you just can't use them during this step.

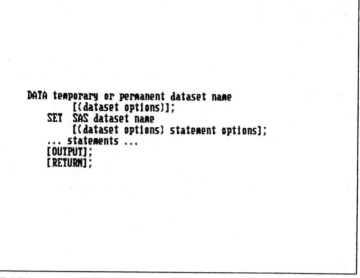

```
DATA temporary or permanent dataset name
        [(dataset options)];
   SET  SAS dataset name
        [(dataset options) statement options];
   ... statements ...
   [OUTPUT];
   [RETURN];
```

Figure 5.1   DATA step with SAS dataset input

KEEP=   The converse of DROP=. It blocks all variables from being
               read except the ones you specify. This form is more convenient
               than DROP= when you are dropping more variables than you
               are keeping.

RENAME=   Renames the specified variables during this step, although
               they retain their original names on the input dataset.

OBS=   Limits the number of input observations.

You can also use these data set options on output datasets by listing
them in parentheses after the dataset name on the DATA statement. In this case, they refer to the variables and/or observations
being added to the output dataset.

Example 5.1 Sample DATA step.   This example illustrates the general
description of the DATA step with SAS dataset input (Fig. 5.1).
Assume your input file is a SAS dataset that contains test records
for a group of students. The dataset (a permanent dataset called
SASPDS.TEST1) contains individual students' test scores for several
different tests. Each test is identified by a unique code (TEST_ID).
You'd like to count the total number of students who took TEST_ID
'A001'. You'd also like to create a smaller dataset (called A001PASS)
containing only the passing grades (over 70) on TEST_ID = 'A001'.

Let's think about what we need to do in our program. First of all,
we need a counter for the number of students who took test A001.
We'll go into detail later in the chapter about creating new varia-

bles; for now, all you need to know is that you can create a counter (we'll call it FOUND) by coding the statement

```
FOUND + 1;
```

The next thing we need to make sure of is that this counter will be displayed after we've read all the input observations. For this purpose, we'll use the END= option which we used in Chapter 3 on the INFILE statement. Now, of course, we'll use it on the SET statement. Recall that this option creates a Boolean variable which is made "true" (i.e., equal to 1) when the final input record is being processed. We'll create an END= variable called DONE, and when DONE is true, we'll use the following statement to print the final value of FOUND:

```
PUT 'Records found: ' FOUND;
```

That takes care of our counter. Now, let's create the new dataset containing only the observations of passing grades on test A001. First, we need to check for TEST__ID = 'A001'. We've used IF statements unofficially in several examples. The SAS IF . . . THEN . . . ELSE construct is similar to that in many programming languages:

```
IF condition
    THEN DO;
        statements;
        END;
    ELSE DO;
        statements;
        END;
```

The semicolons are required, but you can omit the DO; and END; statements when only one statement is included between them. You can also omit the ELSE clause if you don't need it.

If TEST__ID = 'A001' then we know we have an interesting record. We know we have to add to the counter. We also have to output an observation if the grade was above 70. The statement which outputs an observation is OUTPUT.

As one final touch, we'll drop the variable TEST__ID from our output dataset. After all, we know that everything in this dataset came from TEST__ID = 'A001'. Remember that we can block variables from appearing on the output dataset by coding the DROP= option after the dataset name on the DATA statement.

Now let's put this all together into a program. Note that comments begin with an asterisk (*), may flow over several lines, and end with a semicolon (;).

```
* We're creating a temporary dataset named 'A001PASS'.
  It will contain all the variables except TEST_ID;

DATA A001PASS (DROP = TEST_ID);

* The input dataset is called TEST1 in the permanent SAS
  library referenced by the DDname SASPDS.
  When the last record is being processed, set the Boolean
  variable called DONE to true.
  Note that END=DONE is part of the SET statement so there is
  no semicolon before it;

    SET SASPDS.TEST1
        END=DONE;

* When a TEST_ID of A001 is encountered, add 1 to a counter
  called FOUND. Also, if the score is greater than 70, we want
  to include this observation in the A001PASS dataset, so we
  OUTPUT the record;

    If TEST_ID = 'A001' THEN DO;
        FOUND + 1;
        If SCORE > 70 THEN OUTPUT;
    END;

* If we are on the last record, then print the total number of
  A001 records found;

    IF DONE THEN PUT 'Records found: ' FOUND;
```

And that's it! This chapter will explain much of what is introduced in this example.

5.2 CHANGING THE SAMPLE SIZE

Sample size changes can be coded a variety of ways depending on the reason for including or excluding a record:

1. You want to analyze only those observations that have specific values in one or more variables. (Controlling I/O, Using conditionals)

2. You want to test a few observations before submitting a large job. (Controlling I/O, Limiting sequential processing)

3. Your data is sorted and you want to summarize it or remove duplicate records. (Removing duplicates and summarizing, Controlling I/O)

4. You want to expand the sample by outputting multiple observations from one input observation. (Controlling I/O)

5. You want to create many output datasets. (Multiple dataset output)

5.2.1 Controlling I/O

You are already familiar with the implicit I/O found in the DATA step (Chapter 3). The DATA step functions as a read loop, with an implicit "read" at the top of the loop and an implicit "write" at the bottom. The loop is executed once for each record on the input dataset. It is possible to control the looping and the "reads" and "writes" more closely, so that you can specify exactly when and under what conditions they are to occur.

We will introduce two new statements in this section. The RETURN statement says to return to the top of the DATA step loop immediately, without executing any more statements in the current iteration. The OUTPUT statement says to create an output record immediately, rather than waiting till the end of the DATA step loop.

Why would you use RETURN? You may decide early in the DATA step that there is no more work to do with the current observation. Rather than plow through the remaining statements anyway, you can skip them with RETURN. The implicit "write" at the bottom of the loop is still executed, but control then returns immediately to the top of the loop to process the next input observation. The format of this statement is simply

```
RETURN;
```

The OUTPUT statement lets you decide exactly when to create an output observation. When this statement is encountered, an output observation, which contains the current values of all variables (subject, of course, to DROP and KEEP restrictions), is created immediately. The format of this statement is simply

```
OUTPUT;
```

Before we go any further, we need to make one important point about the OUTPUT statement. If there is even one OUTPUT statement anywhere in the DATA step, it completely overrides the automatic output that normally takes place at the bottom of the DATA step loop. In effect, the system washes its hands of responsibility for creating output observations. Whether you proceed normally to the bottom of the loop, or execute a RETURN statement to get there immediately, no implicit "write" takes place.

Example 5.2 Explicit I/O handling. The SAS dataset TOTAL on the FULLSET library contains customer information including a SEX code 'F' for female or 'M' for male. Each observation represents one customer. In this example, we want to collect only those observations (customers) coded as males.

The sample program below creates a new dataset called MALES, with the desired observations. Note the first IF statement: if SEX is neither F nor M (blank or garbage, perhaps), the DATA step is instructed to bypass further processing of this observation and to RETURN immediately to the top of the DATA step to retrieve the next one. Otherwise, the statement

```
IF SEX = 'M' THEN OUTPUT;
```

causes an output observation to be created at that point in the program, but only if SEX is 'M'. It is worth remembering that the output observation will contain all the values that were on the input observation, even though they were not referenced specifically in the step. For example, the FULLSET.TOTAL dataset may include variables for NAME, ADDRESS, PHONE, and so forth; they will all be retained on the output dataset MALES.

What will happen to observations in which SEX is F? They will fail the first IF test, so processing will proceed. They will also fail the second IF test, so output will not occur. At the bottom of the loop, the automatic output is suppressed because we have an OUTPUT statement in the step. So, the answer is that observations with SEX = F are not output, and control returns to the top of the loop.

```
DATA MALES;
   SET FULLSET.TOTAL;
   IF SEX NOT = 'F' AND SEX NOT = 'M' THEN RETURN;
   ELSE
   IF SEX = 'M' THEN OUTPUT;
```

You can use the OUTPUT statement to create multiple observations from one input record. For example, this code will output more observations than it reads in:

```
DATA DOUBLES;
   SET FULLSET.TOTAL;
   IF SEX = 'F' THEN OUTPUT;
   ELSE
   IF SEX = 'M' THEN OUTPUT;
   OUTPUT;
```

One observation is output for each female, one observation is output for each male, and the last statement outputs an additional observation for every input observation encountered. (This additional observation contains the same data as the first one; remember that output observations contain the current values of all variables.) So the dataset DOUBLES has twice as many observations as FULLSET.TOTAL, if we assume that all SEX codes are either 'F' or 'M'.

5.2.2 Removing duplicates and summarizing

The SAS System provides several ways to remove duplicate records from a dataset, or to summarize the information in the dataset. PROC SUMMARY and PROC FREQ can be used if your data is not sorted (see Chapter 10). But if your file is already sorted, or if you run PROC SORT first, you can summarize observations or remove duplicates in a DATA step that lets you keep more control over the processing. Figure 5.2 shows the syntax of a generalized "summarizing DATA step". This DATA step is identical to any other DATA step with SAS dataset input except for the addition of a BY statement and references to the FIRST and LAST keywords in the IF statements.

You remember the use of the BY statement in a PROC from the introduction to PROC PRINT in Chapter 4. It is used similarly in the DATA step: to tell the supervisor to keep track of the changes in value of the "BY variables". The SAS System shares this information with you through two Boolean variables which are created for each BY variable: FIRST.by-variable and LAST.by-variable. ("By-variable" is not a keyword; it is replaced with the name of the BY variable.) These internal flags are used to identify the input observation with the FIRST occurrence of the BY variable or the input observation of the LAST occurrence of the BY variable.

The SAS supervisor finds the FIRST (or LAST) occurrence, it sets the FIRST.by-variable (or LAST.by-variable) to 1. Your program can then use it as a Boolean switch. Unlike COBOL, SAS programs don't have to read a record in the next BY group to find out that the last one is finished. When LAST.by-variable = 1, you're actually pro-

```
DATA fileref;
    SET  SAS dataset;
    BY [descending] by-variable(s);
    (statements)
    If FIRST.by-variable THEN ...;
    (statements)
    IF LAST.by-variable  THEN ...;
    (statements)
```

Figure 5.2 Summarizing DATA step

cessing the last record in the group. (This means you don't have to do things like "MOVE DEPTNUM TO SAVE-LAST-DEPTNUM"!)

Example 5.3 Removing duplicates using the DATA step. Let's see how we can use FIRST.by-variable to remove duplicate records from a SAS dataset. Assume we have a dataset called ROUTINFO, that is supposed to contain one record per route. We know from experience that it may actually contain several records for the same route. The extra records must be removed.

Our first step is to sort the dataset by ROUTE. We'll create a new dataset called SORTED. (Remember that in PROC SORT, the DATA= option names the input dataset and OUT= names the output dataset.)

```
PROC SORT DATA=ROUTINFO OUT=SORTED;
    BY ROUTE;
```

We know that if there are duplicate route records, they will all occur together in dataset SORTED. Now let's consider the values of FIRST.ROUTE. If a route occurs on several observations, FIRST.ROUTE will only be equal to 1 when we process the first one. For the extras, FIRST.ROUTE will be 0. On the other hand, for routes which are not duplicated, FIRST.ROUTE will always be 1 because the first record for each route is the only record for the route.

This means if we keep only those observations which cause FIRST.ROUTE to be equal to 1, we will remove all the duplicates. This is accomplished in the following simple program, which creates a new dataset called UNDUPED containing only one record per route.

```
DATA UNDUPED;        /* NAME OUTPUT DATASET      */
    SET SORTED;      /* NAME INPUT DATASET       */
    BY ROUTE;        /* SAY THAT IT'S SORTED     */
    IF FIRST.ROUTE   /* IF 1ST OR ONLY FOR ROUTE */
        THEN OUTPUT; /* ... THEN OUTPUT          */
                     /* OTHERWISE NO OUTPUT      */
RUN;
```

This example will output only the observation that shows the FIRST occurrence of the by-variable value for ROUTE. If other observations with that by-variable value are read, the program will not output them.

Example 5.4 Summarizing observations using the DATA step. The following example illustrates a way to accumulate totals at the same time you're eliminating duplicates. The input dataset SORTED has been sorted by variable PROM_PLN. We want to count the total number of COPIES for each PROM_PLN. To do this, we will use an an accumulator variable RESPONSE which is set to zero for each new PROM_PLN value. The number of COPIES is accumulated for each record processed. (This is an extension of the type of counter variable we saw earlier, in Example 5.1. Now, instead of adding 1 for each observation, we add the value of a numeric variable.)

We will not write any output until we have processed the last input observation in each PROM_PLN group. By creating an output observation only when the last occurrence of PROM_PLN is detected, we will have only one observation per PROM_PLN value. The value of RESPONSE in that observation will equal the total number of copies found under that particular PROM_PLN value.

```
DATA SUMMED;
    SET SORTED;
    /* THE INPUT IS SORTED BY PROM_PLN             */
    BY PROM_PLN;
    /* CLEAR COUNTER AT START OF A PROM_PLN GROUP */
    IF FIRST.PROM_PLN THEN RESPONSE = 0;
    /* ADD COPIES FROM CURRENT OBS TO COUNTER      */
    RESPONSE + COPIES;
```

```
/* OUTPUT TOTAL RESPONSE AT END OF THE GROUP  */
IF LAST.PROM_PLN THEN OUTPUT;
```

Note that it is the RESPONSE variable which contains the total number of copies. The COPIES variable will still have the number of copies from the last observation in the group. It would probably be wise to specify (DROP=COPIES) on the DATA statement, to get rid of the COPIES variable and avoid confusion.

5.2.3 Limiting sequential processing: FIRSTOBS and OBS

You have already seen how to limit the number of observations in PROC PRINT by naming the input dataset and using the OBS=n dataset option. This same code works in a DATA step on the input dataset named in your SET statement. There is also a FIRSTOBS=n dataset option, which says to skip (n−1) observations before beginning. The syntax of FIRSTOBS and OBS is shown in Fig. 5.3.

FIRSTOBS is used when you want to begin sequential processing at a record other than the first one. OBS is used when you want to end processing at a record other than the last one. FIRSTOBS and OBS can be used together to define a range of records that neither starts at the first record nor ends at the last record.

If you include FIRSTOBS, but not OBS, all observations starting with the "start number" and ending with the last observation in the input dataset will be available to the DATA step statements that follow. If you include OBS, but not FIRSTOBS, the first observations from the input dataset through the "end number" will be available. If you include both FIRSTOBS and OBS, then observations from "start number" through "end number" will be available.

The following code shows how you could create a dataset that contains the first five observations of your input dataset INSET:

```
DATA FIRST_5;
    SET INSET (OBS=5);
```

Suppose you found out later that you also needed a dataset with the next five observations. The code in this case would be:

```
DATA NEXT_5;
    SET INSET (FIRSTOBS=6 OBS=10);
```

5.2.4 Using conditionals to bypass processing

We've used conditional processing numerous times before, without formally introducing it. Conditional processing refers to the common

```
DATA output dataset name;
    SET input dataset name
        ( [FIRSTOBS = start number]
          [OBS      = end number] );
    ...
```

Figure 5.3 Limiting observations with dataset options FIRSTOBS and OBS

IF . . . THEN . . . ELSE found in most programming languages, including the SAS System. Figure 5.4 shows the simple conditional IF.

You can compare character as well as numeric type variables. Character comparison is based on collating sequence, and is a byte-by-byte process (the shorter string is padded with blanks).

Any executable statements may be used in the THEN or ELSE clauses. Executable statements are statements that perform an action during the execution phase. (There are nonexecutable statements too; they're covered later in this chapter.) Right now, we're interested in bypassing observations, or bypassing some of the processing for an observation. Two executable statements that allow you to skip processing of some observations are:

- DELETE: tells the system to stop processing this observation and start the next DATA step iteration.

```
For example,
IF COPIES = 0
    THEN DELETE;
```

- GOTO statement label: tells the system to continue processing at the statement preceded by the statement label indicated. (A statement label is simply a valid SAS name followed by a colon.)

```
        IF condition(s)      THEN
                 executable statement;


A condition consists of a comparison that evaluates to true (1)
or false (0).  The comparison includes these operators (you can
use the symbol or its English abbreviation):

        A = B        or    A  = B
        A^= B        or    A NE B
        A > B        or    A GT B
        A >=B        or    A GE B
        A < B        or    A LT B
```

Figure 5.4   Simple conditional

```
For example,
IF COPIES = 0
    THEN GOTO NOCOPIES;
...
NOCOPIES:
...
```

DELETE acts somewhat like RETURN, which we saw earlier in this chapter. It skips all remaining statements and goes directly to the next loop iteration. Unlike RETURN, though, DELETE turns off the automatic output at the bottom of the DATA step.

Example 5.5 How to bypass processing with DELETE and GOTO. Let's say that your input data is supposed to have valid order codes in the first five bytes, but an earlier PROC FREQ showed that you actually have three types of values: valid order codes (numerics), missing codes (.), and invalid codes (0).

Typical data could be:

```
0---------1---------2---------3
12345 ... plus other fields
23456
00000
.
```

45678
.
67890
00000

You want to output all records with valid or missing order codes. The output observations should include a switch called VALID, which will be set to 1 when the order code is valid, or 0 when the order code is missing. The following DATA step accomplishes this and also illustrates the use of DELETE and GOTO:

```
/* OUTPUT DATASET CALLED ''SAMPLE''                */
DATA SAMPLE;
/* SPECIFY INPUT FILE                              */
   INFILE 'C:\Ordinfo\Order1.dat'
/* ALLOW FOR POSSIBILITY OF MISSING VALUES         */
   MISSOVER;
/* TRY TO GET THE ORDER CODE.                      */
/* HOLD THE INPUT LINE TO GET MORE DATA LATER      */
   INPUT @1 ORDERCD 5. @;
/* THE "VALID" SWITCH DEFAULTS TO 0 (NOT VALID) */
   VALID = 0;
/* IF ORDER CODE IS MISSING, SKIP SOME CODE        */
/* BUT REMAIN WITHIN THIS ITERATION                */
   IF ORDERCD = . THEN GOTO SKIPPIT;
   ELSE
/* IF ORDER CODE IS ZERO, GET OUT OF THIS          */
/* ITERATION IMMEDIATELY AND DON'T OUTPUT          */
   IF ORDERCD = 0 THEN DELETE;
/* IF WE ARE HERE, IT MUST BE A VALID CODE.        */
/* SET THE "VALID" SWITCH.                         */
   VALID = 1;
/* CONTINUE PROCESSING THE VALID AND MISSING       */
/* ORDER CODES.                                    */
   SKIPPIT: INPUT rest of the fields ....;
/* CREATE OUTPUT OBSERVATION.                      */
/* THIS STATEMENT REQUIRED BECAUSE THE PRESENCE    */
/* OF THE "DELETE" STATEMENT TURNED OFF THE        */
/* AUTOMATIC OUTPUT THAT NORMALLY OCCURS HERE      */
   OUTPUT;
RUN;
```

Recall that we use the MISSOVER option to allow for missing values rather than wrapping the input line to look for a value. The

INPUT statement reads in ORDERCD, then holds the line with an '@'.

The VALID = 0 assignment creates a Boolean variable to indicate whether the order code is valid (1) or invalid (0).

If the ORDERCD is missing, we don't set the "VALID" switch, but do read in more fields and OUTPUT the record.

If the ORDERCD is 0, however, we stop processing the observation and go get another record. Only when the ORDERCD is a number do we set the VALID switch on, read in more input fields, and OUTPUT the observation.

Figure 5.5 shows a PROC PRINT of the SAMPLE dataset showing variable ORDERCD. Note that the missing as well as valid order codes are included, but not the zeros. VALID is only set to 1 when the order code is valid; it is 0 when the order code is missing.

5.2.5   How to output multiple datasets

A DATA step can output more than one SAS dataset. This is especially useful if you have a dataset with mixed data that should be analyzed separately. Figure 5.6 shows the general syntax for creating multiple datasets. Although we have numbered both output datasets in Fig. 5.6, you can give them any valid permanent or temporary SAS name.

Creating multiple datasets involves two slight extensions to the

```
┌OUTPUT══════════════════════════════════
│Command ═══>

                        SAS

            OBS     ORDERCD    VALID

             1      12345        1
             2      23456        1
             3        .          0
             4      45678        1
             5        .          0
             6      67898        1
```

Figure 5.5 Bypassing observations with DELETE

```
          DATA Name1 [(dataset options)]
               Name2 [(dataset options)]
               ... ;

          SET input dataset name;
          .... (statements)....

     To output observations to separate datasets:
          IF ... THEN OUTPUT Name1;
          [ELSE]
          IF ... THEN OUTPUT Name2;
          ...
```

Figure 5.6   DATA step that outputs multiple datasets

syntax we've learned so far. The first thing we have to do is specify more than one name on the DATA statement. Remember that the DATA statement is used to name the output dataset; now we are simply naming more than one. Each dataset may have its own set of dataset options.

For example, this DATA statement says that we will be creating two output datasets, PITCHERS and HITTERS, from a (presumably larger) dataset. The PITCHERS dataset will keep only variables NAME, ERA, WINS, and LOSSES. The HITTERS dataset will keep only variables NAME, HITS, RUNS, RBI, and HOMERS.

```
DATA PITCHERS (KEEP =  NAME ERA WINS LOSSES)
     HITTERS (KEEP =  NAME HITS RUNS RBI HOMERS);
```

The other extension we have to make to our syntax is on the OUTPUT statement. We now have the option of specifying a dataset name on the OUTPUT statement. For example,

```
OUTPUT PITCHERS;
```

There are three ways to route observations to the correct output dataset(s).

1. No OUTPUT statement: Each input observation will be output into every output dataset.

2. Unspecified OUTPUT statement: Coding the OUTPUT statement without a dataset name *will output observations to every output dataset wherever the statement appears.* If it is part of a conditional statement, you may only output some of the observations, but *each one will be written to every output dataset.*

3. OUTPUT with dataset name: The system *will output an observation into the specified output dataset only.*

Example 5.6 Routing observations to multiple datasets. In this simple example, we read in the numbers 1 to 5, then attempt to separate them into a dataset of ODD numbers and one with EVEN numbers. Our program specifies two output datasets (ODD and EVEN) on the DATA statement. The MOD function tells us whether the number is even or odd, and then we decide whether to add to the EVEN dataset (OUTPUT EVEN;) or to the ODD dataset (OUTPUT ODD;). Figures 5.7 and 5.8 show the resulting ODD and EVEN datasets.

```
/* CREATE TWO OUTPUT DATASETS            */
DATA ODD EVEN;
/* GET TEST VARIABLE; OUTPUT ONLY ONE DATASET */
INPUT TESTVAR;
    IF  MOD (TESTVAR,2) = 0 THEN OUTPUT EVEN;
                            ELSE OUTPUT ODD;
/* INPUT DATA */
CARDS;
1
2
3
4
5
;
```

Now look what happens when we add an unspecified OUTPUT statement (see Figs. 5.9 and 5.10). The unspecified OUTPUT statement writes every record to both datasets, in addition to the records they've already gotten. So ODD has every record, plus an extra record for each odd value of TESTVAR. EVEN has every record, plus an extra for each even value of TESTVAR.

```
DATA ODD EVEN;
INPUT TESTVAR;
    IF  MOD (TESTVAR,2) = 0 THEN OUTPUT EVEN;
```

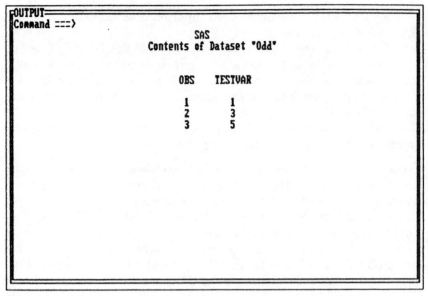

Figure 5.7   Selective output to multiple data sets

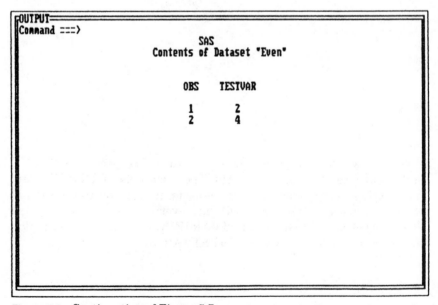

Figure 5.8   Continuation of Figure 5.7

```
                            ELSE OUTPUT ODD;
/* UNSPECIFIED OUTPUT STATEMENT */
OUTPUT;
RUN;
```

5.3   ADDING AND DELETING VARIABLES AND VALUES

The previous sections showed you how to limit the number of observations processed. In this section, you'll learn how to change the number of variables available for processing your new dataset. This is important if you want to:

1. Include new information (create new variables).
2. Save CPU and storage resources by including only the variables needed for current DATA step processes (selecting the variables).
3. Read a multiple record file (retain values across observations).
4. Rename variables (selecting the variables).

5.3.1   Selecting the variables you need: DROP, KEEP, and RENAME

As in limiting observations, there are several ways to limit the number of variables available for processing in the current DATA step. They can be limited through:

```
┌─OUTPUT════════════════════════════════════════════════════╗
│ Command ===>                                               ║
│                              SAS                           ║
│                    Contents of Dataset "Odd"              ║
│                                                            ║
│                     OBS     TESTVAR                        ║
│                                                            ║
│                      1         1                           ║
│                      2         1                           ║
│                      3         2                           ║
│                      4         3                           ║
│                      5         3                           ║
│                      6         4                           ║
│                      7         5                           ║
│                      8         5                           ║
│                                                            ║
│                                                            ║
│                                                            ║
└════════════════════════════════════════════════════════════╝
```

Figure 5.9   Default output to multiple datasets

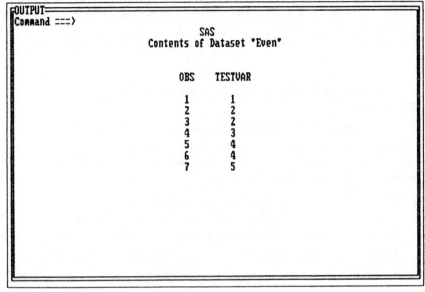

Figure 5.10   Continuation of Figure 5.9

- Dataset options: DROP, KEEP
- Statements: DROP, KEEP

Similarly, there is a RENAME dataset option and RENAME statement that allow you to change the name of a variable.

Dataset options were introduced in Chapter 4 and expanded on in the beginning of this chapter. The options DROP, KEEP, and RENAME let you define a view of the input or specify what variables to include in the output. Figure 5.11 reiterates the format of the DROP, KEEP, and RENAME dataset options.

Don't forget the dataset options follow the dataset they modify, and are enclosed in parentheses. The dataset option must have a keyword (e.g., DROP) followed by the dataset operator = and then one or more variable names or a name range.

There are also statements called DROP, KEEP, and RENAME. They accomplish the same action as their dataset option counterparts, but in this case they're in statement form. Fig. 5.12 shows the syntax of these statements.

These statements are known as "nonexecutable" statements because the action taken is not dependent on values at runtime, but applies to the entire DATA step output. Because of this, nonexecutable statements are position independent: a DROP statement at the end of a DATA step means the same as one at the beginning of a DATA step.

```
DATA output dataset (dataset options);
    SET input dataset (dataset options);

where the dataset options are:

DROP = var1 var2 ...varN
KEEP = var1 var2 ...varN
RENAME = (old1 = new1 old2 = new2...)
```

Figure 5.11   DROP, KEEP, and RENAME dataset options

```
DROP var1 ...varn;
KEEP var1 ...varn;
RENAME old1 = new1 old2 = new2;
```

Figure 5.12   DROP, KEEP, and RENAME statements

Example 5.7 Nonexecutable statements. Because nonexecutable statements are processed for the output data step, they can force you to do some nonintuitive things.

In this example, although POPPCT was renamed to PERCENT, all references to the variable (including the KEEP statement) use the old name (POPPCT). Output dataset SEGMENT1, however, will have the updated values listed under the new variable name PERCENT.

```
DATA SEGMENT1;
   SET LIST;
   KEEP POPPCT INDEX;
   RENAME POPPCT = PERCENT;
   IF POPPCT = . THEN POPPCT = 0;
   IF SRCCODE = 'A1' THEN OUTPUT;
```

5.3.2 Creating new variables

The assignment statement allows you to add new variables to your SAS dataset. Its format is simple: the name of the new variable, an equal sign (=), then an expression which defines the value it is to receive. This is shown in Fig. 5.13 and in the following examples.

```
variable = [other variable]
           [constant]
           [expression];


Note: An expression is a group of variables, constants, SAS
functions and/or punctuation that resolves to a single value
at run time.
```

Figure 5.13 Assignment statement

LEFT = RIGHT;

X = 0;

SUM = SUM + 10;

MSG = 'HELLO';

You don't have to initialize a variable before using it in an assignment statement. The system will automatically type the variable as numeric or character and then initialize it to 0 if numeric, blank if character. For clarity, you can use the LENGTH statement to tell how much storage to allocate for the variable and whether it is character or numeric.

```
LENGTH NUMVAR    4;        /* NUMERIC   */
LENGTH CHARVAR $ 3;        /* CHARACTER */
```

Numeric variables can be used in any common arithmetic operation:

```
A = B + C;
E = M * C**2;
AVGSALES = TOTSALES / NUMSALES;
```

Character variables can be the subject of special operations such as concatenation or taking a substring.

5.3.3   Creating new variables from old variables: SUBSTR and Concatenation

We mentioned that an expression could include SAS functions. Although SAS functions are covered in more detail in Chapter 8, the character function SUBSTR (substring) is introduced now to show you how to build a variable "from the rib" of another.

The SUBSTR function is followed by three arguments, enclosed in parentheses. The first is the character variable from which you would like to extract the substring. The second is the starting position (where the first character is position 1). The third argument is the desired length of the substring. Figure 5.14 shows the syntax of using the SUBSTR function. For example, if MESSAGE contains the value 'HELLO THERE', then

```
SUBSTR(MESSAGE,3,2)   is 'LL'
SUBSTR(MESSAGE,5,4)   is 'O TH'
```

If ZIPCODE contains a nine-digit ZIP code, you can extract the five-

```
new variable = SUBSTR (old variable,
                       start byte,
                       length);
```

Figure 5.14   Building a variable from another using SUBSTR

digit ZIP code by taking a substring as follows. This example assigns the string of the first five characters of ZIPCODE (a nine-digit number) to the new variable named ZIP.

```
ZIP = SUBSTR (ZIPCODE,1,5);
```

Now suppose you needed to build one variable from the values found in two or more variables. That is, you wanted to append one to the other. You can use the concatenation operator ¦¦ to do this. It's syntax is shown in Fig. 5.15.

For example, you might want a list of sales people, with the names of those who surpassed their previous year's average highlighted. The input SALEREPS has the sales person's name, the gross totals for this year (THISYR), and the gross totals for last year (LASTYR). If this year's totals exceed last year's, we'll concatenate an asterisk in front of the name to highlight it. When the report is printed, the asterisk in front of the name indicates those salespeople whose sales figures have improved.

```
DATA REPORT;
   SET SALEREPS;
   IF THISYR > LASTYR THEN '* ' ¦¦ NAME;
```

```
new variable = section1 :: section2 :: ... :: sectionN;

Each section can consist of a:
-  variable name
-  literal
-  expression that evaluates to a character value
   at run time
```

Figure 5.15 Building a variable from another using concatenation

5.3.4 Accumulating values across iterations: the Sum variable

When the SAS supervisor reads an input observation, it brings in the values associated with the variables on the dataset. These values remain the same for the duration of that DATA step iteration.

If you are creating a new variable (using the assignment statement), it is normally initialized to "missing" for each iteration of the DATA step. Your assignment statement is evaluated and then the missing value is overwritten with an actual value. There are two cases when the value will not be set to missing:

- sum variables

- RETAINED variables

The sum variable statement says that you're going to accumulate totals in the sum variable (any valid SAS name) and you're going to do this by adding the values in the accumulator variable (the accumulator variable can be of numeric or numeric-character type). Figure 5.16 shows the format of the sum variable statement. Notice that unlike other assignment statements, it does not include an equal sign. Instead, the plus sign serves as a shorthand indicating that the variable should retain its current value, plus the value to the right of the plus sign.

Only on the very first iteration of the DATA step is the value of the sum variable = 0. Each iteration after that will bring in an observation that can contribute to the accumulation. You can put the sum variable clause as the executable statement in a condition statement to restrict the accumulation. For example,

```
IF TEMP > 90
THEN HOTDAYS + 1;
```

Example 5.8 Conditional accumulation using a sum variable. In this example, we define a sum variable called SALES, which will be used to conditionally count the number of sales in February.

The sum variable SALES will be incremented by 1 when the month is February and revenue is greater than zero. When there are no more observations in the SAS dataset INPUT, the DATA step will output ACCUMFEB. ACCUMFEB contains one observation and one variable (SALES) which has the accumulated count of February sales.

```
DATA ACCUMFEB (KEEP = SALES);
    SET INPUT END=ALLDONE;
    IF  MONTH = 'FEB'
        AND REVENUE > 0 THEN SALES + 1;
    IF ALLDONE THEN OUTPUT;
```

sum variable + accumulator variable

Figure 5.16 Sum variable format

5.3.5 Retaining values across iterations: RETAIN

So far, we've seen that most variables are cleared and initialized to "missing" at the beginning of each iteration of the DATA step. We've seen one exception, sum variables, which are retained across iterations but have a limited, specific purpose. But what if you want to retain a value across observations for some other purpose.

By naming the variable in a RETAIN statement, you can indicate that you do not want the variable reinitialized at each iteration of the DATA step loop. Variables named in RETAIN statements keep their values until you explicitly change them in an assignment statement. Figure 5.17 shows the syntax of RETAIN statements.

You can optionally specify an initial value for a RETAINed variable. Remember though, that this value is set only once, the first time the statement is encountered. For example, the following statement indicates that variable BASEVAL should be initialized to 1200. This value may change, but the current value will always be retained, even across iterations of the DATA step loop. It will not be changed back to either 1200 or "missing".

```
RETAIN BASEVAL 1200;
```

Example 5.9 Accumulating with a nonzero start value. Suppose, in Example 5.8, that we had wanted to initialize ACCUMFEB not with 0, but with the $12,000 sales recorded in January. We could use a RETAIN statement to initialize the value. Note that although a RETAIN statement is not required for a sum variable, you can always include one either to initialize the variable or for clarity.

```
DATA ACCUMFEB (KEEP = SALES);
   SET INPUT END=ALLDONE;
   /* START OFF WITH 12000 SALES */
   RETAIN SALES 12000;
   IF  MONTH = 'FEB'
       AND REVENUE > 0 THEN SALES + 1;
   IF ALLDONE THEN OUTPUT;
```

The ACCUMFEB dataset now contains totals from both January and February.

RETAIN can be especially useful when your input dataset contains two types of records (one relating to parents; the other to a child), and you want to carry over some of the information from one to the output of the other.

Figure 5.17 RETAIN statement syntax

Example 5.10 Retaining values across DATA step iterations. Assume the SAS dataset PRODUCTS is a hierarchical file with a parent segment (identified by REC = 1) and multiple child segments (REC = 2). Assume also that the parent contains a field called PRODTYPE which identifies whether the trailer info is magazine, book, or record data. PRODTYPE is not included in the trailer segments (on these segments, PRODTYPE is "missing"). If you simply separated the two types of records, you would lose the PRODTYPE information that relates to the trailers. RETAIN allows you to "carry over" the value of PRODTYPE so that it is available to every record in the output dataset.

```
/* SPLIT PRODUCTS FILE INTO PARENT & CHILD SEGS */
   DATA PARENT CHILD;
      SET PRODUCTS;
/*    KEEP PRODTYPE FROM PARENT SO IT IS        */
/*    STILL AROUND WHEN WE WRITE CHILD          */
      RETAIN PRODTYPE;
/*    DECIDE WHICH TO OUTPUT.                    */
/*    BOTH WILL CONTAIN THE PRODTYPE.           */
      IF REC=1  THEN OUTPUT PARENT
                ELSE OUTPUT CHILD;
```

6

External File Output

So far, we've described how to get external file data into a SAS dataset. We've also seen how to use a SAS dataset for PROC and DATA step applications. This chapter completes the circle. It describes how to move data out of SAS datasets and back into an external file. The output file can then be read by software outside of the SAS System.

In this chapter, we'll also discuss how to create your own reports. There are times when PROC PRINT is not enough. By using an external PRINT file, however, you can write reports in any format you might want.

Finally, we cover some additional program control statements that are useful in the DATA step applications which create external files.

6.1 CREATING A FILE

SAS software makes a distinction between SAS datasets, which are created and managed exclusively by the SAS System itself, and external files. External files are the normal files managed by your operating system. For example, OS sequential and partitioned datasets, as well as VSAM datasets, are considered to be external files. On a PC, external files are listed in the DOS directory.

You'll want to create an external file if you need your data to be read by any program other than SAS software. This is because SAS datasets are maintained in an internal format which is not recognized by other languages or applications.

External datasets are created in a DATA step, using a combination of the FILE, FILENAME, and PUT statements. These statements are described in this section. Other statements used frequently in the creation of output external files are covered in the remainder of the chapter. (If you need to refresh your mind on external file input, look at Chapter 3.)

6.1.1 Defining the external output file

To identify an external output file in your SAS program, use the FILE statement (see Fig. 6.1). This statement is similar to the INFILE statement we used to define an external input file. It provides a "fileref" for your output file. (Refer to Fig. 3.2 for the general naming conventions.) On OS systems, the fileref is actually a DDname which is allocated in your JCL or TSO session. You can also specify the special name PRINT to direct output to the standard print file.

Example 6.1 External file creation in OS batch. In this example, the SAS program refers to an output file called OUTDATA. The actual dataset to be written is defined in the JCL as a disk dataset called TEST.SAS.OUTDATA.

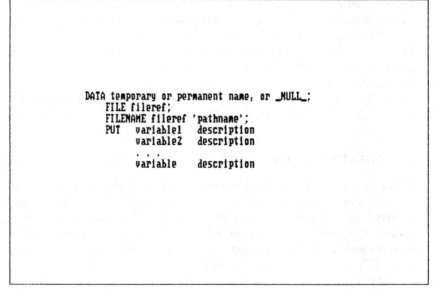

```
DATA temporary or permanent name, or _NULL_;
    FILE fileref;
    FILENAME fileref 'pathname';
    PUT    variable1    description
           variable2    description
            . . .
           variable     description
```

Figure 6.1   DATA step using external file output

```
//SASSTEP EXEC SAS
//OUTDATA   DD DSN=TEST.SAS.OUTDATA,
               DISP=(NEW,CATLG,DELETE)
//SYSIN     DD * (SAS STATEMENTS FOLLOW ...)
  DATA SASDATA;
    FILE OUTDATA; /* REFERS TO DDNAME        */
    (other SAS statements)
/*
```

On a PC, the fileref is associated with an actual dataset by using the FILENAME statement. (You can also use FILENAME on mainframe systems if it's more convenient than using JCL or TSO allocations.) Example 2.6 illustrates file creation on a PC.

Example 6.2 External file creation on a PC. This example shows how to use a SAS program to create an output file called 'OUTDATA.SAS' in the current directory. To create a file in a different directory, you would use the fully qualified path name in your FILENAME statement.

```
DATA SASDATA;
  FILENAME OUTDATA 'OUTDATA.SAS';
  FILE OUTDATA; /* REFERS TO FILENAME STMT */
  (other SAS statements)
```

The FILE statement can appear anywhere in your DATA step, but it must be placed before any PUT statement for the external file. (The PUT statement actually creates each output record; we'll cover it in detail in following Sec. 6.1.2.) In general, the cleanest way to do this is to code the FILE statement immediately before every PUT, even if this means coding the same FILE statement several times.

You can create more than one external file in a DATA step by using a separate FILE statement for each. When you do this, be sure to pair up the FILE statements with the correct PUT statements. Note the difference between Example 6.3 and Example 6.4. In Example 6.3, both PUT statements will direct output to OUTFILE2, whether or not that was the programmer's intention. In Example 6.4, the first PUT is written to OUTFILE1, and the second is written to OUTFILE2.

Example 6.3 Unclear pairing of FILE and PUT. In this example, both PUT statements are directed to OUTFILE2.

```
DATA SASDATA;
  FILE OUTFILE1;
  FILE OUTFILE2; /* OVERRIDES LAST STMT */
```

```
PUT 'TEST PUT #1';
PUT 'TEST PUT #2';
```

Example 6.4 Correct pairing of FILE and PUT. In this example, the first PUT is written to OUTFILE1 and the second to OUTFILE2.

```
DATA SASDATA;
    FILE OUTFILE1;
    PUT 'TEST PUT #1';
    FILE OUTFILE2;
    PUT 'TEST PUT #2';
```

Keep in mind that the DATA step will still be creating a SAS dataset called SASDATA, even though you are also creating an external file. These two processes are completely independent. An output SAS dataset is identified on the DATA statement, and observations are written with OUTPUT statements (or automatically at the end of the DATA step loop). An output external file is identified on the FILE statement, and records are written with PUT statements.

If you do not need to create a SAS dataset (i.e., you are only interested in the output external file), you can specify a "null" DATA statement by replacing the name of the SAS dataset (SASDATA) with the keyword __NULL__. This acts like the "DUMMY" parameter in OS JCL; the output SAS dataset is not created, but the step processes normally in all other respects.

```
DATA _NULL_;
```

6.1.2. Formatting output records

The PUT statement formats and writes output records on the external file. Usually, a PUT statement will include the names of several SAS variables. Most of the time, you'll also want to specify each variable's location within the output record as well as its format. There are many variations on the PUT statement. In this section, we describe a simple formatted approach which will serve for most of your output requirements.

A PUT statement consists of the word PUT followed by a description of each variable you want to output. The description group consists of three parts which are specified together for each variable:

1. the position of the output variable

2. the name of the SAS variable to be output

3. the format of the output variable

Example 6.5 Using the PUT statement. In this example, SAS software is used to reformat an external file. The variables SALESREP, ROUTE, and QUANTITY are extracted from a large external input record, and written to an output external file with smaller records.

Notice that the PUT statement looks similar to the INPUT statement we used to read from an external file. Each variable to be output is represented by its position, name, and format. The position and format do not have to match the original input. Recall that $CHARn. is a standard character format specifying a length of n bytes, and plain n. is a standard numeric format of n bytes.

```
* CREATE SAS DATASET 'INDATA 'FROM
  INPUT EXTERNAL FILE 'BIGFILE';
  DATA INDATA;
      INFILE BIGFILE;
*     READ THE INPUT FIELDS;
      INPUT @152 SALESREP  $CHAR30.
            @217 ROUTE     3.
            @296 QUANTITY  5.;
  DATA OUTDATA;
      SET INDATA;
      FILE MINIFILE;
*     WRITE THE FIELDS AT NEW POSITIONS;
      PUT   @1   SALESREP  $CHAR30.
            @40  ROUTE     3.
            @50  QUANTITY  5.;
```

6.1.3. Specifying output position

The output position of a variable can be specified in several ways. We saw the most direct one in Example 6.5, where the column number is specified explicitly using "@." SALESREP will be output at column 1, ROUTE at column 40, and QUANTITY at column 50. If you need to format several lines at once, you can use # to indicate the relative line number as well as @ to indicate the column. You can also use / to skip to the next line. Note that # specifies a particular line number within the group, while / always goes to the next line.

You can specify fields in any order, even across several records, because the output records are not released until the semicolon at the end of the statement. When the records are released, columns which were not associated with any output fields will contain blanks. This PUT statement creates two records, the first containing NAME and ADDRESS and the second containing CITY, STATE, and ZIP:

```
PUT #1  @1  NAME     $CHAR30.
        @31 ADDRESS  $CHAR30.
    #2  @1  CITY     $CHAR20.
        @21 STATE    $CHAR2.
        @23 ZIP      $CHAR5.;
```

To reduce the dependence on hard-coded column numbers, you can use the + sign in specifying output position. This indicates a position relative to the last column of the previous field.

Example 6.6 Using relative positioning. This program reworks the output step of Example 6.5. It uses relative positioning to reduce the need for counting and hard-coding column numbers.

```
/* CREATE OUTPUT EXTERNAL FILE 'MINIFILE'   */
/* FROM SAS DATASET 'INDATA'                 */
   DATA OUTDATA;
        SET INDATA;
        FILE MINIFILE;
/* FIRST FIELD WRITTEN IN BYTES 1-30         */
        PUT   @1   SALESREP  $CHAR30.
/* THE LAST FIELD ENDED AT BYTE 30, SO THE   */
/* NEXT ONE WOULD NORMALLY START AT BYTE 31. */
/* +10 SAYS TO START INSTEAD AT BYTE 41      */
              +10   ROUTE     3.
/* THE LAST FIELD ENDED AT BYTE 43, SO THE   */
/* NEXT ONE WOULD NORMALLY START AT BYTE 44. */
/* +6 SAYS TO START INSTEAD AT BYTE 50       */
              +6   QUANTITY   5.;
```

The #, @, and + position indicators may use variables in place of the numeric constants we've seen so far. This is useful not only for maintainability, but for situations where the output position may depend on a particular condition.

Example 6.7 Using variable output positioning. In this example, an external name and address file (NAMEADDR) is being created from information on the SAS dataset SASMAST. The output requirements specify that we must create two types of records on the same file. If a record has TYPE = 'A', it should include name and address data beginning at column 10. All other records should begin the name and address at column 100. Within the name and address group, the formatting is identical for both types of records.

Notice also that we omitted the position indicators for all but the first variable. This means that each output variable will immediately follow the preceding one, with no intervening spaces.

```
/* DATA STEP TO CREATE OUTPUT FILE ONLY   */
    DATA _NULL_;
/* INPUT SAS DATASET 'SAS''MAST'          */
SET SASMAST;
/* USE 'TYPE' TO DETERMINE OUTPUT COLUMN  */
/* OF NAME/ADDRESS AREA: BYTE 10 OR 100   */
        IF TYPE = 'A'
            THEN OUTCOL = 10;
            ELSE OUTCOL = 100;
/* IDENTIFY THE OUTPUT FILE AND WRITE IT. */
/* NAME/ADDRESS GROUP HAS CORRECT COLUMN  */
        FILE NAMEADDR;
        PUT @OUTCOL NAME      $CHAR30.
                    STREET1   $CHAR30.
                    STREET2   $CHAR30.
                    CITY      $CHAR20.
                    STATE     $CHAR2.
                    ZIP       $CHAR5.;
```

6.1.4 Specifying output formats

In some cases, you will not need to specify an output format on the PUT statement. This is true when the default format is acceptable or when your input is a SAS dataset and you used the FORMAT statement to assign appropriate formats to the variables (see Chapter 5).

However, you will probably want to specify formats for output variables fairly frequently. For example, numeric variables can be output in packed-decimal or binary formats, "standard" character numeric, with commas and/or dollar signs, and so forth. There is even a SAS output format for Roman numerals! Figure 6.2 shows some common SAS formats.

Most formats include a portion described as "w." or "w.d." The "w" indicates the width, the maximum number of columns to use for the printed field. The "d" indicates the number of decimal places (for numeric fields). For example, DOLLAR15.2 reserves 15 print positions (including the dollar sign, commas, period, and digits) including two positions for decimal digits.

Many other formats are described in the SAS documentation, but these are the most commonly used. When outputting numeric display data, pay particular attention to the difference between w. and Zw. formats. The "Z" must be included if you want leading zeros. You'll probably want to use the Zw. formats when creating nonprint files such as disk or tape files, but w. for most print files.

Also remember that the length portion always specifies the number of output bytes, not the number of numeric digits. Thus, a format of PD3. will output a three-byte, packed-decimal number, which may range as high as +99999.

SAS date formats can also be used to output dates in many common formats. Some of the most common date formats are MMDDYYw., YYMMDDw., and MONYYw. In the date formats, w. controls whether or not extra formatting characters are included; for example, MMDDYY6. will display 022895 while MMDDYY8. will display 02/28/95. To use the date formats, your data must be stored in SAS date form. The date formats must have been used when you created the dataset (see Chapter 3).

Also remember that PROC FORMAT can be used to define special formats customized to your application. This can relieve you of much programming work, while providing professional-looking reports. Example 6.8 shows a simple use of PROC FORMAT in producing an

FORMAT	DESCRIPTION	EXAMPLE	OUTPUT
w.	Standard display numeric	5.	12345
w.d	Numeric with decimals	5.2	12345.67
ZDw.	Zoned decimal	ZD5.	Hex F1F2F3F4F5
PDw.	Packed decimal	PD5.	Hex 000012345C
IBw.	Binary	IB5.	Hex 0000003039
Zw.d	Numeric with leading zeros	Z6.	012345
COMMAw.d	Numeric with commas	COMMA5.2	12,345.67
DOLLARw.d	Numeric with dollar sign and commas	DOLLAR10.2	12,345.67
$w.	Standard character	$5.	HELLO
$CHARw.	Character with blanks	$CHAR11.	HELLO THERE

Figure 6.2   Common SAS output formats

output report. (We'll cover PRINT files more fully in Sec. 6.2.1. For a complete discussion of PROC FORMAT, see Chapter 4.)

Example 6.8 Using PROC FORMAT in creating a report. Suppose your dataset contains information about items in a retail catalog. One of the variables, SRC_SHIP, might indicate the source of each item. For example, large or customized items may be shipped directly from the supplier; these items are marked with SRC_SHIP = X. Items shipped from your company's three warehouses (EAST, WEST, and CENTRAL) are marked with SRC_SHIP A, B, and C respectively. PROC FORMAT can be used to translate these codes into displayable descriptions. Actual data values, saved in a permanent dataset called CATALOG.INFO, include the following:

PART_NUM	SRC_SHIP
019743	X
019882	A
110236	C
181742	C
190163	X
203455	B
694378	Z

Here is a simple report program, using PROC FORMAT to reformat the SRC_SHIP code. This produces the report shown in Fig. 6.3.

```
* DEFINE THE FORMAT TO TRANSLATE 'A' TO 'EAST', ETC.;
  PROC FORMAT;
        VALUE  $SRCFMT
               'A'    = 'EAST'
               'B'    = 'WEST'
               'C'    = 'CENTRAL'
               'X'-'Z' = 'SHIPPED DIRECTLY FROM SUPPLIER';
* DATA STEP TO WRITE REPORT FROM SET CATALOG.INFO;
  DATA_NULL_;
        SET CATALOG.INFO;
        FILE PRINT; /* OUTPUT IS TO STANDARD PRINT FILE */
* WRITE PART_NUM IN STANDARD NUMERIC FORMAT
  WITH 6 DIGITS INCLUDING LEADING ZEROES
  AND SRC_SHIP USING OUR OWN $SRCFMT FORMAT;
        PUT @1  PART_NUM   Z6.
            @10 SRC_SHIP   $SRCFMT.;
```

6.2. CREATING A CUSTOM REPORT WITH PROC FORMAT

A quick look at the output of the last section, Fig. 6.3, will convince you that this is not a particularly good report. There are no mean-

```
┌─OUTPUT═══════════════════════════════════════════════════════════════════┐
│Command ===>                                                               │
│                                                                           │
│                              SAS                                          │
│019743   SHIPPED DIRECTLY FROM SUPPLIER                                    │
│019882   EAST                                                             │
│110236   CENTRAL                                                          │
│181742   CENTRAL                                                          │
│190163   SHIPPED DIRECTLY FROM SUPPLIER                                    │
│203455   WEST                                                             │
│694378   SHIPPED DIRECTLY FROM SUPPLIER                                    │
│                                                                           │
│                                                                           │
│                                                                           │
│                                                                           │
│                                                                           │
│                                                                           │
│                                                                           │
│                                                                           │
│                                                                           │
│                                                                           │
│                                                                           │
│                                                                           │
└───────────────────────────────────────────────────────────────────────────┘
```

Figure 6.3   DATA step report using custom formats

ingful headings, for one thing. In the following sections, you'll learn how to create a full-featured report using SAS basic software.

6.2.1. PRINT files as external files

The SAS System considers printed reports to be simply a special case of external file output. To indicate that you are using the standard print file, use the special name PRINT instead of the normal external file name. You will not have to provide a DD statement if you use the standard print file.

```
FILE PRINT;
```

You can also specify PRINT on named output files. For example, the following statement will treat the OUTRPT file as a print file.

```
FILE OUTRPT PRINT;
```

Even if you do not code PRINT, the supervisor will attempt to determine if you "really" wanted a print file. For example, on OS systems the software will create a print file whenever the file's DD statement includes the SYSOUT parameter. Don't depend on this, though. You may get into trouble if you override the DD to create a permanent dataset and later attempt to print it. If you are creating a print file, code PRINT!

The reason the SAS System distinguishes so carefully between print and nonprint files has to do partly with carriage control characters. SAS print files are automatically created with a carriage control character in column 1 of each line; the printed data does not begin until column 2. Nonprint files do not include the carriage control characters, so data begins immediately in column 1. Of course, this is transparent to your program; you always specify @1 as the first data position.

There are a number of DATA step features that are primarily intended for print files. These include the HEADER, LINESLEFT, PAGESIZE, and N=PAGESIZE options on the FILE statement, as well as __PAGE__ specifications on the PUT statement. These features are introduced in the following sections of this chapter which cover specific report situations.

6.2.2 A simple report with headings

As we saw in Example 6.8, you can produce a simple report by using a DATA step with FILE and PUT statements, just as you would for any external file. However, our example had some problems. One problem we noted is the lack of meaningful headings. When you design your own report by using a DATA step, the system makes no assumptions about headings. Compare the DATA step output in Fig. 6.3 with an equivalent PROC PRINT in Fig. 6.4. You can see that PROC PRINT produces a more meaningful report.

The simplest way to get headings is to use the TITLE statement. We encountered this statement in our discussion of PROC PRINT in Chapter 4, Section 4.6.1. It works just as well here. The TITLE statement allows you to specify a full line of constant text which will be printed at the top of each page. If you require more than one line, you can use TITLE1 through TITLE10, in place of TITLE. Figure 6.5 shows the report with its title and our program, which now includes TITLE statements to produce the three-line constant heading. (PC users can also use the TITLES window to specify titles. We'll cover this in Chapter 12.)

TITLE has several advantages. It is simple to use, and it can also be used in the same format to supply page headings for PROC step output. The bad news is that TITLE only prints constants. If the heading is to contain any variable data or requires positioning, you cannot use TITLE.

This problem is easily remedied. When you use the FILE statement to identify your output file, you can also identify a header rou-

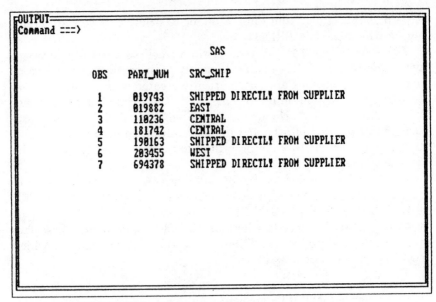

```
┌OUTPUT══════════════════════════════════════════════════════════════════
│Command ===>
│
│                              SAS
│
│              OBS    PART_NUM    SRC_SHIP
│
│               1      019743     SHIPPED DIRECTLY FROM SUPPLIER
│               2      019882     EAST
│               3      110236     CENTRAL
│               4      181742     CENTRAL
│               5      190163     SHIPPED DIRECTLY FROM SUPPLIER
│               6      203455     WEST
│               7      694378     SHIPPED DIRECTLY FROM SUPPLIER
│
│
└─────────────────────────────────────────────────────────────────────────
```

Figure 6.4   PROC PRINT using custom formats

```
┌OUTPUT══════════════════════════════════════════════════════════════════
│Command ===>
│                      AMERICAN CATALOG COMPANY
│                       -- SOURCES OF PARTS --
│
│019743    SHIPPED DIRECTLY FROM SUPPLIER
│019882    EAST
│110236    CENTRAL
│181742    CENTRAL
│190163    SHIPPED DIRECTLY FROM SUPPLIER
│203455    WEST
│694378    SHIPPED DIRECTLY FROM SUPPLIER
├PROGRAM EDITOR═══════════════════════════════════════════════════════════
│Command ===>
│
│00001 data;                      /* Output SAS dataset has default name */
│00002    file print;             /* Output external print file         */
│00003    set info;               /* Input is SAS dataset "info"        */
│00004    put @1 part_num z6.           /* Print part # (6-byte #)       */
│00005       @10 src_ship $srcfmt.;     /* & source w/custom format      */
│00006    title1 'AMERICAN CATALOG COMPANY'; /* First line of title      */
│00007    title2 ' -- SOURCES OF PARTS -- '; /* Second line of title     */
│00008    title3 '                       ';  /* Third line of title      */
└─────────────────────────────────────────────────────────────────────────
```

Figure 6.5   Report headings using TITLEs

tine. The header routine is simply a section of your program that will be executed whenever a new page is started. It can be as long or short, as simple or complicated as you wish. In all likelihood, it will include PUT statements to write the header records, but it may include other DATA step statements as well.

You must give the header routine a statement label. Recall that a SAS statement label is a keyword followed by a colon (e.g., HEADRTN:); it is used to mark a location within the SAS program. In this case, the statement label will be used in two places. First, it is named in the HEADER option on the FILE statement:

```
FILE PRINT HEADER=HEADRTN;
```

Then, it is used as a label just before the header routine statements:

```
HEADRTN:
```

Figure 6.6 shows the program of Fig. 6.5, updated to include page headers. The FILE statement specifies HEADER=HRTN, which means that whenever it is time for a page break, the program will branch to label HRTN. The program statements at HRTN create three header lines. (Recall that "/" in a PUT statement says to skip to the next line.)

Both the main program and the header routine end with RETURN statements. This is necessary for your program to work correctly. We've already seen that the RETURN statement in a main program means to skip to the bottom of the main DATA step loop; here, we are using it to skip the header routine. In the header routine, it does something different: it returns to the main program to process the PUT statement which caused the page break.

Also note that we now have to keep track of page numbers ourselves. We count the pages in a sum variable PGNUM, which is initialized to 0 and incremented only in the header routine. PGNUM is then included in the PUT statement for the header lines.

6.2.3 Forcing page breaks and using page footings

You do not have do anything special to control page breaks. The supervisor will automatically keep track of the number of lines printed and begin a new page when necessary. It will automatically process any HEADER= routine or TITLE statements whenever a new page is started.

However, there will probably be times when you'll want addi-

```
┌─PROGRAM EDITOR══════════════════════════════════════════════════════════════
│ Command ===>
│
│ 00001 data;                            /* Default output SAS dataset     */
│ 00002     file print header=hrtn;      /* Print file with header routine */
│ 00003     set info;                    /* Input SAS dataset              */
│ 00004     put @1  part_num  z6.        /* Write the detail info to print */
│ 00005         @10 src_ship $srcfmt.;
│ 00006     return;                      /* End of main line               */
│ 00007 hrtn:                            /* *** Header routine starts here  */
│ 00008     pgnum + 1;                             /* It ups the page # ... */
│ 00009     put @28 'AMERICAN CATALOG COMPANY'    /* .. prints titles  ... */
│ 00010         @75 pgnum 4.
│ 00011       / @28 ' -- SOURCES OF PARTS -- '
│ 00012       / @28 '                        ';
│ 00013     return;                      /* .. returns to main line        */
│ 00014 run;
│ 00015
│ 00016 /* Note: the return to the main line sends us to the "put" at line 4 */
│ 00017 /* because this is the statement that sensed the need for page break */
│ 00018
│ 00019
│ 00020
│ 00021
│
└──────────────────────────────────────────────────────────────────────────────
```

Figure 6.6 Report headings using header routine

tional control over page breaks. For instance, your pages may be an unusual length, as with special forms. Or you may want to print "footings" at the bottom of some or all of the pages. Or, you may want to force page breaks for readability.

You can control the number of lines per page by using the PAGESIZE option on your FILE statement. PAGESIZE=n means a maximum of n lines will be printed on one page, including the headers. Figure 6.7 shows a report program which has been modified to print only forty lines per page by using the PAGESIZE=40 option.

You may want to force a page break before the actual page limit is reached. For example, a report of sales by department may be more useful if each department is broken out onto a separate page. Whenever you want to force a page break, you can use the special variable __PAGE__ in any PUT statement:

```
PUT _PAGE_;
```

The special variable __PAGE__ alerts the supervisor to begin a new page immediately, regardless of the current line count. Figure 6.8 shows how to produce a sales report with each department on a separate page. Note how FIRST.DEPT is used to recognize the start of each department's data, and PUT __PAGE__ to force the new department to a new page. Of course, the data must have been sorted prior to this step.

```
┌PROGRAM EDITOR───────────────────────────────────────────────────────┐
│Command ===)                                                          │
│                                                                      │
│00001 data; /* Default output SAS dataset  */                         │
│00002     set trans.tuesday; /* Input permanent SAS dataset (2 names)    */│
│00003     file print header=hrtn pagesize=40; /* Print file: 40 lines/page */│
│00004     put @25 tran_id    $2.                 /* Write detail info    */│
│00005         +4  n_units    comma6.                                  │
│00006         +4  dollars    dollar9.2;                               │
│00007     return;                            /* End of main line      */│
│00008 hrtn:                                  /* Header routine        */│
│00009     pgnum + 1;                                                  │
│00010     put @20 'TRANSACTION REPORT FOR WEDNESDAY'                  │
│00011         @75 pgnum 4.                                            │
│00012         /;                                                      │
│00013     return;                            /* End of header routine  */│
│00014                                                                 │
│00015                                                                 │
│00016                                                                 │
│00017                                                                 │
│00018                                                                 │
│00019                                                                 │
│00020                                                                 │
│00021                                                                 │
└──────────────────────────────────────────────────────────────────────┘
```

Figure 6.7   Report with PAGESIZE modified

```
┌PROGRAM EDITOR───────────────────────────────────────────────────────┐
│Command ===)                                                          │
│                                                                      │
│00001 data _null_;               /* Don't need SAS dataset output       */│
│00002     set sales.info;                                            │
│00003     by dept;               /* Input sorted by "dept", we want breaks */│
│00004     file print;                                                │
│00005     if first.dept then     /* Each time the "dept" value changes ... */│
│00006         put _page_;        /* .. we start a new page             */│
│00007     startcol = 40;                                             │
│00008     put @startcol dept     /* Write the detail info             */│
│00009         +2    sales comma9.2;                                  │
│00010     title1 '          SALES BY DEPARTMENT';    /* Title lines    */│
│00011     title3 '          DEPT    SALES';                          │
│00012 run;                                                           │
│00013                                                                │
│00014                                                                │
│00015                                                                │
│00016                                                                │
│00017                                                                │
│00018                                                                │
│00019                                                                │
│00020                                                                │
│00021                                                             I──│
└──────────────────────────────────────────────────────────────────────┘
```

Figure 6.8   Forcing page breaks with PUT __PAGE__

You can also use the LINESLEFT option to control page breaks. LINESLEFT allows you to check how close you are to the bottom of a page, and control your program accordingly. You can use this to add page footings to your report. When you specify LINESLEFT for a print file, you name a variable in which the SAS System will always place the number of lines left on the current page. For example,

```
FILE PRINT LINESLEFT=LLVAR;
```

says to use a variable called LLVAR to hold the number of remaining lines. (You can call the variable anything you want.) You can then use this variable as you would any other SAS variable.

In Fig. 6.9, we use LINESLEFT to place a note at the bottom of each page. Whenever LINESLEFT goes below 2, we assume we are "close enough" to the bottom of the page to force the page footings and a new page.

6.2.4 Full-page formatting

In addition to the line-oriented reports we've seen so far, you can create a report by formatting each page in its entirety before printing. This can be extremely useful. For example, a multicolumn listing is easier to use if the entries read down each column, but it is

```
┌─PROGRAM EDITOR══════════════════════════════════════════════════
│Command ===>
│
│00001 data _null_;
│00002     set sales.info;
│00003     by dept;                              /* Want control breaks by dept  */
│00004     file print linesleft=tobottom;        /* Also want to know ...        */
│00005     if tobottom < 2 then                  /* .. if we are 2 lines from    */
│00006         do;                               /* .. page bottom, for footnote */
│00007         put / @1 'NOTE: Sales figures are subject to verification';
│00008         put _page_;
│00009         end;
│00010     startcol = 40;
│00011     put @startcol dept
│00012         +2        sales comma9.2;
│00013     title1 '          SALES BY DEPARTMENT';
│00014     title3 '          DEPT    SALES';
│00015 run;
│00016
│00017
│00018
│00019
│00020
│00021
│
└══════════════════════════════════════════════════════════════I══
```

Figure 6.9 Adding footnotes using LINESLEFT

difficult to create such a listing unless you can format the entire page as a unit.

To select page-oriented processing, code option N=PAGESIZE (or N=PS) on your PRINT statement. Then code your PUT statements as before. Remember that just as you use @ in the PUT statement to specify a column number, you can also use # to specify a line number. For example, the following statement writes HELLO at line 7, column 23:

```
PUT #7 @23 'HELLO';
```

Example 6.9 creating a multicolumn report. This program illustrates how to create a multicolumn report. Notice the specification of N=PS. The variable LVAR is used to specify the line number and CVAR to specify column. The nested DO loops will be covered in detail in the next chapter, but their use should be clear: we vary the line number from 1 to 5 within each column, creating three columns spaced at 20 positions apart. When the page is complete, we use PUT _PAGE_ to print it. A portion of the output is shown in Fig. 6.10. (Of course, we could also add column headings to make it more readable.)

```
* CREATE MULTICOLUMN REPORT FROM SET 'GRADES';
  TITLE 'LIST OF GRADES';
  DATA _NULL_;
*     CREATE A COLUMN STARTING AT BYTE 15
*     AND THEN EVERY 20 BYTES THEREAFTER;
      DO CVAR = 15 to 55 BY 20;
*         IN EACH COLUMN, CREATE 5 ROWS;
          DO LVAR = 1 to 5;
*             GET OBSERVATION TO BE DISPLAYED;
              SET GRADES;
*             FORMAT DATA AT THE RIGHT ROW/COLUMN.
              THE "N=PS" SAYS THAT WE ARE
              FORMATTING AN ENTIRE PAGE;
              FILE PRINT N=PS;
              PUT #LVAR @CVAR SOC_SEC
                      +3    GRADE;
          END;
      END;
      WHEN ALL ROW/COLUMN POSITIONS HAVE BEEN
      FILLED, OUTPUT THE COMPLETE PAGE;
      PUT _PAGE_;
```

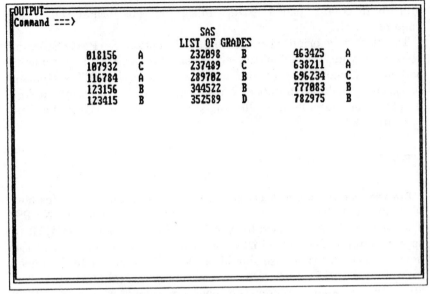

Figure 6.10 Full-page formatted report

6.2.5 Redirecting print files

As we've seen, any output external file can be specified as a PRINT
file. This gives you great flexibility in directing PRINT files created
in a DATA step. However, the assignment must be made again for
every PRINT file in every step. If you would simply like to redirect
all output to a new destination, you can use PROC PRINTTO to
reassign the standard print file. PROC PRINTTO does not create any
output by itself; it is a separate step which you include in your program before the DATA or PROC steps which will create the output.

PROC PRINTTO allows you to assign the standard print file to
any valid fileref (DDname) or pathname. Here's a PC example, which
will direct all standard print file output to the DOS file called
'c:\SASOUT\LIST2.PRT'.

```
PROC PRINTTO PRINT='c:\SASOUT\LIST2.PRT'
```

This example could have been written using a fileref and the
FILENAME option, as follows:

```
FILENAME LIST2 'c:\SASOUT\LIST2.PRT';
PROC PRINTTO PRINT=LIST2;
```

On OS systems, you can use JCL or TSO allocations instead of the

FILENAME statement. You can specify either an output dataset or a particular SYSOUT. The following example creates two copies of all standard print output on SYSOUT class B. This is because PROC PRINTTO specifies DDname LIST2 for all standard print output, and the DD statement for LIST2 includes SYSOUT=B and COPIES=2.

```
//LIST2    DD   SYSOUT=B,COPIES=2
//SAS      EXEC SAS
  PROC PRINTTO PRINT=LIST2;
```

The standard print file includes output from two sources. It receives all output from DATA steps which is directed to FILE PRINT. It also receives all PROC step output. Since PROC steps do not allow you to specify FILE PRINT, if you want to redirect any PROC step output you must use PROC PRINTTO.

In the following example, we route PROC FREQ output to the dataset with fileref FREQOUT. All standard print output from subsequent PROC and DATA steps will also be written to FREQOUT.

```
PROC PRINTTO PRINT=FREQOUT;
PROC FREQ;
   (more SAS statements)
```

To restore the standard print file to its default setting, code

```
PROC PRINTTO PRINT=PRINT
```

Everything we've said about the standard print file applies equally to the SAS log. For example, to route the SAS log to a dataset whose fileref is LOGDD, you can code

```
PROC PRINTTO LOG=LOGDD;
```

To restore the log to its default setting, code

```
PROC PRINTTO LOG=LOG;
```

Finally, your installation may have already defined several print destinations using the filerefs FTnnF001, where nn is a two-digit number. This is not as odd as it sounds. These are the standard filerefs used by the SAS System; the standard print file is FT12F001. To direct your standard print file output to FTnnF001, code

```
PROC PRINTTO UNIT=nn;
```

To restore this setting to its default, code

```
PROC PRINTTO;
```

6.3   ADDITIONAL CONTROL STATEMENTS

This section covers some important SAS statements that are useful not only in creating external files, but in many other situations. They are particularly important for designing "structured" SAS programs that are modular and easy to modify.

6.3.1.   The SELECT statement

The SELECT statement provides a convenient way of choosing one of several processing paths, depending on a particular value. It is similar to the "CASE" statement in other languages. For example, your program may need to select a different processing routine depending on a geographic state code. Missouri residents have one set of rules, Delaware another, and so on.

One way to code this is shown in Example 6.10. Here, we use a series of chained IF . . . THEN . . . ELSE clauses to select the appropriate processing for the current value of STATE.

Example 6.10 Processing selection using IF/ELSE.

```
IF STATE = 'AL' THEN
     (SAS Statement)
ELSE
IF STATE = 'AK' THEN
     (SAS Statement)
ELSE

        . . .
        . . .

ELSE
IF STATE = 'WY' THEN
ELSE
     (SAS Statement);
```

Strings of IF/ELSE conditions such as those in Example 6.10 can become cumbersome and unclear. The SELECT statement can simplify coding. Figure 6.11 shows the general format of the SELECT statement.

The SELECT statement actually begins a statement group that

```
SELECT;      or  SELECT (expression);
    WHEN (expression) statement;
    WHEN (expression) statement;
    . . .
    OTHERWISE statement;
    END;
```

Figure 6.11 SELECT statement syntax

always terminates with an END statement. The WHEN and OTH-
ERWISE clauses are used within the SELECT group to direct processing depending on the value of a variable or expression.

The SELECT group essentially consists of a control value, which
is named in parentheses in the SELECT statement, and a list of candidate values, each named in parentheses in a separate WHEN
statement. The control and candidate values can be variable names,
constants, or expressions. Each WHEN value is associated with a
processing routine. The WHEN values are compared one by one to
the SELECT value. If a match is found, only the associated routine
is performed; all of the rest are ignored.

If no match is found, the SELECT statement performs the routine
associated with the OTHERWISE statement, if it is present. Otherwise, an error condition is created.

There is another form of the SELECT statement, which omits the
control value and replaces the candidate values with full-fledged conditions. In many situations, the two are equivalent; for example,
these two code segments will have the same effect:

```
SELECT (PRODUCT);
    WHEN (02)          LINK PROD02;
    OTHERWISE          LINK PRODXX;
END;
```

```
SELECT;
    WHEN (PRODUCT = 02) LINK PROD02;
    OTHERWISE          LINK PRODXX;
END;
```

Example 6.11 shows Example 6.10, rewritten to use the SELECT statement. Notice that each of the SELECT and WHEN statements names a particular value enclosed in parentheses (the parentheses are required). Each WHEN statement also includes another SAS statement, which is performed if, and only if, the associated WHEN value matches the SELECT value.

Example 6.11 Processing selection using SELECT.

```
SELECT (STATE);
    WHEN ('AL') SAS statement;
    WHEN ('AK') SAS statement;
       . . .
    WHEN ('WY') SAS statement;
    OTHERWISE SAS statement;
END;
```

In Example 6.11, the SELECT value was a single SAS variable and all the WHEN values were constants. This need not be the case. Remember, both SELECT and WHEN may name variables, constants, or expressions of any complexity.

Just as important, the SAS statement associated with each WHEN value does not have to be a single SAS statement. It can be several statements enclosed in a DO/END pair. In fact, each WHEN statement can specify a routine of arbitrary complexity, as long as it is bracketed by a DO/END pair. Both the DO statement and END statement must include semicolons; we'll discuss this in more detail in Chapter 7.

Also, any WHEN value may be associated with a "null" routine by simply not specifying any SAS statement. If the SELECT value matches this WHEN value, no processing will be performed and the OTHERWISE statement will not be activated.

In Example 6.12, we use a SELECT statement to determine counts of one-car, two-car, and multicar households. People with no cars are ignored. (Notice the null statement associated with the WHEN(0) condition.) An appropriate message is also created for each type. Our database does not have a total car figure for each household, so we need to add the figures for domestic cars and foreign cars.

Example 6.12 More complex SELECT.

```
/* ADD DOMESTIC + FOREIGN CARS FOR THE HOUSEHOLD   */
/* AND SELECT PROCESSING BASED ON THE RESULT        */
SELECT (DOMCARS + FGNCARS);
```

```
/* IF NO CARS, DON'T DO ANYTHING                  */
WHEN (0);
/* IF ONE CAR, ADD TO THE "ONE-CAR" COUNTER   */
/* AND SET APPROPRIATE GREETING                  */
WHEN (1) DO;
          ONECAR + 1;
          MSG = 'DEAR SINGLE CAR OWNER';
          END;
/* IF TWO CARS, ADD TO THE "TWO-CAR" COUNTER */
/* AND SET APPROPRIATE GREETING                  */
WHEN (2)  DO;
            TWOCAR + 1;
            MSG = 'DEAR PROUD TWO-CAR OWNER';
            END;
/* OTHERWISE, ADD TO THE "MULTICAR" COUNTER  */
/* AND SET APPROPRIATE GREETING                  */
OTHERWISE DO;
            MULTICAR + 1;
            MSG = 'DEAR PRIVILEGED MULTICAR OWNER';
            END;
END;
```

6.3.2 The LINK statement

The LINK statement allows you to code modular subprograms and call them from your main program. LINK is easy to use, and should be employed when developing production programs of any size. This statement consists of the keyword LINK followed by a SAS statement label. Figure 6.12 shows the general format of the LINK statement. LINK allows you to create a routine of any complexity, give it a name, and then call it from anywhere within your SAS program. For example, the main line of our Example 6.12 could have been coded without knowing the details of each WHEN statement group. Look at Example 6.13 and note that the processing details have been stripped out. LINK statements have been substituted.

Example 6.13 Coding LINK in a main program.

```
SELECT (DOMCARS + FGNCARS);
    WHEN (0) LINK RTNOCAR;
    WHEN (1) LINK RTN1CAR;
    WHEN (2) LINK RTN2CAR;
    OTHERWISE LINK RTNMCAR;
END;
```

The routines named in your LINK statements should be coded

```
DATA;
     LINK label;
     RETURN;

label:
     (SAS statements)
     RETURN;
```

Figure 6.12 LINK statement syntax

after the main program. Each LINKed routine as well as the main program itself should end with a RETURN statement. This prevents incorrect fall-throughs from one routine to another. (We've already seen something like this in our discussion of header routines, Sec. 6.2.2.) Example 6.14 shows the car-counting program with its LINKed routines.

Example 6.14 Adding the LINKed routines.

```
/* ADD DOMESTIC AND FOREIGN CARS FOR HOUSEHOLD */
/* AND SELECT APPROPRIATE SUBROUTINE           */
   SELECT (DOMCARS + FGNCARS);
        WHEN (0) LINK RTNOCAR;
        WHEN (1) LINK RTN1CAR;
        WHEN (2) LINK RTN2CAR;
        OTHERWISE LINK RTNMCAR;
   END;
/* RETURN HERE PREVENTS FALLING THROUGH        */
/* TO THE SUBROUTINES                          */
   RETURN;
/* SUBROUTINE FOR 0 CARS.                      */
/* DOESN'T DO ANYTHING, RETURNS TO MAIN PGM    */
   RTNOCAR:
   RETURN;
```

```
/* SUBROUTINE FOR 1 CAR.                            */
/* ADDS TO COUNTER, SETS MESSAGE, AND RETURNS */
   RTN1CAR:
   ONECAR + 1;
   MSG = 'DEAR SINGLE CAR OWNER';
RETURN;
/* SUBROUTINE FOR 2 CARS.                           */
/* ADDS TO COUNTER, SETS MESSAGE, AND RETURNS */
   RTN2CAR:
   TWOCAR + 1;
   MSG = 'DEAR PROUD TWO-CAR OWNER';
   RETURN;
/* SUBROUTINE FOR MORE THAN TWO CARS.               */
/* ADDS TO COUNTER, SETS MESSAGE, AND RETURNS */
   RTNMCAR:
   MULTICAR + 1;
   MSG = 'DEAR PRIVILEGED MULTICAR OWNER';
   RETURN;
```

Note that each LINKed routine begins with its identifying label, followed by a colon. The SAS statements to be executed follow. You can use any SAS statements in a LINKed routine. Each routine ends with a RETURN statement, as does the main program. When the subroutine's RETURN statement is encountered, execution returns to the main program at the statement following the LINK. This is a little different from the effect of RETURN in a main program, which is to skip to the bottom of the DATA step loop.

You can also LINK from one subroutine to another, with similar syntax. The maximum LINK depth is ten. That is, a main program can LINK to a subroutine, which LINKs to another subroutine, and so on, until ten LINKs have been executed. At that point, the "bottommost" subroutine can no longer LINK. It must complete its processing and issue a RETURN statement.

Example 6.15 Nested LINKs. The program in this example reads dataset SALES.INFO with the purpose of fixing some bad data. It appears that in department A12 some of the sales figures are negative. These must be replaced with zero values.

The "fix" routine has been isolated from the main program in a subroutine called FIXDEPT. Thus, the main program only checks for department A12 and links to FIXDEPT whenever it is found.

The FIXDEPT routine itself links to one of two subroutines. If the sales figure is less than zero, it links to a routine called FIXMINUS, which changes the value to zero, then returns to FIXDEPT. If the sales figure is zero or greater, FIXDEPT links to a routine called SHOWOK, which displays the sales figure and returns to FIXDEPT. After the return from FIXMINUS or SHOWOK, FIXDEPT returns to the main program.

```
/* MAIN PROGRAM, WHICH LINKS TO 'FIXDEPT' ROUTINE */
   DATA;
        SET SALES.INFO;
        IF DEPT = 'A12' THEN LINK FIXDEPT;
        RETURN; /* AVOID FALLTHROUGH TO SUBROUTINES */
/* FIXDEPT ROUTINE, WHICH LINKS TO                 */
/* 'FIXMINUS'  ? 'SHOWOK' ROUTINE                  */
   FIXDEPT:
        IF SALES <   THEN LINK FIXMINUS;
                     ELSE LINK SHOWOK;
        RETURN; /* RETURN TO MAIN PROGRAM */
/* FIXMINUS ROUTINE                               */
   FIXMINUS;
        SALES = 0;
        RETURN; /* RETURN TO FIXDEPT ROUTINE */
/* SHOWOK ROUTINE                                 */
   SHOWOK;
        PUT @1 'SALES OK 'SALES;
        RETURN; /* RETURN TO FIXDEPT ROUTINE */
```

6.3.3 The GOTO statement

Like most programming languages, the SAS language provides a GOTO statement which is similar to GOTOs in other languages. GOTO (which can also be written GO TO) transfers control to a statement label. These labels are the same as those discussed in Sec. 6.3.2 on LINK. However, there is no assumption (as with LINK) that control will be returned to the main program. GOTO does not imply a subroutine structure; thus, the ten-level nesting limit does not apply. You must be careful about mixing GOTO and LINK, because the way RETURN statements are handled is different. A RETURN in a LINKed routine goes back to the statement following the LINK. RETURN following a GOTO acts the same as a main program RETURN; that is, it returns to the beginning of the DATA step.

Example 6.16 Using the GOTO statement.

```
   DATA;
        IF DEPT < 'ZOO' THEN GOTO SKIPPUT;
/*      THIS STATEMENT IS SKIPPED IF DEPT < ZOO     */
```

```
      PUT @1 DEPT
          @8 SALES;
/* THE GOTO BRANCHES TO HERE. WE ALSO FALL THROUGH  */
/* TO HERE WHEN THE GOTO IS NOT TAKEN. SO FOLLOWING */
/* STATEMENTS ARE EXECUTED FOR ALL DEPARTMENTS.     */
   SKIPPUT:
      TOTSALES + SALES;
/* BOTTOM OF DATA STEP LOOP. IMPLIED RETURN HERE     */
/* CREATES OUTPUT OBSERVATION, THEN RETURNS TO TOP   */
/* OF THE LOOP. THIS IS DONE FOR ALL DEPARTMENTS.    */
```

Loops and Table Handling

We have used loops several times without formally introducing them. This chapter discusses the format and usage of program loops in SAS programs. Some of the formats are similar to those in other languages, while some are peculiar to the SAS System.

Loops frequently act on data which is stored in tables. Accordingly, this chapter also introduces the SAS language statements used to create and process data in tables.

7.1 THE LOOP/TABLE RELATIONSHIP

A "loop" generically defines a block of code that is to be repeated based on certain specifications. A "table" is a logical collection of individual elements handled similarly within the table. By defining a block of code as repeatable, table processes such as initialization, loading, and searches can be coded and executed very efficiently.

7.1.1 Delimiting a block of code

A typical SAS statement performs one action and ends in a semi-colon. In order to group multiple statements into a single unit, the SAS language includes the DO . . . END block as a sort of packaging tool.

The keyword DO alerts the DATA step that this is the start of a block of code. The keyword END indicates no more statements are to be included in the block. All statements coded between the DO and END are to be processed as a unit. Both DO and END statements must be terminated by a semicolon, as must each of the statements included between them.

There are several forms of the DO . . . END group. Each format is designed to allow you to specify processing with the minimum number of words. The nonlooping DO block (the simple DO) groups statements into a unit. Looping DO blocks (iterative DO, DO WHILE, DO UNTIL, DO OVER) also specify a repetition rule for the unit.

7.1.2 Nonlooping DO

The DO keyword followed by a semicolon signals that this is the start of a simple (nonlooping) statement block. There are no restrictions as to the type of SAS statement allowed within the block (provided the statement can be performed within the DATA step). You can even nest other DO blocks, including the looping DO blocks. The general format of the simple DO statement is shown in Fig. 7.1.

The basic use of the DO block is to group statements together following an IF clause. This use of the DO block allows you to specify a group of SAS statements to be performed conditionally.

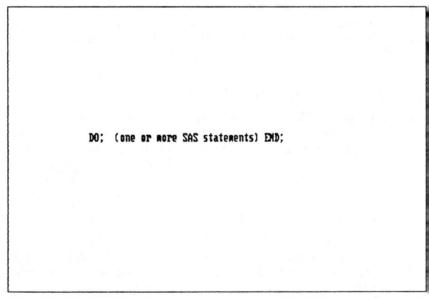

Figure 7.1 Simple DO statement

Example 7.1 Simple DO.

```
IF PAIDDOL  = .  THEN DO;     /* START OF GROUP */
   CASHDUE + BILLAMT;
   OUTPUT UNPAID;
END;                          /* END OF GROUP   */
ELSE DO;                      /* START OF GROUP */
   CASHDUE + (BILLAMT - PAIDDOL);
   OUTPUT PAID;
END;                          /* END OF GROUP   */
```

7.1.3 Iterative DO (pattern type)

To perform the statements in the DO . . . END group multiple times, varying an index variable, you can include a pattern specification. The start and stop values can be figurative constants, numeric or character-numeric variables, or expressions that can be converted to numbers. If the increment is not specified, 1 will be used. Fig. 7.2 shows the general format of the pattern-type iterative DO statement.

Use the pattern-type DO when you need to process a block of program statements a fixed number of times, or when statements within the loop depend on an index defined over a fixed interval.

Example 7.2 Pattern-type DOs.

```
DO I = 1 to 8;
DO I = 2 TO 10 BY 2;
DO COUNT = 20 TO 1 BY -1;
DO INDEX = 1 TO 5, 10 TO 20 BY 2;
DO J = START = 1 TO STOP;
DO J = 1.5 to 3.7;
```

Some syntactically valid patterns may be "impossible" in real life; for example, the following pattern will never be true. This is not considered to be an error, but simply bypasses processing of the loop.

```
DO I = 10 TO 1 BY 1;
```

When the DO is first encountered, the index variable is set to the value of the start variable (or constant). The loop then processes all statements between the DO and END. On reaching the END statement, control returns to the top of the loop (the DO), increments the index, and checks to see if it has passed the stop value. If so, the loop ends and execution resumes processing at the statements following the loop's END; otherwise the loop continues.

Before execution of the first loop, the SAS supervisor evaluates the pattern and freezes the increment and stop values. This means you cannot change any of the boundary values within the loop itself. However, you can change the number of repetitions by modifying the index within the loop.

Example 7.3 Manipulating the index.

```
STOP= 10;                        STOP= 10;
DO I = 1 TO STOP;                DO I = 1 TO STOP;
    Z = X * I;                       Z = X*I;
    IF Z > 5 THEN STOP=I;            IF Z > 5 THEN I=STOP;
END;                             END;


This loop will repeat        Number of repetitions of
10 times regardless of Z     loop depends on Z
```

7.1.4   Iterative DO (list type)

When your index values are not easily patterned, the list-type iterative DO format may be more appropriate. In this format, the actual values of the index are listed in place of the pattern. The block of

```
DO index = start TO stop [BY increment];
    SAS statements
END;
```

Figure 7.2   Iterative DO statement (pattern type)

code is processed one time for each value listed. Index values can be either character or numeric constants or variables. The general format is shown in Fig. 7.3.

Example 7.4 List-type DOs.

```
DO SUBSCRPT = 1;
DO COLOR = 'RED', 'BLUE', 'GREEN', 'YELLOW';
DO I = 1,3,4,8,11;
```

7.1.5 Deliberate exit from the loop

It is possible to leave a DO loop even if you have not completely satisfied all of the conditions in the DO statement. You can leave the loop temporarily (to perform a function you have coded in another part of your program), or you can leave the loop permanently (until the next observation). The simplest way to exit from a loop is to issue a GOTO statement to a label outside the loop.

Example 7.5 Using GOTO to exit the loop. This loop expects to process values of I from 2 to N, counting by twos. However, another variable Y is calculated in the course of the loop. If Y is not positive, an error condition is raised and the loop terminates prematurely.

```
DO index = value, value, ... value;
    SAS statements;
END;
```

Figure 7.3   Iterative DO statement (list type)

```
N = 50;
DO I = 2 TO N;
   Y = X*(I-1);
   IF Y < = 0 THEN GOTO ENDERR;
END;
RETURN;
ENDERR: FILE PRINT;
PUT 'INVALID Y VALUE - RUN ENDED';
```

You can also use the GOTO with a labeled statement inside the loop, including the END statement. This allows you to bypass the current case, while continuing the loop until its normal completion.

Example 7.6 Using GOTO within the loop. In this example, the statements in the loop calculate a variable Y. If Y is zero, the program should bypass the statement that divides by Y, but otherwise proceed normally. Note that the statement label BYPASS is within the loop.

```
N = 50;
DO I = 2 TO N;
   Y = X * (I - 1);
   IF Y = 0 THEN GOTO BYPASS;
   D = D / Y;
BYPASS:  END;
```

You can also code a LINK statement within the loop to perform a routine which is coded in another section of your program. When a RETURN statement is encountered in the performed routine, control returns within the loop to the statement following the LINK.

Example 7.7 LINK to routine outside the loop. This program is similar to Example 7.6, in that it needs to do something special when Y is zero, to avoid division by zero. In Example 7.6, the division was bypassed, but here we will link to a subroutine which "fixes" Y by moving the value saved in YDEFAULT (possibly 1).

```
N = 50;
DO I = 2 TO N;
   Y = X * (I - 1);
   IF Y = 0                   /* GO TO YZERO   */
       THEN LINK YZERO;
   D = D / Y;
END;
RETURN;                       /* END OF MAIN   */
```

```
YZERO: FILE PRINT;                  /* START YZERO   */
       PUT 'ZERO Y VALUE - CHANGED TO DEFAULT';
       Y = YDEFAULT;                /* FIX UP Y      */
       RETURN;                      /* RETURN TO MAIN */
```

7.1.6 Conditional loops

Instead of controlling the loop with a fixed series of values in an index variable, you can use the DO WHILE and DO UNTIL statements to continue the loop indefinitely until a certain condition is met. Their general format is shown in Fig. 7.4.

Use the DO WHILE/UNTIL block when the number of repetitions is dependent upon the condition of one or more variables. The condition can be either a simple or complex expression as long as it simplifies to a true/false condition at run time. Note that the parentheses are required.

DO WHILE performs the comparison before the first iteration is made so it is possible no iteration will be performed. DO UNTIL performs at least one iteration before it evaluates the comparison.

Example 7.8 DO WHILE and DO UNTIL. This program matches two files (MASTER and TRANS), using a DO . . . WHILE group to read through the TRANS file until it finds a match on account number. Then it uses a DO . . . UNTIL group to output the matching records.

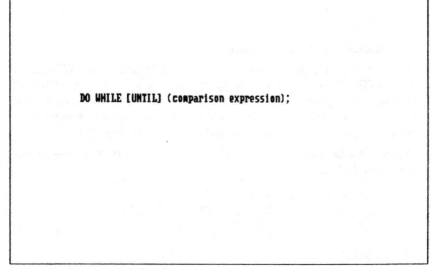

```
DO WHILE [UNTIL] (comparison expression);
```

Figure 7.4 Simple conditional DO loop

```
/* CREATE HISTORY DATASET                          */
   DATA HISTORY (KEEP = TRAN_DT ACCT);
/* READ ACCOUNT NUMBER ON MASTER FILE              */
   INFILE 'C:\SAS\MASTER';
        INPUT @2  ACCT 5.;
/* READ ACCOUNT NUMBER AND DATE FROM TRANS FILE    */
/* UNTIL IT MATCHES THE MASTER ACCOUNT.            */
/* USE DO...WHILE BECAUSE THERE MAY BE NO MATCHES. */
   INFILE 'C:\SAS\TRANS' END = EOF;
   DO WHILE ((ACCT2 NOT = ACCT) AND NOT EOF);
        INPUT @1 ACCT2 5.
              @6 TRAN_DT $CHAR7.;
   END;
/* SECOND LOOP OUTPUTS ALL MATCHING TRANSACTIONS.  */
/* USE DO...UNTIL BECAUSE THE 'IF' ENSURES THERE   */
/* IS AT LEAST ONE MATCH.                          */
   RETAIN ACCT2 TRAN_DT;
   IF ACCT2 = ACCT THEN DO;
        DO UNTIL ((ACCT2 NOT = ACCT) OR EOF);
              /* OUTPUT PREVIOUS TRAN, THEN        */
              /* READ NEXT ONE                     */
              OUTPUT;
              INPUT @1 ACCT2 5.

                    @6 TRAN_DT $CHAR7.;
        END;
   END;
   RETURN;
```

7.1.7 Compound conditional loops

The compound DO combines an iterative DO and a DO WHILE or DO UNTIL. This allows you to control the iteration in a patterned way by varying an index variable, while allowing the loop to terminate at any time based on condition checks on one or more non-index variables. The general format is shown in Fig. 7.5.

Example 7.9 Compound DO. The following are valid examples of the compound DO statement:

```
DO I = 1 TO 10 (UNTIL X > Y);
DO MONTH = 'JAN', 'FEB', 'MAR' (WHILE X = Y);
DO INDEX = ((X - Y)*2) WHILE (X > Y);
```

7.2 TABLES

SAS tables are fixed length, list-type arrays of individually named variables. The individual variables are logically ordered so that you

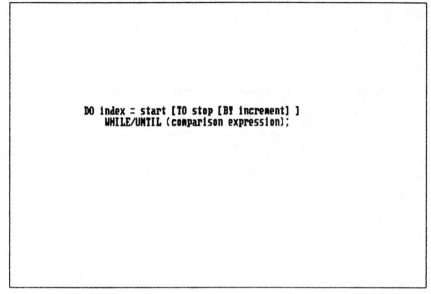

```
DO index = start [TO stop [BY increment] ]
   WHILE/UNTIL (comparison expression);
```

Figure 7.5 Compound conditional DO loop

can refer to each one by an array name and index as well as by its unique individual name.

Although there is only one array structure, the SAS language provides two array constructs: explicit subscript and implicit subscript. The names identify how specific elements in the array will be referenced. The implicitly subscripted array allows for "transparent" array access, where the explicit array always shows the index reference.

7.2.1 Explicit subscript array

Arrays are defined using the ARRAY statement. Explicit subscript arrays are similar in most ways to arrays found in many other programming languages. The array has a simple name, while each element is referred to using the array name plus a subscript. In SAS programs, you can specify that the logical array actually consists of several individual variables, which you name specifically in the ARRAY statement. Figure 7.6 shows the general format of the ARRAY statement for explicit subscript arrays.

The explicit array is processed most frequently using an iterative DO statement. But you can process it with DO WHILE or DO UNTIL statements as well.

Example 7.10 Explicit subscript array examples. The following are valid declarations for explicit subscript arrays.

```
ARRAY name {n} [$][length] [elements];

name    : variable name, unique to the SAS step
n       : the actual number of elements
          ('*' tells SAS to count them)
$       : identifies a character array
length  : length of each element
elements: list or numbered range of the
          individual element names
```

Figure 7.6   Explicit subscript array

```
ARRAY QUARTER {3} $ 3 JAN FEB MAR;
ARRAY VARS    {*}   2 VAR1-VAR12;
ARRAY MIXED   {*} $ 3 VAR1-VAR5 JAN FEB MAR;
```

There are no restrictions as to usage of explicitly subscripted variable references: they can be used in function arguments, condition comparisons, wherever any reference to a single variable is made.

Specific element references can be made either by coding the array name followed by a subscript or by referring directly to the individual element name.

The SAS supervisor considers the individually named elements as "permanent" dataset variables that can be passed between DATA and PROC steps. The array itself, however, is a logical group that only exists for the duration of the DATA step; the array cannot be passed. There are several ways around this dilemma:

1. Recopy the initial array definition into your succeeding program step(s). The supervisor will treat each step exactly as if the array had been passed. (Note: you can change the name of the array in your "new" definition, but as long as you do not change the individual element names, you need not reload the table.)

2. Use only the individual element's name in the program steps rather than in the subscripted array reference.

Example 7.11 Specific element references. Suppose that your program includes the following array declaration. This means that the five elements of EXPLICIT can also be referred to by the names NUM1, NUM2, NUM3, NUM4, and NUM5.

```
ARRAY EXPLICIT {5} 3 NUM1-NUM5;
```

After execution of the following statement, EXPLICIT {2} will contain the value 234, because EXPLICIT {2} is the same as NUM2:

```
NUM2 = 234;
```

Example 7.12 Handling explicit subscript arrays. This example shows how to input multiple array elements using a patterned DO loop, and pass them from one step to another. Our input file (SCORDATA) includes a name and three scores on each record. We first read the name (NAME), using a trailing @ to hold the input record. Then we use a DO loop to read the three scores into SCORES {1}, SCORES {2}, and SCORES {3}, again using the trailing @ to hold the record until all values have been read. Note the use of the variable COL to specify each score's position in the input record.

The ARRAY declaration says that the three elements of SCORES can also be referred to as SCORE1, SCORE2, and SCORE3. This is a good thing, because the output dataset loses all knowledge of the array (PROC CONTENTS will show only the individual variables SCORE1, SCORE2, and SCORE3). To refer to these variables in a later step, we can use the individual names or issue a new ARRAY declaration; the new array name may be different from the original (here it is FNLSCR), but the individual names must be the same.

```
/* CREATE DATASET IN1                        */
     DATA IN1;
/* DEFINE ARRAY "SCORES".                    */
/* THERE ARE 3 ELEMENTS.                     */
/* EACH ELEMENT HAS LENGTH 4.                */
/* NAMES OF THE INDIVIDUAL ELEMENTS          */
/* ARE SCORE1, SCORE2, AND SCORE3.           */
     ARRAY SCORES {3} 4 SCORE1-SCORE3;
/* READ NAME AT POSITION 1, AND THREE SCORES */
/* AT POSITIONS 10, 13, AND 16.              */
     INFILE SCORDATA;
     INPUT @1 NAME @;
     COL = 10;
```

```
    DO I = 1 TO 3;
       INPUT @COL SCORES {I} @;
       COL + 3;
    END;
    DROP COL I; /* (ONLY NEEDED THESE TEMPORARILY) */
    RETURN:
 /* PROC CONTENTS WILL SHOW ONLY SCORE1-SCORE3.    */
    PROC CONTENTS;
 /* NEED TO USE A NEW ARRAY DECLARATION TO REGROUP */
 /* THE INDIVIDUAL VARIABLES INTO AN ARRAY.        */
    DATA FINAL;
    ARRAY FNLSCR {3} 4 SCORE1 - SCORE3;
    SET IN1;
    DO IX = 1 TO 3;
       FNLSCR {IX} = FNLSCR {IX} + 10;
    END;
```

7.2.2 Implicit subscript arrays

In addition to the explicit subscript array, the SAS System also supports an implicit subscript array. The array declaration is similar to that of the explicit subscript array, except that you do not explicitly specify the number of elements and you may associate a specific index variable (much like the INDEXED BY clause in COBOL). If you do not name the index, the system provides an automatic variable called __I__. Figure 7.7 shows the general format of the implicit array declaration.

Example 7.13 Implicit array definitions.

```
 * An implicit array CLASSES with ten elements, called CLS1
   through CLS10;
   ARRAY CLASSES CLS1-CLS10;
 * An implicit character array COLORS with four elements called
   RED,, GREEN, YELLOW, and BLUE. It has an index variable CIX;
   ARRAY COLORS (CIX) $6 RED GREEN YELLOW BLUE;
 * An implicit array MIXED with twenty elements:
   X1 through X8, Y12 through Y24, and Z5.
   It has an index variable I.
   ARRAY MIXED (I) X1-8 Y12-24 Z5;
```

Why would you use an implicit array? One reason is that for multidimensional arrays, explicit arrays are not supported on all operating systems (see Sec. 7.2.4). Another is that there is a special form of the DO statement which only works on implicit arrays. While an

```
ARRAY name [(index)] [$] [length] elements;
  name    :  variable name, unique to the SAS step
  index   :  variable to act as the array index
  $       :  identifies a character array
  length  :  length of each element
  elements:  a list or range of individual
             variable or implicit array names

If you do not specify an index variable name,
SAS will use the automatic index _I_ which you
can reference and update.
```

Figure 7.7 Implicit subscript array

implicit array can be processed using any of the DO statements described earlier in this chapter, the DO OVER statement was designed specifically for implicit array processing.

The DO OVER statement provides a shorthand way of processing all the elements in an array. Every statement in the DO OVER . . . END group will be executed for each element in the array. Moreover, within the group you do not need to use subscripts when you refer to an array element. Within the group, references to the array name actually act on the particular element corresponding to the current iteration. Figure 7.8 shows the general syntax of the DO OVER statement.

Example 7.14 DO OVER vs iterative DO. This example shows how DO OVER is equivalent to a patterned DO which loops through all the elements in the array.

```
ARRAY CODE C1-C12;
DO OVER CODE;
     IF CODE = . THEN CODE = 10;
END;
/* This is the same as the following: */
ARRAY CODE C1-C12;
DO _I_ = 1 TO 12;
IF CODE = . THEN CODE = 10;
```

Figure 7.8 DO OVER statement

```
END;
```

To reference an individual element, either of these forms produces the same result:

```
_I_ = 10;                        ANSWER = C10;
ANSWER = CODE;
```

Note: If you reference more than one array using the automatic __I__ variable, remember that the value of the index is shared. If the arrays are of unequal lengths or if one array is processed after the other, the subscript may go out of range and processing will cease.

Example 7.15 Implicit subscript out of range. In this example, two implicit arrays are defined without index variables. Thus, they will have to share the automatic index variable __I__. After completion of the DO OVER SECOND loop, __I__ has a value of 11. When the attempt is made to PUT FIRST, the subscript __I__ will be out of range.

```
ARRAY FIRST F1-F5;
ARRAY SECOND S1-S10;
DO OVER FIRST;
```

```
DO OVER SECOND;
    PUT SECOND;
END;
PUT FIRST;
END;
```

7.2.3 Multidimensional arrays

Explicit multidimensional arrays can be created by slightly modifying the explicit array statement to add additional dimensions, as seen in Fig. 7.9.

Processing is controlled by nested DO loops. When loading a multidimensional array from a list of values, the DATA step will load the values from the lowest level up. In a two-dimensional table, for example, this means loading row 1 column 1, row 1 column 2, row 1 column 3, and so on.

Implicit arrays can be combined to effect a multidimensional array. Processing is controlled by nested DO loops, including the DO OVER statement.

Example 7.16 Multidimensional implicit arrays. This program defines three separate one-dimensional arrays (STORE1, STORE2, and STORE3) which are then named as the individual elements of array PARTS. In effect, this creates PARTS as a multidimensional implicit array.

```
ARRAY name {...level2,level1} [$] [length]
[elements];

Where the dimension key {...level2, level1 } is:
    level2 = number of rows
    level1 = number of columns

Additional dimensions are added to the left. For
example, a 3 dimension array would be defined with
{depth, rows, columns}.
```

Figure 7.9   Multidimensional explicit array

PARTS itself has only three elements, but since STORE1, STORE2, and STORE3 have five elements each, the PARTS array refers indirectly to (3 * 5) = 15 elements. Our input statement (INPUT P1–P15) obtains values for these fields.

The nested DO loops print the detail elements. The DO OVER statement says to process a block of statements for each occurrence of PART. Remember that at the highest level, PART has only three occurrences. So an inner loop is used to handle the five elements within each of STORE1, STORE2, and STORE3. If you look at the output (Fig. 7.10), you'll notice that the PART number varies from 1 to 5 within each of the three STOREs.

```
DATA REPORT;
ARRAY  STORE1  P1  - P5;  /* DETAIL ARRAYS:     */
ARRAY  STORE2  P6  - P10;  /* EACH IS ONE-      */
ARRAY  STORE3  P11 - P15;  /* DIMENSIONAL       */
/* THE FOLLOWING DEFINES PARTS AS AN ARRAY OF  */
/* THREE ELEMENTS.  SINCE EACH OF STORE1-STORE3 */
/* IS ALSO AN ARRAY, PARTS IS TWO-DIMENSIONAL.  */
ARRAY  PARTS  (IX) STORE1 - STORE3;
/* READ IN THE 15 ELEMENTS.                     */
INFORMAT P1-P15 3.;
INFILE TAPE;
   INPUT P1-P15;
/* PRINT THE 5 PARTS WITHIN EACH OF 3 STORES.  */
DO OVER PARTS;
   DO _I_ = 1 TO 5;
         FILE PRINT;
         PUT @15 '      STORE: ' IX
              '       PART : ' _I_
              '       AMT ON HAND: ' PARTS;
   END;
END;
/* DATA -- SEE FIGURE 7.10 FOR HOW IT ENDS UP  */
CARDS;
100 200 300 10 999 99 100 200 330 888 111 222 . 0 101
;
```

7.2.4 Operating system constraints

Both the implicit and explicit array definitions are available on all supported operating systems for one-dimensional arrays. The explicit

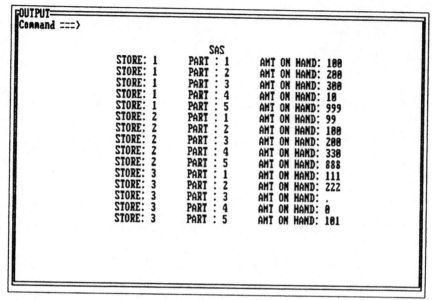

Figure 7.10 Contents of multidimensional implicit array

subscripted array, although a more flexible construct, is not yet fully implemented on all operating systems. As of SAS Version 5, only these operating systems have multidimensional explicit array capabilities: AOS/VS, PRIMOS, and VMS. This means that all other users must define multidimensional arrays using implicit subscripts.

Time/Space Savers

This chapter introduces a number of language features which add useful detail functions and techniques which can save you work. You'll expand your knowledge of automatic variables and learn how to use SAS functions. You'll also learn how to use the SYMPUT and SYMGET functions to store data and pass it between steps.

8.1 AUTOMATIC VARIABLES AND AUTOMATIC DATASET NAMES

Automatic variables are variables that the PROC or DATA step creates for your use. They have standard names and functions and they are always available; you don't have to define them.

In DATA steps, there are automatic variables that allow you to keep track of iterations (_I_ or _N_) or flag processing errors (_ERROR_). Automatic dataset names allow for shorthand processing:

LAST references the last dataset created

DATA tells the system to manage naming of temporary datasets

NULL indicates that no SAS dataset is to be created in a particular DATA step

__INFILE__ contains the entire raw input line (__INFILE__)

__ALL__ allows you to specify processing of all the variables on the dataset

PROC steps can also create automatic variables. For example, in the two PROCs you've learned so far, you can specify that only __NUMERIC__ or __CHARACTER__ variables be processed. (__ALL__ is the default unless you specify otherwise.)

8.1.1   Keeping track of iterations

There are two types of iterations: array iterations and DATA step repetitions. If you are using an explicit type array, no automatic variables are created (because you can access the elements individually by setting your index). But if your array is an implicit one, you can reference an individual element by setting the automatic variable __I__ to a specific number.

Example 8.1 The automatic variable __I__. Suppose you want to read in a questionnaire sheet containing ten answers to questions about book-buying habits (the respondent is instructed to identify the number of each type of books bought over a one-year period). You are especially interested in position 7 which asks about the purchase of a particular book series. The data also includes a code for the type of respondent.

If you wanted to create an analysis file that included the responses of those with activity on the book series, and whose type is "RD" (recent donor), you could use this approach. It creates a SAS dataset called AFFGRP of all questionnaire responses for individuals who have a history of a series purchase and are classed as recent donors. The resulting dataset is listed in Fig. 8.1.

```
DATA AFFGRP;
ARRAY ANSWERS A1 - A10;
INFILE CARDS MISSOVER;
INPUT A1 - A10 @;        /* READ IN THE 10 ANSWERS */
DO OVER ANSWERS;
    IF ANSWERS = .
      THEN ANSWERS = 0;
      ELSE                /* SET SWITCH IF OK        */
    IF _I_ = 7 AND ANSWERS > 0 THEN SERIESOK = 1;
END;
/* INPUT REMAINING DATA INCLUDING CUSTTYPE        */
INPUT CUSTTYPE $2. +1 STATUS $1.;
```

```
/* IF SWITCH SET AND DESIRED CUSTTYPE,        */
/* THEN PUT OBSERVATION ON THE OUTPUT DATASET */
IF SERIESOK AND CUSTTYPE = 'RD' THEN OUTPUT;
CARDS; /* REMEMBER THAT . MEANS A MISSING VALUE */
. . . . . . 1 . 1 . RD D
1 . 1 . 2 . 1 1 1 . XD A
. 1 . . . . . . . . SS A
. . 1 . . 1 2 . . 1 SS A
. . . 4 . . . 4 . . SS A
2 . . . . . 3 . . . XD A
. 2 . . . . 2 . 1 . RD A
. . . . 1 . 3 . . 1 RD A
;
RUN;
/* PRINT THE RESULTING DATASET */
PROC PRINT;
RUN;
```

We have stressed that the DATA step acts as a loop. The automatic variable __N__ tells how many iterations of the DATA step loop have been processed (including the current one). In most cases, this means __N__ also equals the observation number on the input file. (The exception is when extra observations have been read due to wrapping of input lines.)

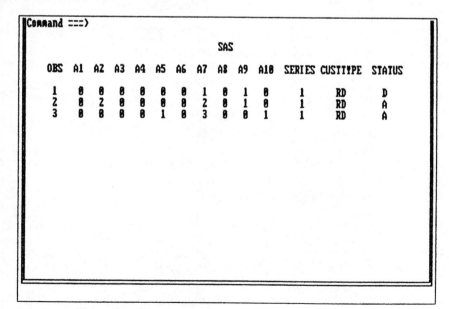

Figure 8.1   Using the __I__ automatic variable

Example 8.2 __N__ counts the number of DATA step repetitions. In this example, we see first how __N__ can be used to count DATA step repetitions. Then we'll analyze a situation in which __N__ is used incorrectly with unexpected results.

Suppose you had a SAS dataset (SCORES) that contained an array containing weighting factors for the ten questions (variables Q1 – Q10). Some questions will be counted more heavily than others, based on the weighting factor. Although we will be processing many sets of answers, we only need to read in the weighting factors once. In the following program, note how __N__ is used to accomplish this; Q1-Q10 are only read when __N__ = 1; that is, on the first iteration of the DATA step. The program's function is to produce weighted results of our questionnaire.

The output is shown in Fig. 8.2. Note that the values of Q1-Q10 are the same for all three observations, because they were read once and then retained.

```
DATA AFFGRP2;
SET AFFGRP;
ARRAY QSCORE {*} Q1 - Q10;
ARRAY ANSWER {*} A1 - A10;
RETAIN Q1 - Q10;
IF _N_ = 1 THEN DO;  /* FIRST TIME ONLY            */
     INPUT Q1 - Q10;  /* GET THE CONSTANT WEIGHTS */
END;
/* FOR EACH CUSTOMER, WEIGHT THE ANSWERS BY        */
/* MULTIPLYING BY THE WEIGHTING FACTORS            */
DO I = 1 TO 10;
     ANSWER {I} = ANSWER {I} * QSCORE {I};
END;
DROP I; /* NO LONGER NEEDED */
/* DATA FOR THE WEIGHTING FACTORS                   */
CARDS;
0.07 0.79 0.50 0.40 0.45 0.76 1.00 0.83 0.55 0.61
;
/* PRINT RESULTS */
PROC PRINT;
RUN;
```

Remember that __N__ refers to the number of iterations of the DATA step (one for each record read) not the number of records you actually used. For instance, in the following example if your very first record had a bad status ('D' = deceased), the weighted scores

```
Command ===)

                              SAS

OBS  A1   A2   A3  A4   A5   A6  A7  A8   A9    A10  SERIES  CUSTTYPE

 1   0  0.00   0   0  0.00   0   1   0  0.55  0.00     1       RD
 2   0  1.58   0   0  0.00   0   2   0  0.55  0.00     1       RD
 3   0  0.00   0   0  0.45   0   3   0  0.00  0.61     1       RD

OBS  STATUS   Q1     Q2     Q3    Q4    Q5     Q6    Q7    Q8    Q9    Q10

 1     D     0.07   0.79   0.5   0.4  0.45   0.76   1   0.83  0.55  0.61
 2     A     0.07   0.79   0.5   0.4  0.45   0.76   1   0.83  0.55  0.61
 3     A     0.07   0.79   0.5   0.4  0.45   0.76   1   0.83  0.55  0.61
```

Figure 8.2   Using the __N__ automatic variable

array (Qscore) would not be loaded because it would be skipped when __N__ = 1 (see Fig. 8.3).

```
          DATA AFFGRP2;
          SET AFFGRP;
          ARRAY QSCORE {*} Q1 - Q10;
          ARRAY ANSWER {*} A1 - A10;
          RETAIN Q1 - Q10;
          /* THIS BAILS OUT OF THE OBS WHERE _N_ = 1  */
          IF STATUS = 'D' THEN DELETE;
          /* DON'T GET HERE TILL _N_ = 2              */
          IF _N_ = 1 THEN DO;
              INPUT Q1 - Q10;
          END;
          DO I = 1 TO 10;
              ANSWER {I} = ANSWER {I} * QSCORE {I};
          END;
          DROP I;
          CARDS;
   0.07 0.79 0.50 0.40 0.45 0.76 1.00 0.83 0.55 0.61
          ;
          PROC PRINT;
          RUN;
```

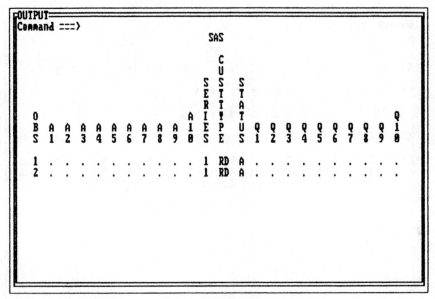

Figure 8.3   Example of __N__ versus DELETE

8.1.2   Processing checks (__ERROR__)

If you've been experimenting with SAS programs, you've probably become acquainted already with __N__ and __ERROR__. These automatic variables and their values are printed on the SAS log when an error is encountered.

__ERROR__ is a Boolean variable. It is set on when a processing error is detected. When __ERROR__ is equal to 1, the system prints on the log the values of all the variables (including __N__ and __ERROR__) of the current observation.

Example 8.3 __ERROR__ and __N__.   In this example, we attempt to read an external data file, one of whose fields is social security number (SSNUM). We set the MISSOVER option on to allow missing social security numbers, but what if we get a non-numeric value? This raises an error condition. __ERROR__ is set to 1 and a message is printed on the log along with the current values of all variables. In this case, the offending input record is also printed on the log and SSNUM is set to "missing", as you can see in Fig. 8.4. An error condition is raised again on the following record, as the non-numeric value FF is encountered for STRT__MON; here, STRT__MON will be set to "missing".

```
DATA ERRORZ;
INFILE CARDS MISSOVER; /* ALLOW MISSING VALUES */
INPUT @1 SSNUM @11 STRT_MON @14 PROJECT $CHAR12.
```

```
          @26 RANK;
/* IN THE FOLLOWING INPUT, CARD #5 WILL RAISE AN ERROR */
/* CONDITION DUE TO THE BAD VALUE FOR SSNUM. CARD #6 */
/* WILL RAISE AN ERROR CONDITION DUE TO BAD STRT_MON. */
          CARDS;
123456789 03 City Bank      8
123456789 05 Blue Visa      3
123456789 06 AP Notes       2
220343445 02 Research       9
220343445 06 Title Search 4
Department 505
317329001 FF Fast Foods    10
   ;
```

In addition to the errors recognized by the system, you can do your own checking and set __ERROR__ = 1 for your own error conditions. Suppose in our previous example, we knew that RANK > 9 was an invalid condition. The system will not automatically detect this error, because it is peculiar to this application. However, we can raise the error condition ourselves by checking the value of RANK and setting __ERROR__ to 1 if RANK is greater than 9. The following program adds this additional line to our previous example. In the output shown in Fig. 8.5, notice that the problem record and con-

```
┌LOG══════════════════════════════════════════════════════════════════════
│Command ===)
│
│   189
│   110          DATA Errorz;
│   111          INFILE CARDS MISSOVER;
│   112          INPUT @1 SSnum @11 Strt_mon @14 Project $CHAR12. @26 Rank;
│   113          CARDS;
│NOTE: Invalid data for SSNUM in line 119 1-10.
│RULE:----+----1----+----2----+----3----+----4----+----5----+----6----+----7---
│ 119 Department 505
│SSNUM=. STRT_MON=505 PROJECT=5 RANK=. _ERROR_=1 _N_=6
│NOTE: Invalid data for STRT_MON in line 120 11-12.
│ 120 317329001 FF Fast Foods  10
│SSNUM=317329001 STRT_MON=. PROJECT=Fast Foods RANK=10 _ERROR_=1 _N_=7
│ 121    ;
│NOTE: The dataset WORK.ERRORZ has 7 observations and 4 variables.
│NOTE: The DATA statement used 17.00 seconds.
│
│
│
│
└──────────────────────────────────────────────────────────────────────────
```

Figure 8.4 SAS-generated __ERROR__

tents of all variables were listed on the log, just as if a standard error condition were present.

```
DATA ERRORZ;
INFILE CARDS MISSOVER;
INPUT @1 SSNUM @11 STRT_MON @14 PROJECT $CHAR12.
    @26 RANK;
IF RANK > 9
    THEN _ERROR_ = 1;
```

There is another way to signal an error condition. Instead of simply setting _ERROR_ to 1, you can use the ERROR statement. This statement includes all the processing associated with setting _ERROR_ to 1—the current record contents are dumped on the log, along with the current values of all variables. But the ERROR statement has an advantage. You can also specify an error message to be printed. In general, the ERROR statement looks like this:

```
ERROR 'message to be printed';
```

In a new version of our program, we use the ERROR statement to define an error message "Rank value is out of range". This message will be printed on the log whenever RANK > 9. If you compare the

```
┌LOG═══════════════════════════════════════════════════════════════════════
│Command ===>
│
│    46
│    47          DATA Errorz;
│    48          INFILE CARDS MISSOVER;
│    49          INPUT @1 SSnum @11 Strt_mon @14 ProJect $CHAR12. @26 Rank;
│    50          IF Rank > 9 then _ERROR_ = 1;
│    51
│    52
│    53          CARDS;
│RULE:----+----1----+----2----+----3----+----4----+----5----+----6----+----7---
│    59 317329001 02 Fast Foods  10
│SSNUM=317329001 STRT_MON=2 PROJECT=Fast Foods RANK=10 _ERROR_=1 _N_=6
│    60        ;
│NOTE: The dataset WORK.ERRORZ has 6 observations and 4 variables.
│NOTE: The DATA statement used 16.00 seconds.
│
│
└═══════════════════════════════════════════════════════════════════════════
```

Figure 8.5 User-generated _ERROR_

new log in Fig. 8.6 with our previous results in Fig. 8.5, you'll see
that they are identical except for the message we just added.

```
DATA ERRORZ;
INFILE CARDS MISSOVER;
INPUT @1 SSNUM @11 STRT_MON @14 PROJECT $CHAR12.
      @26 RANK;
IF RANK > 9 THEN
    ERROR 'Rank value is out of range';
```

8.1.3   Automatic dataset names (__LAST__ and __DATA__)

In DATA steps and most PROC steps (for example, PROC PRINT),
you can use the output dataset of the previous step without referring
to it by name. The default processing selects the dataset last created
if a SET statement or DATA= option is not provided.

You can specifically reference the last dataset created by using the
automatic variable __LAST__. __LAST__ always contains the name
of the last dataset created. These three code segments will produce
identical output:

```
┌LOG═══════════════════════════════════════════════════════════════
│Command ===>
│
│    61
│    62              DATA Errorz;
│    63              INFILE CARDS MISSOVER;
│    64              INPUT @1 SSnum @11 Strt_mon @14 Project $CHAR12. @26 Rank;
│    65              IF Rank > 9 then ERROR 'Rank value is out of range';
│    66              CARDS;
│Rank value is out of range
│RULE:----+----1----+----2----+----3----+----4----+----5----+----6----+----7---
│   72 317329001 02 Fast Foods  10
│SSNUM=317329001 STRT_MON=2 PROJECT=Fast Foods RANK=10 _ERROR_=1 _N_=6
│   73       ;
│NOTE: The dataset WORK.ERRORZ has 6 observations and 4 variables.
│NOTE: The DATA statement used 16.00 seconds.
│
│
│
│
│
└═══════════════════════════════════════════════════════════════════
```

Figure 8.6 Using the ERROR statement

```
  DATA dataset1;
... SAS statements ...
  * BY DEFAULT, THE FOLLOWING PROC PRINT USES
    THE OUTPUT OF THE PREVIOUS STEP; i.e. dataset1;
    PROC PRINT;
    DATA dataset1;
... SAS statements ...
  * HERE, WE EXPLICITLY TELL PROC PRINT
    TO USE dataset1;
    PROC PRINT DATA=dataset1;
    DATA dataset1;
... SAS statements ...
  * HERE, WE EXPLICITLY TELL PROC PRINT TO USE
    THE OUTPUT OF THE PREVIOUS STEP; i.e. dataset1;
    PROC PRINT DATA=_LAST_;
```

We have seen how to name an output dataset using the DATA statement. If you want to create a dataset, but don't really need to name it, you can let the system name it for you by using the automatic dataset name __DATA__. When you code __DATA__ in place of the dataset name on the DATA statement, you are instructing the system to create a new temporary dataset and to keep it on the workfile during your SAS session. The system keeps track of each dataset by naming the first one created "WORK.DATA1", the second one, "WORK.DATA2", and so on. You can also get the same results by omitting the dataset name altogether.

Example 8.4 __DATA__ usage. In this example, PROC PRINT will be performed on the data in WORK.DATA2 :

```
* THIS STEP CREATES WORK.DATA1;
  DATA _DATA_;
  DO I = 1 TO 10;
     OUTPUT;
  END;
* THIS STEP CREATES WORK.DATA2;
  DATA _DATA_ (DROP = J);
  DO J = 1 TO 10;
     I = J * 100;
  END;
* BECAUSE _LAST_ NOW INDICATES WORK.DATA2,
  WORK.DATA2 WILL BE THE INPUT TO PROC PRINT;
  PROC PRINT DATA = _LAST_;
```

8.1.4 The null dataset (__NULL__)

As you learned in Chapter 6, the SAS language can be used to perform utility functions such as creating external files from either SAS datasets or raw input. If your DATA step is creating an external file and you do not want to create a SAS dataset, you can code your DATA step with the __NULL__ automatic dataset name.

Example 8.5 SAS DATA step that creates SAS code, but no dataset. Suppose you have a list of data that contains the name, byte position, and SAS format for financial variables on a sales file. You want to read the list and create a program that will generate SAS code to read this file. Here is the contents of your list which is stored in 'A;\Sales.var'.

```
DEPT     1   $CHAR3.
WEEK     5   $CHAR2.
SALES    10  10.
RETURNS  30  7.
CGS      40  8.
```

The following program reads the list and generates a DATA step that can be used to read the data file 'a:\rawsales.dat'. Because the program itself will be created as an external file ('a:\sasread.pgm') you don't need to create a SAS dataset, so you use the __NULL__ automatic dataset name. In the log shown in Fig. 8.7, note that we do not see the usual message "The dataset has n observations and v variables." This shows that no SAS dataset was created. However, the external file 'a:\sasread.pgm' did receive ten lines of output. In example 8.6, we'll get a look at what we created.

```
* THIS DATA STEP WILL READ THE LIST OF VARIABLES IN
  'a:\sales.var'.
  IT WILL USE THE LIST OF VARIABLES TO BUILD A SAS PROGRAM
  WHICH READS THESE VARIABLES FROM DATA FILE
  'a:\rawsales.dat'.
  THE PROGRAM ITSELF WILL BE CREATED AS FILE
  'a:\sasread.pgm'.
  NO SAS DATASET WILL BE CREATED DUE TO _NULL_ KEYWORD.;
DATA _NULL_;
    INFILE 'a:\Sales.var' EOF=Done;
    FILE 'a:\sasread.pgm';
    INPUT @1  VARNAME $CHAR8.
          @10 BYTELOC 2.
          @15 SASFMT $CHAR7. ;
```

```
* FIRST TIME THRU, CREATE THE DATA STEP HEADER
  AND START OF THE INPUT STATEMENT;
  IF _N_ = 1 THEN DO;
      PUT @5  'DATA Sales;' /
          @5  'INFILE ''a:\rawsales.dat;''' /
          @5  'INPUT';
      END;
* ADD EACH VARIABLE TO THE INPUT STATEMENT
  BY REFORMATTING THE INFO WE GOT FROM THE VARIABLE LIST;
  PUT @10 '@'
          @11 BYTELOC 2.
          @15 VARNAME $CHAR8.
          @25 SASFMT  $CHAR7.;
  RETURN;
* WHEN ALL VARIABLES HAVE BEEN ADDED TO THE INPUT
  STATEMENT, APPEND THE FINAL SEMICOLON AND THE
  RUN STATEMENT;
  DONE: PUT @5 ';' / @5 RUN;';
RUN;
```

8.1.5 How to output a line of raw data
(_INFILE_)

The INPUT statement always gets one record as defined by the INFILE statement and the external file's DCB. When you want to

```
┌─LOG─────────────────────────────────────────────────────────────┐
│Command ===>                                                      │
│                                                                  │
│  55   DATA _NULL_;                                               │
│  56   INFILE 'a:\Sales.var' EOF=Done;                            │
│  57   FILE 'a:\sasread.pgm';                                     │
│  58   INPUT @1 Varname  $CHAR8. @10 Byteloc 2. @15 Sasfmt    $CHAR7. ; │
│  59   IF _N_ = 1 THEN DO;                                        │
│  60       PUT @5  'DATA Sales;' /                                │
│  61           @5  'INFILE ''a:\Rawsales.dat;''' /                │
│  62           @5  'INPUT';                                       │
│  63       END;                                                   │
│  64   PUT @10 '@'                                                │
│  65           @11 Byteloc 2. @15 Varname $CHAR8. @25 Sasfmt $CHAR7.; │
│  66   RETURN;                                                    │
│  67   Done: PUT @5 ';' / @5 'RUN;';                              │
│  68   RUN;                                                       │
│NOTE: The infile 'a:\Sales.var' is file A:\SALES.VAR.            │
│NOTE: 7 records were read from the infile A:\SALES.VAR.          │
│      The minimum record length was 0.                            │
│      The maximum record length was 21.                           │
│NOTE: The file 'a:\sasread.pgm' is file A:\SASREAD.PGM.          │
│NOTE: 10 records were written to the file A:\SASREAD.PGM.        │
│      The minimum record length was 5.                            │
└──────────────────────────────────────────────────────────────────┘
```

Figure 8.7 Log output when _NULL_ is used

see or write the entire contents of that record (you don't care about variables at this point), __INFILE__ allows you to treat the defined line as one variable.

For example, you could copy one file to another with the following SAS program:

```
DATA _NULL_;          /* EXTERNAL FILES ONLY */
    INFILE INDD;      /* DDNAME OF INPUT      */
    INPUT;            /* GET INPUT RECORD     */
    FILE OUTDD;       /* DDNAME OF OUTPUT     */
    PUT _INFILE_;     /* COPY AS IS TO OUTPUT */
```

This technique can be extended to allow you to fix portions of a file, while leaving the rest unaltered. This program corrects the field PROBVAR at position 32, by changing blank characters to zeros:

```
DATA _NULL_;          /* EXTERNAL FILES ONLY */
    INFILE INDD;      /* DDNAME OF INPUT      */
    INPUT             /* GET INPUT RECORD     */
      @32 PROBVAR $1.;
    IF PROBVAR = ' '   /* FIX BAD VALUES       */
      THEN
        PROBVAR = '0';
    FILE OUTDD;       /* DDNAME OF OUTPUT     */
    PUT _INFILE_      /* COPY AS IS TO OUTPUT */
      @32 PROBVAR $1.; /* BUT OVERLAY PROBVAR */
```

Example 8.6 write the contents of the input line. In this example, we read an external file and write each record to the log. The external file input will be 'a:\sasread.pgm', which we created in the last example. This file contains a SAS program, but this same technique will work on any external data file as well. Take a look at the output in Fig. 8.8. The step we're executing is listed as lines 76 through 80. Then another program appears to be listed, but without line numbers. This is actually the contents of 'a:\sasread.pgm' being listed on the log using the PUT __INFILE__ statement.

```
* READ CONTENTS OF EXTERNAL FILE;
  DATA _NULL_;
  INFILE 'a:\sasread.pgm';
  INPUT;
* WRITE EACH LINE TO THE LOG IN ITS ORIGINAL FORMAT;
  PUT _INFILE_;
  RUN;
```

The INFILE statement defines the line read as one complete record from the file 'a:\sasread.pgm'. The INPUT statement with no other specifications tells the SAS supervisor to get the next line, but to create no SAS variables. The PUT __INFILE__ writes the contents of that line to the log (see Fig. 8.8). (You could have directed the contents to another external file by using the FILE statement prior to the PUT.)

In the previous example, we printed the entire data record. It is also possible to read only a specified portion. The INFILE statement has two options that allow you to do this: START= and LINESIZE=. START= identifies a variable whose value is the starting byte position for the line. LINESIZE identifies the variable whose value is the maximum length of the line.

In this step, we will only read in bytes 11 through 60 of the input record, so __INFILE__ contains only a portion of the input record. PUT __INFILE__ will print only these bytes.

```
DATA _NULL_;
    INFILE RAWDATA START=BEGIN LINESIZE=FINISH;
    INPUT;
    BEGIN = 11;    /* START POS = 11           */
    FINISH = 50;   /* INPUT 50 BYTES (11-60) */
    PUT _INFILE_;  /* DISPLAY WHAT WE GOT     */
```

```
┌LOG────────────────────────────────────────────────────────────────────────┐
│Command ===>                                                                 │
│                                                                             │
│   76      DATA _NULL_;                                                       │
│   77      INFILE 'a:\sasread.pgm';                                          │
│   78      INPUT;                                                            │
│   79      PUT _INFILE_;                                                      │
│   88      RUN; /* Log output follows, showing _INFILE_ recs read        */ │
│        DATA Sales;                                                           │
│        INFILE 'a:\Rawsales.dat;'                                            │
│        INPUT                                                                 │
│            @ 1  Dept      $CHAR3.                                            │
│            @ 5  Week      $CHAR2.                                            │
│            @10  Sales     10.                                               │
│            @30  Returns   7.                                                │
│            @40  CGS       8.                                                │
│        ;                                                                    │
│        RUN;                                                                  │
│NOTE: The infile 'a:\sasread.pgm' is file A:\SASREAD.PGM.                     │
│NOTE: 10 records were read from the infile A:\SASREAD.PGM.                    │
│        The minimum record length was 5.                                      │
│        The maximum record length was 31.                                     │
│NOTE: The DATA statement used 13.00 seconds.                                  │
│                                                                             │
└─────────────────────────────────────────────────────────────────────────┘
```

Figure 8.8   Printing input records using __INFILE__

8.1.6   How to output a line of SAS data (__ALL__)

Another useful "automatic variable" is __ALL__. When you use __ALL__ as the object of a PUT statement, it is shorthand for "display the current values of all variables known in the step." We saw in Fig. 8.4 that you get this sort of display automatically when an error condition arises, but you can use PUT __ALL__ to get it at any time. This can be very helpful when testing or debugging a program.

Example 8.7 printing the __ALL__ variable on the log.   This program demonstrates the use of PUT __ALL__. As you can see in the output in Fig. 8.9, all variables in the dataset are displayed when "PUT __ALL__" is encountered. The display includes both variables you have created (ALPHA, NUMBER) and automatic variables created by the SAS supervisor (__ERROR__, __N__).

```
* READ IN PAIRS OF ALPHA/NUMBER VALUES.
  REMEMBER THAT THE TRAILING @@ HOLDS THE RECORD
  ACROSS MULTIPLE ITERATIONS OF THE DATA STEP LOOP;
  DATA FIRST;
     INPUT ALPHA $ NUMBER @@;
     CARDS;
A 1 B 2 C 3 D 4 E 5 F 6 G 7 H 8 I 8 J 8
;
  * NOW READ THE DATASET, AND DISPLAY ALL VALUES FOR
    EACH OBSERVATION USING "PUT _ALL_";
  DATA SECOND;
     SET FIRST;
     PUT _ALL_;
  RUN;
```

8.1.7   A few PROC step automatic variables

Not all automatic variables are available to all PROCs. However, the automatic dataset names __LAST__ and __DATA__ can be referenced by most PROCs. Remember that in PROC steps, the input dataset is identified using the DATA= option and the output dataset using the OUT= option. This PROC SORT will read in the last dataset created, and create a temporary dataset whose name will be automatically assigned as WORK.DATAn:

```
PROC SORT DATA=_LAST_ OUT=_DATA_;
```

PROC FREQ and PROC PRINT both allow you to specify __NUMERIC__ when you want to process only numeric variables or __CHARACTER__ if you want only character variables.

```
┌─LOG────────────────────────────────────────────────────────────────────┐
│Command ===>                                                             │
│                                                                          │
│NOTE: The DATA statement used 14.00 seconds.                              │
│   36      DATA Second;                                                   │
│   37      SET First;                                                     │
│   38      PUT _ALL_; /* Each time thru, we'll display every variable  */ │
│   39      RUN;       /* Following log output shows the PUT _ALL_ results */│
│ALPHA=A NUMBER=1 _ERROR_=0 _N_=1                                          │
│ALPHA=B NUMBER=2 _ERROR_=0 _N_=2                                          │
│ALPHA=C NUMBER=3 _ERROR_=0 _N_=3                                          │
│ALPHA=D NUMBER=4 _ERROR_=0 _N_=4                                          │
│ALPHA=E NUMBER=5 _ERROR_=0 _N_=5                                          │
│ALPHA=F NUMBER=6 _ERROR_=0 _N_=6                                          │
│ALPHA=G NUMBER=7 _ERROR_=0 _N_=7                                          │
│ALPHA=H NUMBER=8 _ERROR_=0 _N_=8                                          │
│ALPHA=I NUMBER=8 _ERROR_=0 _N_=9                                          │
│ALPHA=J NUMBER=8 _ERROR_=0 _N_=10                                         │
│NOTE: The dataset WORK.SECOND has 10 observations and 2 variables.        │
│NOTE: The DATA statement used 15.00 seconds.                              │
│                                                                          │
│                                                                          │
│                                                                          │
└──────────────────────────────────────────────────────────────────────┘
```

Figure 8.9 Log output using __ALL__

Example 8.8 PROC FREQ with _NUMERIC_ tables only. The DATA step in this program is the same as we saw in the previous example: it reads pairs of values into variables called ALPHA and NUMBER. Normally, the PROC FREQ step would produce a table for each variable in the dataset; however, by specifying TABLES _NUMERIC_ we request tables for only the numeric variables. Thus, we get a table for NUMBER but not ALPHA, as shown in Fig. 8.10.

```
DATA FIRST;
    INPUT ALPHA $ NUMBER @@;
CARDS;
A 1 B 2 C 3 D 4 E 5 F 6 G 7 H 8 I 8 J 8
;
PROC FREQ;
TABLES _NUMERIC_;       /* SHOW ONLY NUMERIC VARIABLES */
RUN;
```

8.2 SAS FUNCTIONS

Functions are routines used in the DATA step that perform a specific unit of work at the observation level. They usually do this by receiving a variable, constant or expression, then operating on it to produce a single result. When you "nest" functions, the system performs the innermost function first, and then works outward.

```
┌OUTPUT════════════════════════════════════════════════════════════
│Command ===>
│
│                              SAS
│
│                                     Cumulative  Cumulative
│          NUMBER    Frequency   Percent  Frequency    Percent
│          ----------------------------------------------------------
│             1          1       10.0        1        10.0
│             2          1       10.0        2        20.0
│             3          1       10.0        3        30.0
│             4          1       10.0        4        40.0
│             5          1       10.0        5        50.0
│             6          1       10.0        6        60.0
│             7          1       10.0        7        70.0
│             8          3       30.0       10       100.0
│
│
│
│
│
│
│
│
└
```

Figure 8.10 PROC FREQ output using __NUMERIC__

The SAS System has many built-in functions within a few general categories. The following sections will introduce you to a sample of each of the following:

- arithmetic and math functions
- character functions
- date functions

8.2.1 Arithmetic and math functions

The SAS System includes many common arithmetic and mathematical functions, such as these:

ABS   (arg) is the absolute value function
EXP   (arg) raises e to the power 'arg'
INT   (arg) truncates arg to an integer
MOD   (quotient,divisor) returns the remainder
ROUND   (value,rounding unit) returns your rounded value
TAN   (arg) returns arg's tangent

You can use these functions in assignment statements or conditionals:

```
* HOURS_WK WILL BE THE ROUNDED VALUE OF TIMECARD:
  HOURS_WK = ROUND (TIMECARD,.5);
* CHECK REMAINDER OF DIVISION BY 2 TO SEE IF ODD;
```

```
  IF MOD (NUM1,2) = 1 THEN ODD + 1;
* TAKE THE LOG OF THE ABSOLUTE VALUE OF Y, AND
  ASSIGN THE RESULT TO X;
  X = LOG (ABS (Y));
```

8.2.2   Character functions

Character functions manipulate strings and words. These functions can be particularly useful when your SAS program is reading text, or examining positions within an existing variable, or removing blanks or other unwanted characters from a value.

COMPRESS   (arg) returns arg with the blanks removed

COMPRESS   (arg1,arg2) returns arg1 with the letters common to arg1 and arg2 removed.

Example: Result = COMPRESS ('12345',EVENS);
Result = COMPRESS ('12345','24');

If EVENS = '24', then RESULT is the same for both: RESULT = '135';

INDEX   (arg1, arg2) returns the relative position within arg1 of the value in arg2. If the pattern in arg2 is not found in arg1, the value returned by this function is zero.

Example: POS = INDEX ('ABCDEFG',TESTME);

If the variable TESTME contains the value 'D', then POS will be set to 4.

INPUT   (arg1,input format) allows you to change the input format of variable arg1. arg1 must be a character variable, but the result may be either character or numeric, depending on the input format you specify.

Example: If variable ALPHANUM were read in with the input format 5. and you wanted it stored on the current dataset as $CHAR5, you would code:

```
ALPHANUM = INPUT (ALPHANUM,$CHAR5.);
```

PUT   (arg1,output format) allows you to change the output format for a variable arg1.

Example: If variable NUM were read in with the input format 5.
and you wanted to format it using the COMMA6. for-
mat and create a new variable FORMATTED to contain the formatted value, you could code the following
assignment:

```
FORMATTED = PUT (NUM,COMMA6.);
```

If NUM contained the value 12345, then FORMAT-
TED would contain the character value "12,345".

LEFT   (arg) left aligns arg. This function is especially useful when
used with the other string manipulators such as SUBSTR and
INDEX.

RIGHT   (arg) right aligns arg.

REVERSE   (arg) returns a string containing the characters of arg, but
with their order reversed.

Example: Suppose you were interested in printing values of a
product code PRODCODE, but only if they end with
the letter A. The code does not have a fixed length, so
you don't know the end byte position.
One way to do this would be to code:

```
REV = REVERSE(PRODCODE);
LFT = LEFT(REV);
X   = SUBSTR(LFT,1,1);
IF X = 'A' THEN OUTPUT;
```

The first function processed is the REVERSE of
PRODCODE. This reverses its contents so that what
was previously the last byte is now the first byte of
REV. Next, left-align the result into LFT, so you don't
have to worry about the blank padding. Finally, check
the first byte of LFT (which is the last nonblank byte
of PRODCODE) to see if it is "A". If so, then create
an output observation.

SCAN   (arg,n,delimiters) first breaks up arg into "words" separated
by the delimiters you specify. This assumes that arg is a
string including both words and delimiters. Then it counts
the words and returns the value of the nth word, not including the delimiter.

If no delimiter(s) are specified, the following are used
* (¦ % $ + − , ˆ ; < . & !) blank

Example: TEXT has the value 'The quick brown fox'.

MIDDLE = SCAN (TEXT,3);
The value of MIDDLE is 'brown'.

SUBSTR   (arg,start position,length). Finds the start position in arg, then returns characters for a length of 'length')

Example: BYTE3TO8 = SUBSTR(ORIG,3,6);

SUBSTR can also be used to replace characters within a string.

Example: If variable CHARZIP = ' 1234' and you wanted to replace the blank first byte with a zero:

```
SUBSTR(CHARZIP,1,1) = '0';
/* NOW CHARZIP CONTAINS '01234' */
```

8.2.3   Two functions that let you pass and retrieve data from other DATA steps (SYMPUT and SYMGET)

We mentioned earlier that the DATA step receives information through the input dataset named in the SET statement. Although in most cases this is the way you'll pass data, there may be times when you want only one value from a variable in a previous step.

The SAS System provides several ways to do this, one of which is to use the SYMPUT subroutine paired with the SYMGET function. (Other methods, as well as more extensive use of SYMPUT/SYMGET, are covered in Chapter 11.) SYMPUT creates a new variable and stores a specified value. It is actually a subroutine, so its format is new:

```
CALL SYMPUT ('passing-argument', step1-variable);
```

SYMGET is the function that retrieves the passed value:

```
step2-variable = SYMGET ('passing-argument');
```

Example 8.9 SYMPUT and SYMGET usage.   You want to compare expected CPU usage dollars with the actual totals from run 'FM480'. This DATA step reads the file; when it finds RUNCODE = 'FM480' it creates a new variable CPU__USE whose value can be retrieved after the DATA step is executed.

```
DATA TTLS;
INFILE 'a:\symparms.dat';
INPUT RUNCODE $
      TOTALS;
IF RUNCODE = 'FM480' THEN
      CALL SYMPUT ('CPU_USE',TOTALS);
```

The next step retrieves the value of CPU__USE by using the SYMGET function. The result is written to the SAS log (see Fig. 8.11).

```
DATA ACTUALS;
FORECAST = 39904;
ACTUAL = SYMGET ('CPU_USE');
RATIO = ACTUAL  / FORECAST;
PUT 'Ratio of Actual / Forecast  ' RATIO;
```

8.2.4   Other functions

The SAS System has many other functions including:

```
┌LOG────────────────────────────────────────────────────────┐
│Command ===>                                                │
│NOTE: The infile 'a:\Symparms.dat' is file A:\SYMPARMS.DAT. │
│NOTE: 6 records were read from the infile A:\SYMPARMS.DAT.  │
│      The minimum record length was 11.                     │
│      The maximum record length was 11.                     │
│NOTE: Numeric values have been converted to character       │
│      values at the places given by: (Number of times) at (Line):(Column). │
│      1 at 4:53                                             │
│NOTE: The dataset WORK.TTLS has 6 observations and 2 variables. │
│NOTE: The DATA statement used 22.00 seconds.               │
│    6        DATA Actuals;                                  │
│    7        Forecast = 39904;                             │
│    8        Actual = symget ('CPU_use'); /* RETRIEVE VALUE SAVED IN    */ │
│    9        Ratio = Actual  / Forecast; /* PRIOR STEP USING SYMPUT    */ │
│   10        PUT 'Ratio of Actual / Forecast  ' Ratio;     │
│   11        RUN;                                           │
│Ratio of Actual / Forecast  1.0297463913                   │
│NOTE: Character values have been converted to numeric       │
│      values at the places given by: (Number of times) at (Line):(Column). │
│      1 at 9:12                                            │
│NOTE: The dataset WORK.ACTUALS has 1 observations and 3 variables. │
│NOTE: The DATA statement used 16.00 seconds.              │
└────────────────────────────────────────────────────────────┘
```

Figure 8.11   Log output showing SYMGET value

DATE( ), otherwise known as TODAY( ), which returns the current date. The result of this function is what is known as a SAS date (the number of days from January 1, 1960). To print out the absolute date, you must use a SAS date output format (see Chapter 6). Note that the parentheses are required in DATE( ), but no argument is required between them.

Example: RPT__DT = PUT(DATE( ),DATE7.);

TIME ( ) returns the current time.

ZIPFIPS ( ) converts ZIP codes to FIPS state codes.

ZIPNAME ( ) converts ZIP codes to state names.

SYSPARM( ) returns the value of the OS parm field. The following jobstream will pass the value 'PUTNAM' from the JCL to a SAS variable called COUNTY:

```
//RUNSAS   EXEC SAS,PARM='SYSPARM=PUTNAM'
//SYSIN     DD *
  DATA;
  COUNTY = SYSPARM();
/*
```

Joining Datasets

There are times when information you need resides on separate files and you need to access both, or all at once. Examples include transaction updates of a master file, normalized database processing, and routine separation and rejoining of different views of the data for performance or convenience considerations.

9.1 ADDING OBSERVATIONS

You may need to append observations or interleave them. You may want to capture only one variable or combine many variables from one dataset with the variables from another to produce a merged observation with contributions from both input datasets.

9.1.1 Adding observations from one dataset to another

The simplest way to add observations to a dataset is to include the names of all the datasets you wish to combine on a single SET statement in the DATA step. The output will be a single combined dataset. The format for appending several datasets is shown in Fig. 9.1.

The SET statement, as you learned in Chapter 5, defines input from a SAS dataset. When you include a second (or more) dataset name, it appears to the DATA step as if the datasets were concatenated. The order of concatenation is the same as the order of the dataset names on the SET statement.

Each iteration of the DATA step loop processes an observation from one (and only one) of the input datasets. You can keep track of which dataset contributed the current observation by using the IN= dataset option immediately following each dataset name. This option allows you to identify a Boolean variable that is set to 1 when the associated dataset's observation is being used in a DATA step iteration. For example, each iteration of this DATA step can check INJAN and INFEB to see whether JAN or FEB is the source of the current observation:

```
* COMBINE JAN AND FEB DATASETS INTO 'TWOMONS';
  DATA TWOMONS;
      SET JAN (IN=INJAN) FEB (IN=INFEB);
      IF INJAN = 1 THEN
          DO;
          /* special processing for January record  */
          END;
      ELSE DO;
          /* special processing for February record */
  END;
```

```
DATA output dataset name (options);
SET dataset1 (options)
    dataset2 (options)  ... [END=e of boolean] ;


Options include the dataset options DROP, KEEP, and RENAME
plus the IN= boolean dataset option (for input datasets)
that allow you to detect when an observation from the
dataset is being used in an iteration of the DATA step.

The END=end of file boolean allows you to detect when the
last observation is read.
```

Figure 9.1   Appending SAS datasets

Example 9.1 Concatenating two datasets. Let's see how to concatenate two SAS datasets (called FIRST and SECOND) and create a third (THIRD) containing all the observations of FIRST, followed by all the observations of SECOND.
Dataset FIRST contains this data:

OBS	VAR1	VAR2	VAR3
1	A	5	0.00
2	B	6	.
3	C	7	1.99

Dataset SECOND contains this data:

OBS	VAR1	VAR2	VAR3
			313
1	D	8	2.00
2	E	9	3.10
3	F	.	4.40

This simple DATA step will combine the observations into a single dataset called THIRD:

```
DATA THIRD;
    SET FIRST SECOND;
```

The contents of dataset THIRD will be as follows. Note that there are six observations: the first three copied from FIRST, and the remaining three from SECOND:

OBS	VAR1	VAR2	VAR3
1	A	5	0.00
2	B	6	.
3	C	7	1.99
4	D	8	2.00
5	E	9	3.10
6	F	.	4.40

In other words, your output dataset will have a total number of observations equal to the sum of both input datasets. The order of those observations is a complete list of all observations of the first dataset listed followed by the complete list of all observations in the second data set.
You don't have to restrict your concatenations to datasets with common variables. If you combine datasets with different variables, the output dataset will contain all the variables present on all of the

input files. (You can modify this with a DROP or KEEP dataset option or statement.)

Variables which are present in one input dataset but not in another are set to "missing" on observations taken from the latter. The DATA step will first set up the internal table with a column for each unique variable on every input dataset. Before each read, it sets the value of each variable to missing. When an observation is read, the variable names are matched, and nonmissing values are saved for output.

Example 9.2 Concatenating two datasets with different variables on them. If dataset FIRST contained this data:

OBS	VAR1	VAR2	VAR3
1	A	5	0.00
2	B	6	.
3	C	7	1.99

and dataset SECOND contained this data (note that VAR1 and VAR2 have been replaced by VAR4 and VAR5):

OBS	VAR4	VAR5	VAR3
1	D	8	2.00
2	E	9	3.10
3	F	.	4.40

then this DATA step

```
DATA THIRD;
    SET FIRST SECOND;
```

would produce dataset THIRD as follows:

OBS	VAR1	VAR2	VAR3	VAR4	VAR5
1	A	5	0.00	.	.
2	B	6	.	.	.
3	C	7	1.99	.	.
4	.	.	2.00	D	8
5	.	.	3.10	E	9
6	.	.	4.40	F	.

Note how on observations 1, 2, and 3, VAR4 and VAR5 have missing values. This is because these variables are not present on dataset FIRST and so could not contribute an actual value. Similarly VAR1 and VAR2 are not present on dataset SECOND, so observations 4, 5, and 6 can only have missing values for these variables.

When several input datasets contain the same variable, the variable should have consistent attributes on all datasets. If the DATA step finds a name match, but type or attribute mismatch, any of the following will occur, depending on the mismatch:

- Type mismatch: If the types (character or numeric) don't match, the supervisor will issue an error message.

- Length mismatch: For character variables, the length on the output dataset will be the same as that on the first input dataset that has it. For numeric variables, the dataset will keep a length that is stated in an explicit LENGTH statement. Values are truncated if necessary.

- Format (input or output) or Label mismatch: the dataset will always keep explicit definitions over any created by default processing.

Example 9.3 Concatenating two datasets with length attribute mismatches. In this example, we try to match two files having variables (one character and one numeric) with the same names, but with mismatched lengths.

Dataset FIRST was created with the following statements. There are no default lengths in dataset FIRST.

```
DATA FIRST;
    LENGTH CODE 3;
    INPUT CODE NAME $5.;
    CARDS;
    123 HOOD
    345 SMED
    567 WYSTE
    ;
```

Dataset SECOND was created with the following statements. The default length for the numeric variable CODE is 8 bytes. NAME is given an explicit length (9). Note how both CODE and NAME are larger in size than they were in FIRST.

```
DATA SECOND;
    INPUT CODE NAME $9.;
    CARDS;
    1234567890 ARCHIBALD
    4567890123 MOSINSSKI
    7890123456 JELLINECK
    ;
```

Now we create dataset THIRD, concatenating FIRST and SECOND:

```
DATA THIRD;
    SET FIRST SECOND;
```

Let's examine the output (Fig. 9.2). Notice first that NAME has been truncated in all the observations from SECOND. This is because a length conflict for character variables is resolved in favor of the length defined in the first dataset. In this case, dataset FIRST indicates a length of 5 for NAME, so this is the value used throughout the DATA step.

Note, too, how the values of CODE in the last three observations are unreliable. This occurs because an explicit LENGTH overrides the default storage length for numeric variables. Hence, the explicit length 3 was taken from dataset FIRST and used throughout. With only three bytes in which to store CODE, the values had to be truncated in the observations from SECOND. PROC PRINT attempted to re-expand the values, with erroneous results; these errors will occur in any step which tries to use the dataset THIRD.

9.1.2 PROC APPEND

PROC APPEND allows you to add observations from one SAS dataset to the end of another. The basic format is shown in Fig. 9.3. You specify a base dataset with the BASE= option and use the DATA= option to name a dataset containing additional observations. You can

```
┌OUTPUT══════════════════════════════════════════
│Command ===)
│                           SAS
│                OBS         CODE    NAME
│
│                 1           123    HOOD
│                 2           345    SMED
│                 3           567    WYSTE
│                 4     1234436896    ARCHI
│                 5     4567597856    MOSIN
│                 6     7889485824    JELLI
│
│
│
└──────────────────────────────────────────────────
```

Figure 9.2 Concatenating with fields of unequal length

use the FORCE option to restrict the output dataset to variables that are defined in the base file.

As usual, if you do not specify the DATA= option to identify the input dataset, the assumption is that you want to append the last created SAS dataset.

The FORCE option forces the appended observations to match the variables present on the base dataset:

- variables not present on the base dataset are not included on the output

- variables on the base file that are not present on the appending file are set to missing

- the length of an appended dataset's variable will be truncated if it is longer than the same named variable on the base file

- a type mismatch occurs if same named variables are not both character or both numeric

The supervisor will issue warnings for these conditions.

Example 9.4 PROC APPEND with FORCE key. In this example, we append a file called SUPPLY to a base file called MASTER. Both files contain fields called NUM and ALPHA; however, ALPHA has different lengths on the two files. Also, MASTER contains one variable (LAST)

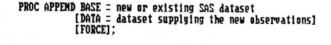

```
PROC APPEND BASE = new or existing SAS dataset
          [DATA = dataset supplying the new observations]
          [FORCE];
```

Figure 9.3 PROC APPEND syntax

that is not on SUPPLY, and SUPPLY has one variable (ANY) that is not on MASTER.

We use the FORCE option to limit our output dataset (a new copy of MASTER) to only those variables which were present in the original MASTER. Look at Fig. 9.4, which includes the log output of PROC APPEND. It informs us first of the length mismatch between the two ALPHA variables: ALPHA has length 3 on the base file and 5 on the data file. Because the base file takes precedence, the output ALPHA fields will have length 3.

The next thing we see in the log is a warning that variable LAST (defined on the base file) was not found on the data file; the appended observations will all have missing values for LAST. Notice that there is no message warning that variable ANY was not found on the base file. This is because the FORCE option dictates that variables not on the base file will simply be ignored.

The output MASTER has six observations (three from MASTER, and three from SUPPLY). It has three variables, corresponding to the original MASTER. Its contents are shown in the PROC PRINT in Fig. 9.5. Note that ALPHA has been restricted to three bytes, and that the appended observations have blank values for LAST. (For character variables, missing values are converted to blanks.)

```
    * CREATE BASE FILE "MASTER"
      CONTAINING NUM, ALPHA (3 BYTES), AND LAST;
      DATA MASTER;
      INPUT @1 NUM      3.
            @5 ALPHA $CHAR3.
            @9 LAST  $Char1.
        ;
        CARDS;
123 ABC Z
345 DEF Z
567 GHI Z
 ;
      RUN;
    * CREATE DATA FILE "SUPPLY"
      CONTAINING NUM, ALPHA (5 BYTES), AND ANY;
      DATA SUPPLY;
      INPUT @1 NUM        5.
            @7 ALPHA  $CHAR5.
            @13 ANY   $CHAR1.
        ;
        CARDS;
78901 JKLMN X
89012 OPQRS 1
```

```
90123 TUVWX 0
;
      RUN;
   * APPEND "SUPPLY" OBSERVATIONS TO THE END OF
     "MASTER" DATASET. THE FORCE OPTION LIMITS
     VARIABLES TO THOSE WHICH WERE ORIGINALLY IN
     MASTER;
     PROC APPEND BASE=MASTER DATA=SUPPLY FORCE;
     RUN;
```

9.1.3   Interleaving observations from other datasets

We have seen how to concatenate observations from several input datasets by using a SET statement with multiple dataset names. You can cause the observations to be interleaved, rather than concatenated, simply by adding a BY statement following the SET statement. The general format is shown in Fig. 9.6.

The BY statement is not new to you. You were introduced to it in Chapter 4 as a way to perform control-break processing in PROC PRINT. When you use the BY variable in a DATA step, you're promising that the input datasets are sorted in order by the BY variable(s). You can sort the datasets by using PROC SORT on each, with the same BY statement (see Chapter 4).

```
┌LOG════════════════════════════════════════════
│Command ===)
│
│   47    PROC APPEND BASE= Master  DATA = Supply FORCE;
│   48    RUN;
│NOTE: Appending WORK.SUPPLY to WORK.MASTER.
│WARNING: Variable ALPHA has different lengths on BASE and DATA files
│         (BASE 3 DATA 5).
│WARNING: Variable LAST was not found on DATA file.
│NOTE: The dataset WORK.MASTER has 6 observations and 3 variables.
│NOTE: The PROCEDURE APPEND used 10.00 seconds.
│   49    PROC PRINT DATA = Master;
│   50    RUN;
│NOTE: The PROCEDURE PRINT used 9.00 seconds.
```

Figure 9.4   Log output of PROC APPEND

```
┌OUTPUT════════════════════════════════════════════════════
│Command ===)
                            SAS
                OBS    NUM    ALPHA    LAST

                 1     123     ABC      Z
                 2     345     DEF      Z
                 3     567     GHI      Z
                 4   78901     JKL
                 5   89012     OPQ
                 6   90123     TUV
```

Figure 9.5 Output of PROC APPEND

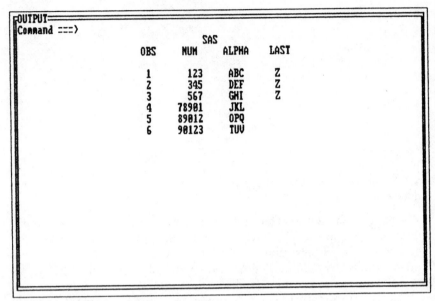

```
DATA Output dataset name (options);
SET dataset1 (options)
    dataset2 (options)... [END=e of boolean];
BY by-variable1 by-variable2...by-variable;

Options include:
-   IN= boolean identifies when an observation from the
    dataset is contributing information to a
    particular iteration of the DATA step

-   other dataset options like KEEP, DROP, RENAME
    can be used to limit/change the variables
    available to the interleave

-   the END= boolean allows you to detect
    when the last observation has been read
```

Figure 9.6 Interleaving observations

As we saw when we looked at concatenating two datasets, each iteration of the DATA step loop processes an observation from one and only one of the input datasets. You can identify the source of the current observation by defining IN= variables for each input.

Example 9.5 Interleaving datasets. In this example, we want to use ZIP code to interleave fund-raising letters to contributors with the regular monthly sweepstakes in order to gain a postal discount. We'll include a forms code on the output dataset to identify the type of letter required.

```
* INTERLEAVE SWEEPS AND CONTRIBS DATASETS
  BY ZIP CODE;
  DATA COMBINED;
    * SW_IN WILL = 1 WHEN CURRENT OBS IS FROM SWEEPS;
      SET SWEEPS (IN=SW_IN) CONTRIBS;
      BY ZIPCODE;
    * IF CURRENT OBS IS FROM SWEEPS, USE FORM 'A01X2',
      OTHERWISE USE FORM 'MXX01';
      IF SW_IN THEN FCODE = 'A01X2';
              ELSE FCODE = 'MXX01';
```

We define a Boolean IN= variable called SW_IN, which is associated with dataset SWEEPS. The supervisor will set SW_IN to 1 when an observation from SWEEPS is being used and will set it to 0 when CONTRIBS is being used.Thus, we can test whether a given observation came from SWEEPS or CONTRIBS by testing SW_IN, and this is used to determine the FCODE value to output. Remember that "IF SW_IN" is equivalent to "IF SW_IN = 1", since the values can only be 1 (true) or 0 (false).

9.2   COMBINING OBSERVATIONS

In the previous sections we saw how to add observations from one dataset to another, thereby increasing the total number of observations in your output dataset. Although these techniques allowed us to combine observations into a single dataset, each observation contained data from only one of the input datasets. We could not create an observation containing data which was merged from several datasets.

In this section, you'll learn how to use the MERGE statement to merge information from several datasets into a single observation, and create a dataset containing the merged information.

9.2.1 The merge operator

The MERGE statement replaces the SET statement as the input statement in a DATA step. The syntax is similar to SET. However, MERGE implies that information will be combined from observations on several datasets to create single records on the output dataset. Apart from using the MERGE statement in place of SET, the DATA step is otherwise unchanged. A DATA step using the MERGE statement can include all the statements and observations available in other DATA steps; e.g., RETAIN, LENGTH, DROP, KEEP, FORMAT.

There are two uses for a MERGE statement:

- to combine variables from positional related observations (positional merge)
- to combine variables from observations that match on one or more keys (match merge)

9.2.2 Positional merge

In the positional merge you want to combine the variables in the first observations of every input datasets, then combine the second observations, then the third, and so on. The assumptions are that all datasets have the same number of observations and that the position of each observation is meaningful. Figure 9.7 shows the MERGE statement for a positional merge.

For example, you might have a number of datasets, each with four observations representing European, Asian, African, and American sales in that order. You could quickly combine them into a single, four-observation dataset by using a positional merge.

By default, all variables from all input datasets are included in the output. If the same variable is present on several input datasets, the supervisor must make a decision as to which one to keep. We saw a similar situation in the concatenating type of DATA step earlier in this chapter. But now we not only have to decide on the attributes of the variable, we also have to decide which of several values to keep.

The rule is: When identically named variables are merged, the resulting value on the output dataset is the value for the variable as it appears on the dataset listed last on the MERGE statement.

Example 9.6 Positional merge with nonunique variables. In this example, we attempt to merge two text files (PART1 and PART2). In both files, the data is in a single variable named TEXT. Each file has two observations. When we attempt to merge both parts, we discover that the merged file also has two observations containing variable TEXT.

```
MERGE dataset1 [(options)]
      dataset2 [(options)] ... [END=e of boolean]
      ;

Options include:
 -  IN= boolean identifies when the dataset
    contributes information to the DATA step

 -  other dataset options like KEEP, DROP, RENAME
    can be used to limit/change the variables
    available to the merge.

 -  END=e of boolean allows you to detect when the
    last observation has been read
```

Figure 9.7   Positional merge syntax

But the value of TEXT is only that contributed by PART2 (the dataset listed last on the MERGE statement). What happened to the data from PART1?

The answer lies in the MERGE statement, which lists PART1 and PART2 in that order. In a positional merge, any conflicts between dataset values are resolved in favor of the last-named dataset. The positional merge first attempts to merge observation #1 from PART1 with observation #1 from PART2. Both contain a variable called TEXT, so the output observation #1 will contain TEXT with the value taken from the last-named dataset; i.e., PART2. Then it merges observation #2 from PART1 with observation #2 from PART2, with similar results.

```
      DATA PART1;  /* PART1 CONTAINS TWO LINES    */
           INPUT TEXT  $CHAR30.;
           CARDS;
Mary had a little lamb
And everywhere that Mary went
      ;
      DATA PART2;  /* PART2 CONTAINS TWO LINES    */
           INPUT TEXT  $CHAR30.;
           CARDS;
Its fleece was white as snow
The lamb was sure to go
```

```
          ;
/*   THE MERGE OUTPUT WILL ALSO CONTAIN 2 LINES. */
/*   CONFLICTS ARE RESOLVED IN FAVOR OF PART2.   */
     DATA MERGED;
          MERGE PART1 PART2;
     RUN;
/*   PRINT THE RESULTS.                          */
/*   "NOOBS" MEANS THE OUTPUT WILL NOT           */
/*   CONTAIN OBSERVATION NUMBERS.                */
     TITLE 'Poetry 101';
     PROC PRINT NOOBS;
     RUN;
```

One way to make sure that you won't lose any information is to RENAME one of the variables. We will rename the TEXT value coming from PART2; its new name will be TEXT2. Hence, there should be no conflict between PART1 and PART2. Observe the difference between the output in Fig. 9.9 and in Fig. 9.8. We still have only two output observations; that is the nature of the positional merge. But now each observation has two variables: TEXT, which comes from PART1, and TEXT2, which comes from PART2.

```
DATA MERGED;
     MERGE PART1 PART2 (RENAME = (TEXT = TEXT2));
RUN;
```

Figure 9.8 Merge with non-unique variables

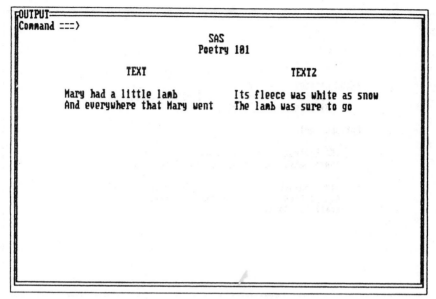

Figure 9.9 Correcting positional merge with RENAME

9.2.3 Match merge

The match merge is more sophisticated than the positional merge. In the match merge, we combine observations from several datasets only if there is a match on the values of specified key variables. This implies that there must be at least one common variable and the datasets must be in order by that variable. You probably have already guessed how to code a match merge: it looks just like the positional merge, with the addition of our old friend the BY statement. Fig. 9.10 shows the general format for the matching MERGE statement.

As with the positional merge, when identically named variables are merged, the resulting value for the output observation is the value that appears on the last listed dataset in the MERGE statement. This does not matter in the BY variables (by definition, observations to be combined always have matching BY variables).

It is possible for one dataset to have a BY value which is not matched in another. In this case, the observation will be created with missing values representing the variables of the unmatched dataset.

9.2.4 Match merge with no duplicates

The simplest match merge is that performed on files with no duplicates. This means that on each of the input datasets, every value of the BY variable is unique.

```
MERGE dataset1 (options)
      dataset2 (options)  .... [END=e of boolean];
      BY [descending] var1 ... varN;

Options include:

-   IN= boolean identifies when the dataset
    contributes information to the DATA step

-   other dataset options like KEEP, DROP, RENAME
    can be used to limit/change the variables
    available to the merge
```

Figure 9.10 Match merge syntax

Example 9.7 "Bare Bones" match merge. In this example, we have two files that we've already read into SAS datasets. Both files are in account number sequence. The first file (SPNDNP) contains a list of credit customers suspended for nonpayment. A sample of its contents is shown in Fig. 9.11. ACCT is the account number, MATCODE is a match code based on name and address, WO is the amount that will be written off, and DTLAST is the date of last activity on the account.

The second file (TRANS) contains a list of transactions for the week. It contains the account number (ACTN), the transaction ID (TRAN) and the amount associated with the transaction. For this simple example, we assume that there can be no more than one transaction per account. A sample is shown in Fig. 9.12.

We'd like to find out if there are any transactions for the suspended customers. Our solution is to match the suspended customer file against the transaction file. Since the data is already in order by account number, this simple DATA step performs the merge. The RENAME is necessary only because the BY variable must be the same in both datasets (had we had the foresight to call it ACCT in both datasets, the RENAME could be omitted).

The output in Fig. 9.13 shows the results of the match merge. We see that it did properly combine data from the two datasets when there were matching keys (e.g., observation #3). Observations were also created for unmatched values; observation #1 has only data from TRANS, while observation #2 has only data from SPNDNP. We'll see how to suppress the unmatched observations in Example 9.8.

```
* MERGE 'SPNDNP' AND 'TRANS' datasets;
  DATA VERIFY;
      MERGE SPNDNP
            TRANS (RENAME = (ACTN = ACCT));
*     ONLY MERGE OBSERVATIONS WITH MATCHING ACCOUNTS;
      BY ACCT;
```

We saw that the MERGE outputs an observation for each match as well as for each nonmatch. To keep only the matching observations, you need two additional pieces of code: an IN= dataset option for both files (so that you know when a match occurs) and an OUTPUT statement to indicate explicitly when the observation should be written.

We have come across the IN= option before. It associates a Boolean variable with a particular dataset. The variable is set to 1 when the associated dataset is contributing to the current observation. When we used the IN= option in concatenating datasets, only one of the IN= variables could be set to 1 for a given observation; each observation came from one dataset or another, but not a combination.

Now any combination of the IN= variables is possible. (Well, not exactly; they can't all be zero because this would mean that none of the input datasets is contributing to the current observation.) In par-

```
┌OUTPUT═══════════════════════════════════════════════════════════
│Command ===>
│                              SAS
│                   Contents of dataset: Spndnp
│
│        OBS    ACCT     MATCODE       WO        DTLAST
│
│         1      918    Fedr10112a    22.50     03MAR87
│         2     1123    Wrth53124x   109.10     04MAR87
│         3     1234    Znda60017a    11.45     19MAR88
│         4     2133    Ader92112a    49.22     01AUG87
│         5     3324    Jhns78773a    23.20     11OCT88
│         6     5551    Dgas01182x    89.02     19JUL88
│
└
```

Figure 9.11 Contents of Credit Customer File

```
┌OUTPUT══════════════════════════════════════════════════
│Command ===>
│                             SAS
│                   Contents of dataset: Tran
│
│              OBS     ACNT    TRAN     AMT
│
│               1       14     PAYT    15.88
│               2      1123    PAYT    75.88
│               3      1234    ORDR    11.95
│               4      3324    RETN    23.28
│               5      6732    CNCL    18.95
│               6      7889    ORDR   156.48
│               7     19934    ORDR    25.89
│               8     23345    ORDR    39.82
│
│
│
│
│
│
│
└────────────────────────────────────────────────────────
```

Figure 9.12   Contents of Transaction File

```
┌OUTPUT══════════════════════════════════════════════════
│Command ===>
│                             SAS
│                Contents of merged dataset: Verify
│                    Default output processing
│
│ OBS    ACCT    MATCODE      WO      DTLAST    TRAN     AMT
│
│  1      14                    .        .      PAYT    15.88
│  2     918    Fedr18112a    22.58   83MAR87
│  3     1123   Wrth53124x   189.18   84MAR87   PAYT    75.88
│  4     1234   Znda68817a    11.45   19MAR88   ORDR    11.95
│  5     2133   Ader92112a    49.22   81AUG87
│  6     3324   Jhns78773a    23.28   110CT88   RETN    23.28
│  7     5551   Dgas81182x    89.82   19JUL88
│  8     6732                    .        .      CNCL    18.95
│  9     7889                    .        .      ORDR   156.48
│ 18    19934                   .        .      ORDR    25.89
│ 11    23345                   .        .      ORDR    39.82
│
│
│
└────────────────────────────────────────────────────────
```

Figure 9.13   Output of match merge

ticular, we can tell when there is a match because all of the IN=
variables will be set to 1. We can test for this condition and only
create output if it is true.

Example 9.8 Match merge (output only matches). In this example, we modify the program of Example 9.7 to output only observations for accounts which were matched on both files. The last statement tests
the two Booleans to see if both datasets have provided data available to the current output observation. Remember that once we include an OUTPUT statement, all automatic output is turned off, so
these are the only observations which will be written. You can see
in Fig. 9.14 that only the matching observations were written, and
only three observations had matching account numbers on both files.

```
DATA VERIFY;
MERGE SPNDNP (IN = SP)
      TRANS  (IN = TR RENAME = (ACTN = ACCT));
BY ACCT;
* OUTPUT MATCHES ONLY.
THIS IS SHORTHAND FOR SAYING:
IF SP = 1    (MATCHED ON THE SPNDNP DATASET)
AND TR = 1   (MATCHED ON THE TRANS DATASET)
THEN OUTPUT  (CREATE OUTPUT OBSERVATION);
IF SP AND TR THEN OUTPUT;
```

```
┌OUTPUT══════════════════════════════════════════════════════
│Command ===)
│                              SAS
│                Contents of merged dataset: Verify
│                Controlling output of matches only
│
│     OBS    ACCT    MATCODE      WO      DTLAST    TRAN    AMT
│
│      1     1123    Wrth53124x   109.10  04MAR87   PAYT    75.00
│      2     1234    Znda60017a    11.45  19MAR88   ORDR    11.95
│      3     3324    Jhns78773a    23.20  11OCT88   RETN    23.20
│
│
│
│
│
│
└─────────────────────────────────────────────────────────────
```

Figure 9.14 Selecting only matched observations

Example 9.9 Match merge with a simple update. This example illustrates that a MERGE is also a normal DATA step and you can perform more than just a merge in it. The code is similar to Example 9.8, except that when a match is found, further checks and a simple update are made in the LINKed section of code (starting at UPDT). The output is shown in Fig. 9.15.

The UPDT routine uses a SELECT statement (see Chapter 6) to determine the current transaction ID. We do not want to accept new orders from suspended customers who have had a writeoff, so when the transaction is 'ORDR' we flag a status code. On payments ('PAYT') and returns ('RETN'), we reduce the outstanding writeoff by the value of the payment or return; if there is still a writeoff amount, we flag the status.

Note that in this version of the program, we are allowing both matched and unmatched observations to be output (we removed the OUTPUT statement, restoring the automatic output default.) Also note that we have dropped the DTLAST variable.

The program concludes with a PROC PRINT with titles and footnotes. Take a look at Fig. 9.15, which reproduces a portion of the output. Note that two of the matched observations have been flagged according to the rules we stated. The third (observation #6) was not flagged, because the value of the return (AMT = \$23.20) was equal to the old writeoff amount (WO = \$23.20, in Fig. 9.13) so the writeoff is now reduced to zero.

```
DATA VERIFY;
MERGE SPNDNP (IN = SP DROP=DTLAST)
      TRANS  (IN = TR RENAME = (ACTN = ACCT));
BY ACCT;
IF SP AND TR THEN LINK UPDT; /* UPDATE MATCHED RECS */
RETURN;
/* UPDATE ROUTINE                                     */
UPDT: SELECT;
   * FOR ORDER TRAN, SET FLAG IF THERE IS WRITEOFF;
     WHEN (TRAN = 'ORDR') IF WO > 0 THEN STATUS = '*';
   * FOR PAYMENT AND RETURN, FIRST REDUCE WRITEOFF
     BY VALUE OF PAYMENT OR RETURNED ITEM,
     THEN SET FLAG IF THERE IS STILL WRITEOFF;
     WHEN (TRAN = 'RETN' OR TRAN = 'PAYT') DO;
        WO = WO - AMT;
        IF WO > 0 THEN STATUS = '*';
        END;
        OTHERWISE;
     END;
   RETURN;
```

```
* PRINT THE RESULTS;
  FOOTNOTE10 '  ORDR tran not applied if WO > 0';
  TITLE 'Contents of merged dataset: Verify';
  PROC PRINT;
```

9.2.5 Match merge of input datasets with duplicates

In some cases, multiple observations with the same BY variable cannot be deleted because to do so would cause the loss of detail information. For instance, a more realistic version of our last example would have had to allow for multiple transactions on the same account. We'll refer to a group of observations on one dataset having the same BY value as a BY group.

When the merge encounters a BY group, it attempts to match the observations one-for-one against members of a corresponding BY group on the other dataset(s). This is strictly one-for-one if the BY groups have the same number of observations. However, if a BY group on one dataset runs out of observations to match against another BY group, the merge will retain the values of variables as they're found on the last member in that BY group. It will combine the retained values with the remaining members in the nonexhausted BY group.

```
┌─OUTPUT═══════════════════════════════════════════════════════════════════╗
│ Command ===>                                                              │
│                                SAS                                        │
│                 Contents of merged dataset: Verify                       │
│                                                                          │
│     OBS    ACCT    MATCODE      WO      TRAN     AMT      STATUS         │
│                                                                          │
│      1      14                   .      PAYT    15.00                    │
│      2     918    Fedr10112a   22.50            .                       │
│      3    1123    Wrth53124x   34.10    PAYT    75.00        *           │
│      4    1234    Znda60017a   11.45    ORDR    11.95        *           │
│      5    2133    Ader92112a   49.22            .                       │
│      6    3324    Jhns78773a    0.00    RETN    23.20                    │
│      7    5551    Dgas01182x   89.02            .                       │
│      8    6732                   .      CNCL    10.95                    │
│      9    7889                   .      ORDR   156.40                    │
│     10   19934                   .      ORDR    25.89                    │
│                                                                          │
│                   ORDR tran not applied if WO > 0                        │
│                                                                          │
│                                                                          │
└══════════════════════════════════════════════════════════════════════════╝
```

Figure 9.15 Updating observations in a match-merge

Example 9.10 Match merge with one input dataset having duplicate BY variable values. One example of a file with multiple observations with the same BY variable is a file of customer accounts sorted by ZIP code. Obviously, there will be more than one customer per zip code. We will, however, be matching the customer file (INDIVIDS) against a file (ZIPS) which contains only one observation per ZIP code.

The situation is that each ZIP code has been given a "score" related to the likelihood that customers who live there will order from our company. Each customer has also been given an individual score, which reflects the individual's characteristics and buying pattern. The merge combines ZIP scores with individual scores to determine the likelihood that a customer will place an order.

Figure 9.16 shows a sample from the INDIVIDS file that includes duplicate observations of a BY variable (e.g., ZIP = 90654). Figure 9.17 shows corresponding observations on the ZIPS file; note that there are no duplicates.

Do we have to do anything special to handle the duplicates? In this case (where there are duplicates on only one input dataset), the answer is no. If we code a normal match merge, we will get the desired results. Remember that the duplicates (which are all in INDIVIDS) will always be matched against the last matching observation in ZIPS. This means that the single observation in ZIPS for each ZIP code will be correctly matched against all matching ZIP codes in INDIVIDS. First we get the observation from the file that

```
┌OUTPUT════════════════════════════════════════════
│Command ===>
│                           SAS
│                    Individual scores
│
│         OBS    ZIP     ACCT    TESTXY    INDSCORE
│
│          1    10045    s7529     21       1.118
│          2    12987    q2229     21       1.643
│          3    88765    q8345     22       1.883
│          4    88765    z1764     22       1.883
│          5    90654    a1543     22       1.878
│          6    90654    e2336     21       1.149
│          7    90654    d7632     22       1.331
│
└═══════════════════════════════════════════════════
```

Figure 9.16 Contents of Individuals File

has the lowest ZIP value (ZIPS). Since there is no matching ZIP on INDIVIDS, the DATA step simply outputs the observation with missing values for the missing variables.

So far, it's just like the match merge described above. The difference occurs when we process the customers who have ZIP code "88765". These people belong to what is known as a BY group. That is, each member in the group has the same value for the BY variable.

When the merge encounters a BY group, it attempts to match them one-for-one against members of the matching BY group on the other dataset(s). This is strictly one-for-one if the BY groups have the same number of observations (members), but in our example, ZIPS has only one observation that matches the ZIP = 88765 BY group. (We can say it has a BY group with only one member in it.) This observation is retained as long as there are matching observations in the INDIVIDS dataset. In particular, the observation with ZIPSCORE = 1.334 is retained for the remaining members after the initial match in the BY group ZIP = 88765. Similarly, ZIPSCORE = 1.448 was retained for the remaining members in the BY group ZIP = 90654.

The output is shown in Fig. 9.18. Note that the correct ZIPSCORE was associated with each INDSCORE. In particular, note that the two individuals in ZIP code 88765 picked up the correct ZIPSCORE of 1.334, and the three individuals in ZIP code 90654 all picked up the correct ZIPSCORE of 1.448. The only potential problem is that we added an observation for ZIP code 00245, which had no matching

```
┌─OUTPUT════════════════════════════════════════════════════════
│Command ===>
│                              SAS
│                           Zip scores
│
│                   OBS     ZIP     ZIPSCORE
│
│                    1      245      1.009
│                    2     10045      1.101
│                    3     12987      1.035
│                    4     88765      1.334
│                    5     90654      1.448
│
│
│
│
│
│
└───────────────────────────────────────────────────────────────
```

Figure 9.17 Contents of ZIP Code File

```
┌OUTPUT════════════════════════════════════════════════════════════════════════
│Command ===>
│                                      SAS
│                                The Merged scores
│
│          OBS      ZIP     ZIPSCORE     ACCT     TESTKY    INDSCORE
│
│           1       245      1.009                   .          .
│           2     10045      1.101      s7529       21        1.118
│           3     12987      1.035      q2229       21        1.643
│           4     88765      1.334      q0345       22        1.003
│           5     88765      1.334      z1764       22        1.003
│           6     90654      1.448      a1543       22        1.078
│           7     90654      1.448      e2336       21        1.149
│           8     90654      1.448      d7632       22        1.331
│
│
│
│
│
│
│
│
│
│
│
│
└───────────────────────────────────────────────────────────────────────────────
```

Figure 9.18   Match merge with duplicate BY values

individual records (note that ACCT, TESTKY, and INDSCORE are all missing), but we could always refine our program with IN= variables to prevent this from happening.

```
DATA SCORES;
    MERGE ZIPS INDIVIDS;
    BY ZIP;
RUN;
```

Example 9.11 BY-group processing on more than one input dataset. In Example 9.10, we had duplicates on only one dataset. What if there are BY groups on more than one file? Let's see what happens if we modify our ZIPS dataset to include an area code within each ZIP code (AREACD). Figure 9.19 shows a sample of the new ZIPS dataset. Notice that several ZIP codes are now duplicated because of the area codes. For example, there are two different areas within ZIP code 90654.

If we reran the program of Example 9.10, we would get results like those shown in Fig. 9.20. These results are strange! We now have fifteen observations, as opposed to the seven individuals we started out with (Fig. 9.16). Several accounts appear multiple times (e.g., account s7529). It seems that we have created even more duplicates than we started out with. How did this happen, and what can we do about it?

```
┌─OUTPUT══════════════════════════════════════════════════════════════┐
│ Command ===>                                                         │
│                               SAS                                    │
│                            Zip scores                                │
│                                                                      │
│               OBS     ZIP     ZIPSCORE     AREACD                     │
│                                                                      │
│                1      245      1.009        11                       │
│                2      245      1.009        23                       │
│                3     10045      1.101        31                      │
│                4     10045      1.101         9                      │
│                5     10045      1.101         3                      │
│                6     12987      1.035         .                      │
│                7     88765      1.334        72                      │
│                8     88765      1.334        44                      │
│                9     88765      1.334        21                      │
│               10     88765      1.334         1                      │
│               11     88765      1.334        43                      │
│               12     88765      1.334        29                      │
│               13     90654      1.448         1                      │
│               14     90654      1.448         2                      │
│                                                                      │
│                                                                      │
└──────────────────────────────────────────────────────────────────────┘
```

Figure 9.19   Contents of ZIP Code File with duplicate BY values

```
┌─OUTPUT══════════════════════════════════════════════════════════════┐
│ Command ===>                                                         │
│                               SAS                                    │
│                         The Merged scores                            │
│                                                                      │
│   OBS    ZIP    ZIPSCORE    AREACD    ACCT    TESTKY   INDSCORE       │
│                                                                      │
│    1      245    1.009        11                 .        .          │
│    2      245    1.009        23                 .        .          │
│    3    10045    1.101        31     s7529      21      1.118         │
│    4    10045    1.101         9     s7529      21      1.118         │
│    5    10045    1.101         3     s7529      21      1.118         │
│    6    12987    1.035         .     q2229      21      1.643         │
│    7    88765    1.334        72     q0345      22      1.003         │
│    8    88765    1.334        44     z1764      22      1.003         │
│    9    88765    1.334        21     z1764      22      1.003         │
│   10    88765    1.334         1     z1764      22      1.003         │
│   11    88765    1.334        43     z1764      22      1.003         │
│   12    88765    1.334        29     z1764      22      1.003         │
│   13    90654    1.448         1     a1543      22      1.078         │
│   14    90654    1.448         2     e2336      21      1.149         │
│   15    90654    1.448         2     d7632      22      1.331         │
│                                                                      │
└──────────────────────────────────────────────────────────────────────┘
```

Figure 9.20   BY-group processing on more than one input dataset

Our results go back to the fact that SAS default processing outputs all matches and all nonmatches. This means you'll get at least as many observations as in your largest input file (ZIPS has fourteen observations), plus any nonmatching observations from the other files, plus any "extra" matching observations from the other files.

In our example, we have duplicate ZIP codes on both datasets. Whenever we reach the end of a BY group on one dataset, the last observation is retained until all matching observations are used up on the other file. We could get away with this when there were more individuals than areas within a ZIP code, but it doesn't make sense to repeat an individual's values just to "fill up" an area record. In our example, we have picked up an additional observation in ZIP code 90654. Since this BY group on the ZIPS file contains only two members, the third member on the INDIVIDS file can't be matched. But this is not strictly a nonmatch. Note how the value of ZIPSCORE was retained from the last matching member of the ZIPS BY group.

The bottomline is that you must be careful when two datasets contain duplicate BY values. If the BY groups do not have exactly the same number of members in both datasets, you may get unexpected results. One observation in the shorter group will have its data repeated over and over until all observations in the larger group have been matched. We'll see how to get around this in the next example.

Example 9.12 Removing duplicates in BY groups. In Example 9.11, the default output processing created a dataset with fifteen observations. How can we create an unduplicated file of all the accounts that matched the ZIP codes?

The answer is something we have already worked with. As with the match merge on data with no duplicates, you use the IN= dataset option and the OUTPUT statement. But when processing duplicate BY values, we take a bit more care.

Let's look closely at the function of the IN= variable. Earlier, we said that it is set to 1 when the dataset is contributing information to the current DATA step iteration. It retains this 1 to signify that a contribution is being made even when that contribution is just the retained values from the last matched members in a BY group.

You can manipulate the Boolean so that it switches on only when a new value occurs. You can do this *by zeroing the Boolean prior to the MERGE statement.* (Don't put it after the MERGE statement or you'll never meet the "true" condition.) This ensures that the 1 will not be retained so that you can avoid repeating the data multiple times.

Here is a sample of the coding that you would use to output a dataset that contains the accounts that have ZIPSCORES. The code is similar to that used in Example 9.8 (match merge outputting only matches), except for the assignment statement I_IN = 0; coded

immediately before the MERGE statement. This allows us to avoid
repeating an individual score.

Figure 9.21 shows the output of this program. Note that we now
have only one observation per individual, and that the observation
for the unmatched ZIP code has also been removed.

```
* MERGE ZIP SCORES AND INDIVIDUAL SCORES WITHOUT CREATING
  DUPLICATES; DATA SCORES;
* THIS STATEMENT MAKES SURE THAT WHEN I_IN = 1, WE REALLY HAVE
  A NEW INDIVIDUAL SCORE AND NOT A RETAINED ONE; I_IN = 0;
* IDENTIFY THE MERGE RULES;
  MERGE ZIPS (IN=Z_IN)
        INDIVIDS (IN=I_IN);
  BY ZIP;
* WE DON'T REALLY CARE ABOUT AREACD (FOR US, ALL AREAS WITHIN
  A ZIP ARE EQUIVALENT).
  SO DROP THE VARIABLE FROM OUTPUT DATASET; DROP AREACD;
* ONLY OUTPUT IF WE HAVE A MATCH. BY INITIALIZING I_IN TO 0,
  WE MADE SURE NOT TO REPEAT ANY INDIVIDUAL SCORES. (IT'S OK
  TO REPEAT ZIP SCORES); IF Z_IN and I_IN THEN OUTPUT; RUN;
```

9.3   UPDATING A DATABASE

The UPDATE is a specialized type of merge that follows these rules:

```
┌OUTPUT════════════════════════════════════════════════
│Command ===>
│                            SAS
│                 The Merged Unduped Scores
│
│      OBS    ZIP     ZIPSCORE   ACCT    TESTKY   INDSCORE
│
│       1    18045     1.181    s7529     21      1.118
│       2    12987     1.835    q2229     21      1.643
│       3    88765     1.334    q8345     22      1.883
│       4    88765     1.334    z1764     22      1.883
│       5    98654     1.448    a1543     22      1.878
│       6    98654     1.448    e2336     21      1.149
│       7    98654     1.448    d7632     22      1.331
```

Figure 9.21   BY-group processing with duplicates removed

1. Only two datasets can be used: a master and a update (or transaction) file.

2. The master file must not contain duplicates, but the update file can have duplicates.

3. Variables that have missing values on the update file will not be applied to the master file (this means you don't have to worry about which dataset is listed last in the MERGE statement).

The UPDATE statements are very similar to those in the MERGE. See Fig. 9.22 for the syntax.

Example 9.13 How to UPDATE a master file. The abbreviated master file (MASTER) contains the account number (ACCT), the date of the last order (LSTORD), and the amount paid to date (AMT). Its contents are shown in Fig. 9.23.

The update file (TRAN) contains the account number (ACCT), the Tran Id (TRAN), the amount paid (AMT), and, if the tran is an order, the date (LSTORD). Its contents are shown in Fig. 9.24.

The UPDATE is very simple:

```
DATA UPDATED;          /* NAME OF UPDATED DATASET */
   UPDATE Master Tran; /* MASTER AND TRAN FILES   */
   BY ACCT;            /* KEY FIELD FOR MATCH     */
```

```
UPDATE  MASTER dataset   (options)
        TRANS  dataset   (options)
        [END=e of boolean];
        BY [descending] var1 ... varN;
```

Figure 9.22 UPDATE syntax

```
┌OUTPUT══════════════════════════════════════════════════════
│Command ===>
│                           SAS
│                        MASTER FILE
│
│              OBS      ACNT     LSTORD      AMT
│
│               1         14    05SEP89       .
│               2       1123    11OCT89       .
│               3       2787    01APR89    25.95
│               4       3324    22SEP89       .
│               5       6732    30SEP89       .
│               6       7889          .    12.35
│               7      19934          .     5.90
│
│
└──────────────────────────────────────────────────────────
```

Figure 9.23 Contents of Master File

```
┌OUTPUT══════════════════════════════════════════════════════
│Command ===>
│                           SAS
│                        TRAN FILE
│
│         OBS     ACNT    TRAN     AMT     LSTORD
│
│          1        14    PAYT    15.00         .
│          2      1123    PAYT    75.00         .
│          3      1234    ORDR    11.95    05NOV89
│          4      3324    RETN       .          .
│          5      6732    CNCL       .          .
│          6      7889    ORDR   156.40    06NOV89
│          7     19934    ORDR    25.89    07NOV89
│          8     23345    ORDR    39.02    05NOV89
│
│
└──────────────────────────────────────────────────────────
```

Figure 9.24 Contents of Transaction File

The result (shown in Fig. 9.25) shows that when the TRAN dataset has a value for a variable, that value is written over the value in the MASTER dataset. But if the TRAN dataset has a missing

```
┌OUTPUT══════════════════════════════════════════════════════════
│Command ===)
│                            SAS
│                      THE UPDATED MASTER
│
│          OBS     ACNT     LSTORD      AMT     TRAN
│
│           1        14    05SEP89     15.00    PAYT
│           2      1123    11OCT89     75.00    PAYT
│           3      1234    05NOV89     11.95    ORDR
│           4      2787    01APR89     25.95
│           5      3324    22SEP89        .     RETN
│           6      6732    30SEP89        .     CNCL
│           7      7889    06NOV89    156.40    ORDR
│           8     19934    07NOV89     25.89    ORDR
│           9     23345    05NOV89     39.82    ORDR
│
│
│
│
│
│
│
└──────────────────────────────────────────────────────────────────
```

Figure 9.25   Output of UPDATE

value for the variable, no update occurs.

When a variable is found on the TRAN dataset that is not on the MASTER dataset, that variable is added to the updated MASTER. It gives the variable a missing value on any unmatched MASTER records.

10

Basic Statistical and Reporting Procedures

Although we have stressed in this book that the SAS System is "more than just statistics", it is also true that statistical analysis is one of the most fully-developed sides of the SAS System. The statistical procedures available run the gamut from simple descriptive statistics (e.g., PROC FREQ and PROC SUMMARY) to complex techniques in multivariate analysis. Functions are available in base SAS software to calculate simple statistics, such as mean, standard deviation, and Chi-square. Or, advanced statistical procedures are contained in SAS/STAT® software which is licensed separately from base SAS software. For example, SAS/STAT includes procedures for analysis of variance, regression, and factor and cluster analysis. We will not cover SAS/STAT software in this book.

In this chapter we cover the basic statistical procedures, from a nonstatistician's point of view. "Descriptive statistics" is nothing more than counting and classifying data—tasks which are certainly familiar to programmers in every area. The procedures presented in this chapter are basically prepackaged summary reports, useful to even the most statistics-shy.

10.1 GRAPHIC REPORTING PROCEDURES: PROC CHART AND PROC PLOT

PROC CHART and PROC PLOT do exactly what you would expect from their names. PROC CHART creates graphic summary charts such as bar charts. PROC PLOT provides a graphic display of individual data values in two dimensions, enabling you to see patterns which may not be apparent in a nongraphic listing. Both PROC CHART and PROC PLOT use SAS datasets as input. (For information on getting external data into a SAS dataset, see Chapter 3.)

Although PROC CHART and PROC PLOT both produce graphic output, you do not have to use specialized graphics devices or even the SAS/GRAPH® software. This is because they produce simple output using ordinary characters to "draw" the graphs. (SAS/GRAPH software, which is licensed separately from the base SAS software, allows you to add sophisticated color graphics to your system. We will not cover the SAS/GRAPH software in this book.)

10.1.1 Summary graphics using PROC CHART

PROC CHART can produce several different types of output. Depending on your preference, PROC CHART will generate bar charts (vertical or horizontal). You can request several different charts in a single PROC CHART step.

Figure 10.1 shows the basic syntax of PROC CHART. As you can see, it is quite simple. The PROC CHART statement introduces the step and specifies the input SAS dataset. One or more chart definition statements follow; each one completely describes the chart to be produced. If you want to see separate charts for certain groups (e.g., male and female), you can use the optional BY statement.

The chart definition statement is the heart of PROC CHART. It identifies the format of the chart and the variables to be charted. Each chart definition statement has the form

```
chartform variables/options;
```

The chartform specifies the format of the chart to be displayed. Valid chartforms (shown in Figs. 10.2 and 10.3) include:

VBAR   Vertical bar chart (histogram)

HBAR   Horizontal bar chart (histogram)

```
PROC CHART
     DATA=SAS dataset name;              Input to the procedure

     BY variables;                       Optional; separate chart
                                         produced for each value
                                         of the BY variables

     chartform1 variables / options;     Identifies the desired
     chartform2 variables / options;     charts
     . . .
     chartform variables / options;
```

Figure 10.1 PROC CHART syntax

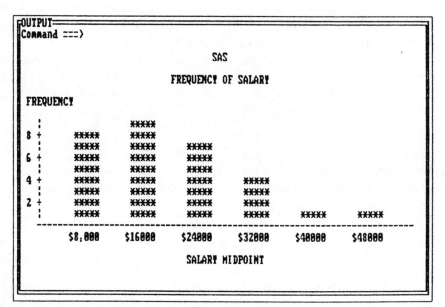

Figure 10.2 Sample vertical bar chart

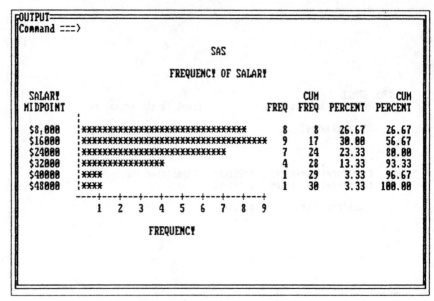

Figure 10.3   Sample horizontal bar chart

The variables and options are used to determine the specifics of each chart to be displayed. Visually, each chart is distinguished by the number of sections it contains and the relative size of each section. For each chart, you specify a class variable which will be used to section the data, and options to determine how many sections will be used and how to calculate the size of each. Note that the variables and options must be separated by a slash ("/").

Each chart is defined primarily by its class variable. You can choose any variable in your SAS dataset. The values of this variable are used to define the sections of your chart. Code the name of the class variable immediately after the chartform.

For example, consider a SAS dataset which contains variables SALARY, AGE, and JOBTITLE. To produce a chart whose sections represent different salary ranges, you would use SALARY as the class variable. The following statements will produce a horizontal bar chart with each bar representing a different salary range (such as the one shown in Fig. 10.3).

```
PROC CHART;
    HBAR SALARY;
```

These statements will produce a horizontal bar chart with each bar representing a different job title.

```
PROC CHART;
    HBAR JOBTITLE;
```

If you specify more than one class variable, each one will be graphed on a separate chart. No attempt is made to combine or cross-tabulate them. For example, the following chart definition statements will produce a vertical bar chart by SALARY, followed by three separate horizontal bar charts. The first horizontal bar chart will be by JOBTITLE, the second by SALARY, and the last by AGE.

```
PROC CHART;
    VBAR SALARY;
    HBAR JOBTITLE SALARY AGE;
```

This is equivalent to coding

```
PROC CHART;
    VBAR SALARY;
    HBAR JOBTITLE;
    HBAR SALARY;
    HBAR AGE;
```

10.1.2 Controlling the number of sections in a chart

Each section represents either a single value of the class variable or a range of values. Having selected your class variable, the next thing you need to do is to determine how these sections will be defined. For example, consider the vertical bar chart by salary in Fig. 10.2. Each section defines an $8,000 salary range.

The LEVELS, MIDPOINTS, and DISCRETE options let you control the choice of sections. Code any or all of these in the options area of the chart specification, after the class variable and a required slash ("/").

Code LEVELS=n to tell PROC CHART that the chart should be divided into *n* sections. For example, LEVELS=8 will produce eight bars on a horizontal bar chart. This option is only meaningful if the class variable is numeric. The HBAR chart in Fig. 10.4 was produced using LEVELS=8.

You can also use the MIDPOINTS option to specify the number of sections. In addition, MIDPOINTS lets you control the specific values to be included in each section. With MIDPOINTS, you specify the midpoint value for each section. PROC CHART then determines appropriate start- and end-points for each section. For example, we

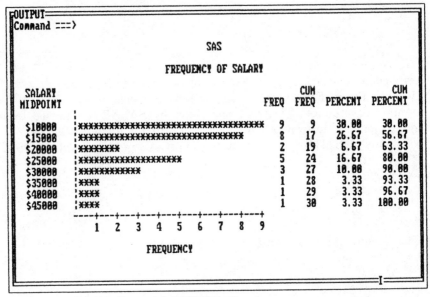

Figure 10.4   HBAR chart with LEVELS=8

can replace our LEVELS option with the following MIDPOINTS specification:

```
MIDPOINTS=10000 20000 30000 40000 50000
```

This will produce a chart with five sections as does LEVELS=5. However, instead of letting PROC CHART completely determine the five ranges, we have specified them ourselves. One section will contain values whose midpoint is $10,000. The second will contain values whose midpoint is $20,000, and so on. The HBAR chart of Fig. 10.5 was produced using this MIDPOINTS specification.

Both LEVELS and MIDPOINTS are optional. If you do not code them, PROC CHART will develop what it thinks is an appropriate breakdown.

The last of our sectioning options is DISCRETE. Code DISCRETE whenever you are using a numeric class variable whose values are not continuous. For example, "number of children" might be a discrete variable. This means that PROC CHART will expect only whole number values and will format the output appropriately.

10.1.3   Controlling the meaning of sections
in a chart

Look at Fig. 10.4 again. Notice that each bar is a different size, indicating its relative contribution to the whole SAS dataset. However,

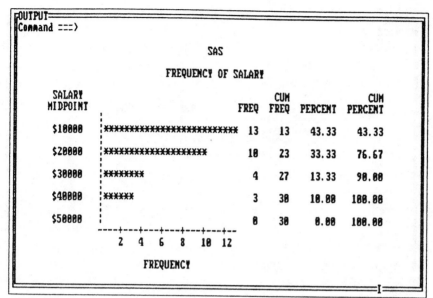

Figure 10.5   HBAR chart with MIDPOINTS

there are several ways to determine the relative contribution of each section. You can use a simple count of the observations or a percent relative to total observations. You can also add the actual values contained in the dataset.

By default, each section represents simply the number of observations in a particular range. This is the assumption used in Fig. 10.5. You can make this assumption explicit by coding TYPE=FREQ in the options section of the chart specification. Look at the following statements:

```
VBAR GRADE / DISCRETE;
VBAR GRADE / DISCRETE TYPE=FREQ;
```

They are equivalent. Both will produce a vertical bar chart, one bar for each value of GRADE. The height of each bar will indicate the number of students who received that grade.

One alternative to simply counting the observations in each class is to show the percent of total observations. To indicate this, code TYPE=PERCENT rather than TYPE=FREQ. Figure 10.6 is the chart of Fig. 10.5 recreated using TYPE=PERCENT. Of course, the relative sizes of the bars are the same, but the labeling now reflects percent rather than frequency.

In some situations, you may wish to actually add the observed val-

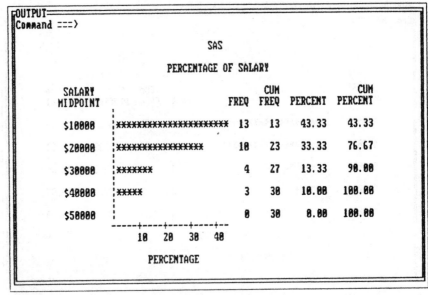

Figure 10.6   HBAR chart with TYPE=PERCENT

ues rather than count them. For example, consider the SALARY/
AGE/JOBTITLE dataset we discussed in Sec. 10.1.1. We have seen
how to chart the data by SALARY and display the number of individuals in each SALARY class—see Fig. 10.2 which was produced
with the following specification:

```
PROC CHART;
    VBAR SALARY / TYPE=FREQ;
```

However, suppose our intention is to show the total salary of individuals in each class. When a class includes ten individuals, its bar
should be determined by adding together the ten salaries. (We would
expect this to produce a chart that is noticeably different from the
frequency chart, because a salary of, say, $250,000 will contribute
more "height" to a bar than one of $10,000.)

Use TYPE=SUM to base the size of each section on the sum,
rather than the count, of some variable. TYPE=SUM should be used
along with the SUMVAR=variable option, which tells PROC
CHART which variable to use for the computation. The following
code produces our "total salary" chart, which is shown in Fig. 10.7.

```
PROC CHART;
    VBAR SALARY / TYPE=SUM SUMVAR=SALARY;
```

If we compare this output with Fig. 10.2, we find that the group con-

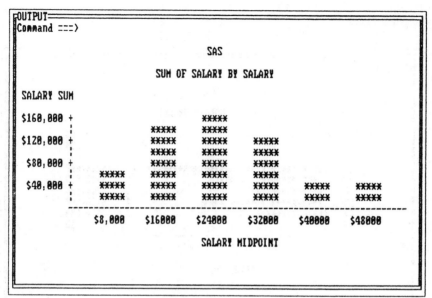

Figure 10.7 VBAR chart with TYPE=SUM and SUMVAR

tributing the greatest total salary is neither the most highly paid group (because there are so few individuals) or the most numerous group (because the salaries are relatively low). Instead, it is the group right in the middle, with salary midpoint $24,000.

The SUMVAR variable does not have to be the same as the class variable. For instance, Fig. 10.8 shows total salary by age, and is produced with the following specification:

```
PROC CHART;
    HBAR AGE / TYPE=SUM SUMVAR=SALARY
                MIDPOINTS = 20 30 40 50 60 70;
```

10.1.4   Grouping sections in a chart

You can specify that sections within a chart be grouped according to some other variable. For example, if our SALARY/AGE/JOBTITLE dataset also included a variable CITY, we might wish to group together the chart sections for each city. This does not affect the size of each section, but it will their arrangement on the page.

Use the GROUP=variable option to provide such grouping. Figure 10.9 shows the data of Fig. 10.3, grouped by city. It was produced using the following specification:

```
PROC CHART;
     HBAR SALARY / TYPE=FREQ GROUP=CITY;
```

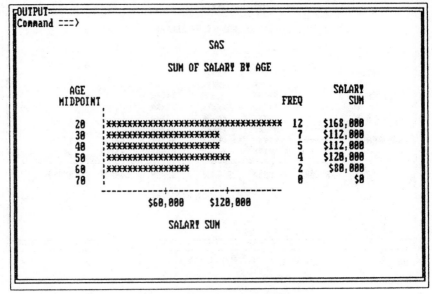

Figure 10.8   Different SUMVAR and class variables

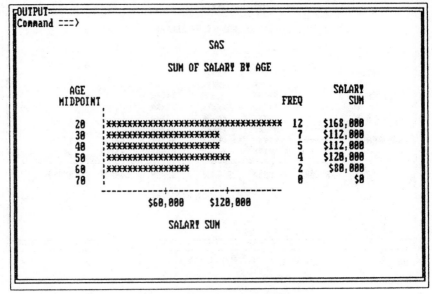

Figure 10.9   Grouping data within a chart

10.1.5   Detail graphics using PROC PLOT

PROC PLOT provides a graphic display of two variables in a SAS dataset, using a specified horizontal and vertical axis. Each observation in the SAS dataset produces a point on the plot.

Figure 10.10 shows the basic syntax of PROC PLOT. The PROC PLOT statement introduces the step and specifies the input SAS dataset. One or more plot definition statements follow; each one completely describes a plot to be produced. If you want to see separate plots for certain groups (e.g., male and female), you can use the optional BY statement. Figure 10.11 illustrates common PROC PLOT output.

The plot definition statement defines the variables to be charted, and may provide some specific display options. Each plot definition statement has the form

```
PLOT requests/options;
```

A single plot definition statement may request one or more plots. Each request has the form

```
YVAR*XVAR=SHOWVAR
```

YVAR is the variable which defines the vertical axis; XVAR defines the vertical axis. Of course, you will use the names of variables in your SAS dataset rather than YVAR and XVAR.

```
PROC PLOT
        DATA=SAS dataset name;     Input to the procedure

        BY  variables;             Optional; separate chart
                                   produced for each value of
                                   the BY variables

        PLOT requests / options;   Identifies the desired plots
        PLOT requests / options
        . . .
        PLOT requests / options;
```

Figure 10.10   PROC PLOT syntax

SHOWVAR is optional. It is used to tell PROC PLOT what character to print at the point determined by YVAR and XVAR in each observation. You may use a constant (for instance, TEMP*HRS='@') or a variable in your SAS dataset (e.g., TEMP*HRS=RESPCODE). If you use a variable, only the first character of its formatted value will be displayed. To use the default, omit the SHOWVAR specification and the preceding equal sign (e.g., TEMP*HRS).

The default display character is an "A" if the plotted point represents one observation. If two observations generate the same point, a "B" is printed, and so on. In Fig. 10.11, each point represents one observation, except the one at HRS=3.1, TEMP=300. There were five observations with HRS=3.1 and TEMP=300, so a letter "E" was printed.

Various options are available to control the coordinates along the horizontal and vertical axes. These options are entered on the plot request specification following the requests and a required slash ("/"). The VZERO and HZERO options will force the vertical and horizontal axes, respectively, to begin at zero:

```
PROC PLOT;
    PLOT WEIGHT*WEEKS / VZERO HZERO;
```

The HAXIS option tells PROC PLOT explicitly how to scale the horizontal axis:

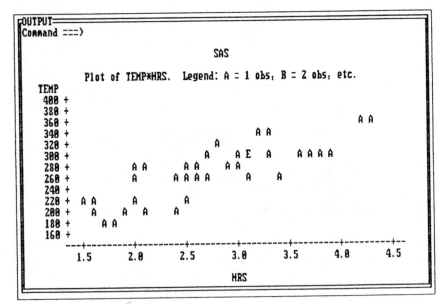

Figure 10.11 Sample PROC PLOT output

```
PROC PLOT;
    PLOT SATSCORE*INCOME / HAXIS=0 TO 250000 BY 10000;
    PLOT WEIGHT*FEEDX / HAXIS=.05 .10 .25 .90;
    PLOT PCB*DEPTH / HAXIS=10 TO 500 BY 10;
```

Similarly, the VAXIS option tells PROC PLOT how to scale the vertical axis:

```
PROC PLOT;
    PLOT LBSLOST*MILESRUN / VAXIS=0 TO 20;
    PLOT INCOME*BIRTHWT / AXIS=0 to 250000 BY 10000;
```

(Of course, both VAXIS and HAXIS options may be used on the same plot.)

You can also use the VPOS and HPOS options to specify the number of print positions available on the vertical and horizontal axes. The following specification restricts the plot to twenty vertical and fifty horizontal positions:

```
PROC PLOT;
    PLOT SYSTOLIC*INCOME / VPOS=20 HPOS=50;
```

10.2 SUMMARIZING A DATASET IN TABLE FORM: PROC FREQ

PROC FREQ provides a summary of the actual values present within a SAS dataset. The analysis is printed in table format. In its simplest form, PROC FREQ works with one variable in the dataset. Every observed value is displayed, along with a count of how many times the value was encountered. We've already seen some uses of the simple PROC FREQ (in Chapter 4), but we'll learn some more sophisticated uses in this chapter.

PROC FREQ can also provide cross-tabulation tables of two or more variables. It can perform statistical analysis on the resulting tables, and it creates an output SAS dataset which contains a summary picture of the detailed input dataset.

PROC FREQ is often the first step in analyzing a large dataset whose contents are unknown or unreliable. You do not need to know anything about the dataset to run PROC FREQ on it. In particular, you do not have to SORT it or identify any BY variables. PROC FREQ will tell you what is in the dataset, while reducing it to manageable size.

10.2.1   One-way frequency tables using PROC FREQ

Example 10.1 Using PROC FREQ to summarize an unknown file. In this example, we are faced with a tape of transactions from an outside source. The documentation lists various transaction codes, ranging from 01 to 50. However, we are not sure all of them are represented on the tape, and we suspect there may be others. Noting that the transaction code is in positions 1 and 2, the following program will provide a convenient summary of the dataset. Note that invoking PROC FREQ takes only one line of the program. The remainder is a DATA step that reads the external file into a SAS dataset.

```
DATA SASDATA;
     INFILE TRANTAPE;
     INPUT @1  TRANID $2.;
PROC FREQ;
```

The output is displayed in Fig. 10.12. Each value of TRANID is listed, along with the following information.

Frequency: How many times it appeared in the dataset

Percent: Its percentage of the total observations

Cumulative Frequency: Total frequency of this value and all values listed above it

Cumulative Percent: Total percent of this value and all values listed above it

As we suspected, not all of the transaction codes are present, and there are two (60 and 61) which were not documented.

In the previous case, the SAS dataset contained only one variable: TRANID. (Note that the INPUT statement disregarded the remainder of the record.) In most cases, SAS datasets will have several variables. Unless you specify otherwise, PROC FREQ will produce a separate frequency list for each variable. For example, if we change the program of Example 10.1 to specify two variables, two lists are produced. The first is identical to the one we saw in Fig. 10.12. The second is shown in Fig. 10.13.

```
DATA SASDATA;
     INFILE TRANTAPE;
     INPUT @1  TRANID $2.
           @4 AMOUNT  6.2;
     FORMAT AMOUNT DOLLAR8.2;
PROC FREQ;
```

```
┌OUTPUT════════════════════════════════════════════════════════
│Command ===>

                                SAS

                                      Cumulative  Cumulative
             TRANID   Frequency  Percent  Frequency   Percent
             ─────────────────────────────────────────────────
             01          10       45.5      10        45.5
             02           2        9.1      12        54.5
             10           1        4.5      13        59.1
             11           2        9.1      15        68.2
             60           4       18.2      19        86.4
             61           3       13.6      22       100.0

```

Figure 10.12   Summarizing an unknown file with PROC FREQ

```
┌OUTPUT════════════════════════════════════════════════════════
│Command ===>

                                SAS

                                      Cumulative  Cumulative
             AMOUNT   Frequency  Percent  Frequency   Percent
             ─────────────────────────────────────────────────
             $1.00        1        4.5       1         4.5
             $7.95        7       31.8       8        36.4
             $13.95      10       45.5      18        81.8
             $16.95       4       18.2      22       100.0

```

Figure 10.13   Second variable summarized

To specify exactly which variables you want PROC FREQ to report on, use the TABLES statement:

```
PROC FREQ;
    TABLES TRANID;
```

This statement is used to name only the variables of interest and will produce output similar to Fig. 10.12, while:

```
PROC FREQ;
    TABLES TRANID AMOUNT;
```

will produce output similar to Fig 10.12 and 10.13.

You can specify that a particular column not be printed. For example, option NOCUM will suppress the cumulative frequency and percentage. NOFREQ suppresses the frequency column, and NOPERCENT suppresses the percent column. These options are coded on the TABLES statement after the variable list and a required slash ("/"). Figure 10.14 shows our transaction tape data generated with the following code:

```
OUTPUT
Command ===>

                        SAS

              TRANID   Frequency
              -------------------
              01          10
              02           2
              10           1
              11           2
              60           4
              61           3
```

Figure 10.14 Suppressing columns in PROC FREQ

```
PROC FREQ;
    TABLES TRANID / NOPERCENT NOCUM;
```

If you need to generate several tables, you have two alternatives. Either name the multiple tables in one TABLES statement, or use multiple TABLES statements under the PROC FREQ heading. If you use a BY statement in addition to the TABLES statement, a separate table will be produced for each value of the BY variable.

You can also specify several different ways of ordering the values. The default is to list them in order of value, as in the previous examples. Another option is to list them in order of frequency. This is very useful when you need to know the most common or least common values.

For example, if you wanted to take the tape of Example 10.1 and determine which transaction IDs occurred most often (possibly so you could work on them first), you would write:

```
PROC FREQ ORDER=FREQ;
    TABLES TRANID;
```

This would produce the output of Fig. 10.15.

You can also use the formatted representation of each data value to order PROC FREQ output. In this case, use the

```
┌OUTPUT══════════════════════════════════════════════
│Command ===)
│
│                              SAS
│
│                                  Cumulative  Cumulative
│         TRANID  Frequency   Percent  Frequency    Percent
│         ----------------------------------------------------
│           81        18      45.5       18         45.5
│           68         4      18.2       14         63.6
│           61         3      13.6       17         77.3
│           82         2       9.1       19         86.4
│           11         2       9.1       21         95.5
│           18         1       4.5       22        100.0
│
│
│
│
│
│
│
└────────────────────────────────────────────────────
```

Figure 10.15   PROC FREQ output in order of frequency

ORDER=FORMATTED option on your PROC FREQ header. This is useful when your TABLES variable is actually a code, and you would prefer to see the full formatted value.

For example, consider an automobile parts dataset which includes a variable MFGR which represents the automaker. MFGR 01 is National Motors, MFGR 02 is Dependable Motors, MFGR 03 is Classic Motors, and there are codes for all the possible automakers. Unless we specify otherwise, PROC FREQ will list MFGR 01 first, followed by MFGR 02, and so on. However, we can produce a list in alphabetical order of the automakers by using PROC FORMAT together with the ORDER=FORMATTED option as follows. The output is shown in Fig. 10.16. Note that the coded values 01, 02, and 03 have been replaced by the formatted values, and these are shown in order.

```
PROC FORMAT;
    VALUE MFGRFMT$
        '01' = 'National Motors'
        '02' = 'Dependable Motors'
        '03' = 'Classic Motors'
            . . .
        ;
DATA step to associate MFGRFMT format with MFGR
variable;
PROC FREQ DATA=PARTS ORDER=FORMATTED;
    TABLES MFGR;
```

By default, PROC FREQ assumes all observations should be weighted equally. If this is not true, you should include a weight variable in your dataset. The weight variable indicates, in effect, how many times the observation should be counted. You can then specify this variable in a WEIGHT statement in your PROC FREQ.

For example, you might run PROC FREQ against a customer dataset to gather information on some characteristic such as number of children (N_KIDS). Rather than count all customers equally, you would prefer to give more weight to frequent customers. If the number of purchases for each customer is in variable N_SALES, you can use this to weight each customer as follows. Note that WEIGHT is a separate statement rather than an option on the TABLES statement.

```
PROC FREQ:
    TABLES N_KIDS;
    WEIGHT N_SALES;
```

```
┌OUTPUT══════════════════════════════════════════════════════════════
│Command ===>
│
│                              SAS
│
│                                       Cumulative  Cumulative
│     MFGR              Frequency  Percent  Frequency   Percent
│     ------------------------------------------------------------
│     Classic Motors      195      35.3      195       35.3
│     Dependable Motors   251      45.4      446       80.7
│     National Motors     107      19.3      553      100.0
│
│
│
│
│
│
│
│
└─────────────────────────────────────────────────────────────────
```

Figure 10.16   PROC FREQ output in formatted order

Actually, WEIGHT can be used with any numeric variable in the SAS dataset. The effect is that PROC FREQ replaces its frequency count for each cell with the total weight variable for observations in that cell.

To display the total income for each sex/age combination, you would write:

```
PROC FREQ;
    TABLES SEX*AGE;
    WEIGHT INCOME;
```

10.2.2   Cross-tabulations using PROC FREQ

So far, we have seen PROC FREQ used to count values of a single variable. A more powerful use of PROC FREQ is to produce cross-tabulations of two or more variables in the SAS dataset.

In a cross-tabulation, the values of one variable correspond to rows, while the values of a second variable correspond to columns. This produces a two-dimensional array of boxes or cells. Each observation is counted in only one cell.

You request a cross-tabulation in the TABLES statement, in the format ROWVAR*COLVAR. Of course, you would use variables in your SAS dataset rather than ROWVAR and COLVAR. The "*" is required as this is what requests PROC FREQ to produce a cross-tabulation rather than two separate tables.

For example, suppose we were analyzing response to a new hair conditioner. Variable RATING indicates each customer's overall rating of the product, on a scale of 1 to 5 (1 being strongly positive). Since we suspect that individuals with different hair colors may respond differently, we would like to cross-tabulate RATING with a COLOR variable. Figure 10.17 shows the output from this analysis. It was produced using a two-way cross-tabulation in PROC FREQ as follows:

```
PROC FREQ;
    TABLES COLOR*RATING / NOCUM NOPERCENT;
```

Notice that values for COLOR are listed down the side, while values for RATING are listed across the top. Each cell contains the number of individuals with that combination of COLOR and RATING. Also notice that row and column totals are provided.

Of course, all the options we discussed for one-way frequency analyses are equally valid for cross-tabulations. For example, we could format the COLOR and RATING variables, or weight each observation by a third variable which indicates how often the individual purchases hair products.

```
┌OUTPUT════════════════════════════════════════════════════════╗
│Command ===>                                                   ║
║                                                               ║
║                            SAS                                ║
║                   TABLE OF COLOR BY RATING                    ║
║                                                               ║
║      COLOR      RATING                                        ║
║                                                               ║
║      Frequency│     1│     2│     3│     4│     5│ Total      ║
║      ---------+------+------+------+------+------+             ║
║      Blonde   │   6  │  11  │  28  │   9  │   5  │   59       ║
║      ---------+------+------+------+------+------+             ║
║      Brunette │  13  │  37  │  36  │   7  │   6  │   99       ║
║      ---------+------+------+------+------+------+             ║
║      Red      │   5  │   5  │   9  │  13  │   5  │   37       ║
║      ---------+------+------+------+------+------+             ║
║      Total       24     53     73     29     16     195       ║
║                                                               ║
║                                                               ║
║                                                               ║
╚═══════════════════════════════════════════════════════════════╝
```

Figure 10.17   Two-way cross-tabulation

It is also possible to request cross-tabulations with more than two variables. For instance, the following TABLES statement requests a four-way cross-tabulation. Every combination of variables CITY, AGE, COLOR, and RATING will be represented.

```
TABLES CITY*SEX*COLOR*RATING;
```

PROC FREQ presents cross-tabulations with more than two variables in a special way. It produces multiple pages, each containing a two-way cross-tabulation of the last two variables listed (in our case, COLOR and RATING). Each page represents a different combination of the other variables. If page 1 included the COLOR*RATING table for Boston females only, page 2 would include Boston males only; then page 3 would include Cincinnati females, and so on.

If you prefer to see a single list rather than the two-way or n-way cross-tabulation tables, use the LIST option on your TABLES statement.

10.2.3 Statistical analysis in PROC FREQ

PROC FREQ provides our first taste of statistical analysis. If you request, PROC FREQ will calculate chi-square statistics for any table, along with other related statistics.

Essentially, chi-square is used to measure whether the rows and columns of your table reveal some strong relationship in the data. For example, we would expect a table of HEIGHT*SEX to show higher values in the "male" column than in the "female" column. However, we would be surprised to find such a relationship in a table of HEIGHT*NUM_PETS, or BIRTHDAY*SEX.

The question we ask is: Are the groups identified by the rows of the table somehow related to the groups identified by the columns? Or do they measure two completely independent factors in the data?

In most cases, we do not know if our rows and columns identify groups which are significantly different. More importantly, if we suspect that there is a correlation, we cannot prove it. Just as it is possible to flip a penny 50 times and get 50 heads, it is possible that the difference we saw between female and male heights was a fluke. By sheer chance, we might have selected a group of tall men and short women.

The chi-square test is designed to provide some help in this situation. It measures your data against the "expected" numbers you would have gotten if your rows and columns were totally unrelated. The result is a single number, called chi-square, which indicates how strongly your actual values differ from the expected values.

The lowest chi-square value is zero. This means that your rows and columns are probably completely independent. The higher the chi-square value, the more likely it is that your table reveals some relationship between the row and column variables.

In fact, statisticians know enough about this statistic to be able to say how likely it is that such a relationship exists. For example, in a two-by-two table, a chi-square value of 3.841 or higher will occur by chance only 5% of the time. Another way of saying this is that if your table determines a chi-square value of 3.841 or higher, you can be 95% sure that this did not occur by chance.

Of course, you can never be 100% sure. Even the most striking relationship (i.e., the highest chi-square) may be due to chance, just as it is theoretically possible to flip an honest penny 3,000 times and get 3,000 heads. The chance of 3,000 heads may be very small indeed, but it does exist. The same is true of any chi-square value.

The accepted statistical procedure is to decide in advance what condition you want to test, and how certain you want to be of your results. For example, we may want to test the statement.

```
"SEX AND NUM_PETS are independent".
```

If we do detect a difference, we want to be 95% sure that it is real, and not just an accident of the particular sample we took.

From this statistical digression, we now return to PROC FREQ. PROC FREQ will perform a chi-square test if you specify option CHISQ on the TABLES statement. For example, our hypothesis about SEX and NUM__PETS could be tested with the following request:

```
TABLES SEX*NUM_PETS / CHISQ
                NOCUM NOPERCENT NOROW NOCOL;
```

Figure 10.18 shows the table produced by this request; it is exactly as it would have been without the CHISQ option. What is new is a second page, shown in Fig. 10.19, which displays the chi-square calculation.

We will discuss only the first line of Fig. 10.19, labeled "Chi-Square". The other statistics are beyond the scope of this book. Three values are shown for the chi-square statistic. The last one, labeled "Prob", is the important one. This is the probability that your observed results could have occurred if the row and column variables were completely independent.

In our case, since we said that we wanted to be 95% certain of any apparent differences, we need this probability to be 5% (that is, .05)

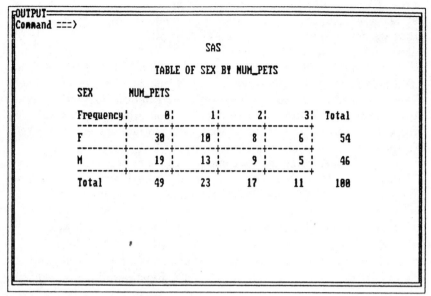

Figure 10.18 Cross-tabulation example

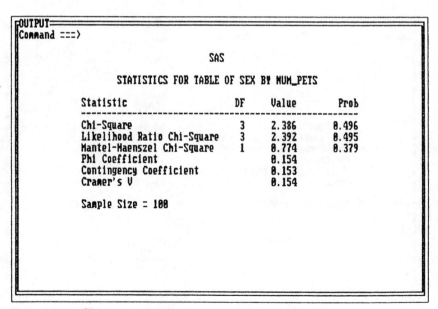

Figure 10.19 Chi-square statistics

or less. In fact, the value 0.496 not only fails this test, it tells us that we could have seen results like this purely by chance in 49.6% of samples we might have chosen.

Our output also includes columns labeled "DF" and "Value". "Value" is the calculated value of the chi-square statistic itself. "DF" stands for "degrees of freedom"; it is determined by the number of rows and columns in your table. For practical purposes, you can concentrate on the "Prob" value, as the others have already been factored into the statistics.

The chi-square calculations come out the same regardless of which is the row and which is the column variable. We would have seen the same statistics if the TABLES request had been

```
TABLES NUM_PETS*SEX / CHISQ;
```

Let's consider another example. Consider the statistical analysis in Fig. 10.20. This table was produced using the following request:

```
TABLES HEIGHT*SEX / CHISQ;
```

Observe that the chi-square probability is now 0.021, well within the 5% limit we set for ourselves. Thus, we could conclude that our results show a definite relationship between sex and height.

```
┌OUTPUT════════════════════════════════════════════
│Command ===>
│                          SAS
│
│             STATISTICS FOR TABLE OF HEIGHT BY SEX
│
│         Statistic              DF     Value      Prob
│         --------------------------------------------------
│         Chi-Square             6     14.848     0.021
│         Likelihood Ratio Chi-Square  6  14.917  0.021
│         Mantel-Haenszel Chi-Square   1  11.439  0.001
│         Phi Coefficient              0.200
│         Contingency Coefficient      0.196
│         Cramer's V                   0.200
│
│         Sample Size = 371
│
└──────────────────────────────────────────────────
```

Figure 10.20   Chi-square showing significant value

How does PROC FREQ react to a CHISQ request for a cross-tabulation in more than two variables? Recall that in a case such as the CITY*SEX*COLOR*RATING request we saw in the previous section, PROC FREQ presents the results as a series of two-way tables, one per page. The chi-square analysis is performed separately for each of these tables.

In concluding our discussion of PROC FREQ, we should point out several things that PROC FREQ will not do. It will not collect statistics for each cell other than frequency and percent. It will not compute summary statistics other than chi-square and its related measures. And, most interesting, it will not permit you to collect statistics on variables other than those being used to classify the data (although you can trick it in a limited way by using WEIGHT). For any of these functions, you will want to use PROC SUMMARY.

10.2.4 Using PROC FORMAT with PROC FREQ

One problem you may have anticipated in PROC FREQ has to do with ranges in the classification variables. In a table by age, you probably will not want to see a separate cell for each age. Rather, you will want to see one cell for age 0–9 years, a second cell for age 10–19, and so on.

You can create ranges in your classification variables by using PROC FORMAT along with PROC FREQ. The idea is to use PROC FORMAT to define the ranges, then use ORDER=FORMATTED in PROC FREQ to use the formatted ranges, rather than raw values of the variable, to perform the classification.

The following code will cause PROC FREQ to use age ranges. It assumes AGE is already recorded in a SAS dataset called OLDDATA. It first creates a format called AGERANGE, then associates this format with the AGE variable in a new SAS dataset called NEWDATA. PROC FREQ is then invoked, using NEWDATA as the input dataset.

```
PROC FORMAT;
     VALUE AGERANGE
          0-9      = '0-9'
          10-19    = '10-19'
          20-29    = '20-29'
          30-39    = '30-39'
          40-49    = '40-49'
          50-59    = '50-59'
          60-69    = '60-69'
```

```
             70-79   = '70-79'
             80-89   = '80-89'
             90-HIGH = '90 and Over'
             ;
DATA NEWDATA;
    SET OLDDATA;
    FORMAT AGE AGERANGE.;
PROC FREQ ORDER=FORMATTED DATA=NEWDATA;
    TABLES AGE;
```

10.3 CREATING A SUMMARY DATASET: PROC SUMMARY

Like PROC FREQ, PROC SUMMARY is used to classify observations in a SAS dataset according to the values of certain variables. Unlike PROC FREQ, PROC SUMMARY does not explicitly produce cross-tabulations or perform chi-square tests.

What PROC SUMMARY does do is output a single SAS dataset that summarizes the input data in every conceivable way. This one list includes a record equivalent to each cell of PROC FREQ, plus a record for each row total and column total, plus records for higher-level totals not shown explicitly in PROC FREQ.

10.3.1 Contents of the PROC SUMMARY output dataset

A dataset which produces a 2-by-2 table in PROC FREQ will produce nine output records in PROC SUMMARY: four for the individual cells, two for the row totals, two for the column totals, and one for the grand total. With larger tables or more variables the number of observations grows very quickly.

What makes this all usable, and useful, is that each record is coded as to the "type" of record it is. Along with the variables you specify, PROC SUMMARY adds a variable called __TYPE__ to the output dataset. __TYPE__ can be used by any subsequent step to select exactly the records it needs.

We will go into more detail in this section. For the moment, just consider the advantages of a procedure which will automatically compute all desired totals and statistics for a dataset and make them available as needed to any reporting step.

In addition to __TYPE__, PROC SUMMARY also automatically adds a variable called __FREQ__ to the output dataset. On each record, __FREQ__ equals the number of observations falling into this classification.

Note that the total __FREQ__ across the entire output dataset does not equal the original number of observations. This is because there are records containing totals and subtotals mixed in with the detail records. This would cause each observation to be counted several times if we added up all the __FREQ__ values.

Most importantly, PROC SUMMARY permits you to include summary statistics on any input variable in the output dataset. The possible summary statistics include the sum, mean, standard deviation, variance, range, minimum, maximum, and others. Any combination of these statistics may be carried for any and all input variables.

For example, suppose we wanted to classify our data by age, education level, and city of residence. For each combination of the three classification variables, we wanted to compute the total income, average income, average disposable income, total number of VCRs owned, and average number of magazine subscriptions. Assuming, of course, that all the data has been collected and saved in a SAS dataset, this can be done very simply using PROC SUMMARY:

```
PROC SUMMARY;
    CLASS AGE ED_LEVEL CITY;
    VAR INCOME DISP_INC N_VCRS N_MAGS;
    OUTPUT OUT=NEWDS
        SUM  (INCOME)   = TOT_INC
        MEAN (INCOME)   = AVG_INC
        MEAN (DISP_INC) = AVG_DISP
        SUM  (N_VCRS)   = TOT_VCRS
        MEAN (N_MAGS)   = AVG_MAGS;
```

Note that there are three key statements in PROC SUMMARY:

1. The CLASS statement names the classification variables. These variables are used to group the input observations into a limited number of classes, determined by the observed values of the classification variables. (This is roughly analogous to the variable specification in the TABLES statement of PROC FREQ.)

The order of the variables is not important for the calculations, but it does determine the sequence in the output dataset, so keep track of it. In our case, we are classifying our data by age (AGE), education level, (ED__LEVEL), and city of residence (CITY).

2. The VAR statement names any variables for which we will want to keep summary statistics. You must list every variable you intend to use. Order is not important. Each variable only has to be named once, even if you are computing several statistics for it (e.g.,

sum, mean, and variance). We list INCOME (because we want the sum and mean), DISP_INC (because we want the mean disposable income), N_VCRS (sum), and N_MAGS (mean). Note that we have not yet identified which statistics to keep.

3. The OUTPUT statement names the output dataset, and specifies all of the statistics to be included in the output record. We will be creating an output SAS dataset called NEWDS. Each record will contain several statistics in addition to the default _TYPE_, _FREQ_, and the classification variables AGE, ED_LEVEL, and CITY. They are TOT_INC, which is the sum of all the INCOME values in this class, AVG_INC (mean of the INCOME values), AVG_DISP (mean of DISP_INC), TOT_VCRS (sum of N_VCRS) and AVG_MAGS (mean of N_MAGS).

We mentioned the _TYPE_ variable briefly earlier in this section. This variable is puzzling at first, because it appears to add a meaningless numeric variable to each output record. After all, isn't each class completely determined by the CLASS variables? What information does _TYPE_ contribute?

To understand _TYPE_, we first need to recall that PROC SUMMARY includes not only records for each class, but all possible subtotals and totals. In our summary by age, education level, and city, PROC SUMMARY will not only create "detail" records for each class, but a record containing the overall totals for the dataset. Also, it will create subtotal records for every age, education level, and city. Finally, subtotals will be created for every age*education level combination (across all cities), every age*city combination (across all education levels), and every city*education level combination (across all ages). In short, PROC SUMMARY creates an output record for every possible combination of the class variables. The function of the _TYPE_ variable on each record is to identify what type of combination is being summarized.

The second thing we need to keep in mind when discussing _TYPE_ is that its numeric value is more confusing than helpful. The reason for this is that _TYPE_ is actually a series of bits, which are used as switches. There is one bit for each class variable. Like any other series of bits, _TYPE_ can be interpreted as a number, but this only muddies the water.

Throughout this discussion, we will always use the SAS binary representation, and we recommend that you do so in your programs. For example, we will say "IF _TYPE_ = '110'B", rather than "IF _TYPE_ = 6".

Since _TYPE_ is a series of bits, it can range from '00 . . . 0'B to '11 . . . 1'B. The _TYPE_ with all zeros appears on the single grand total record. The __TYPE__ with all ones appears on each of the detail records for classes determined by all the class variables.

For instance, to pick up the grand totals after running PROC SUMMARY, you could code the following:

```
PROC SUMMARY;
   CLASS AGE ED_LEVEL CITY;
   ⋮
DATA GR_TOTAL;
   IF _TYPE_ = '000'B THEN OUTPUT;
```

To pick up only the detail classification records, you could code:

```
PROC SUMMARY;
   CLASS AGE ED_LEVEL CITY;
   ⋮
DATA GR_TOTAL;
   IF _TYPE_ = '111'B THEN OUTPUT;
```

Recall that __TYPE__ has as many bits as there are class variables. If we had four class variables, we would have coded '1111'B rather than '111'B. (Although we are using this technique for demonstration purposes, you should know that there is an option called NWAY on the PROC SUMMARY statement itself which will cause only these most detailed observations to be created.)

As you have probably guessed, the remaining values of __TYPE__ correspond to the various subtotals we have described. For example, '101'B appears on every record for an age*city class, combining all education levels.

The way these __TYPE__ values work for subtotals is simple. Each bit corresponds to one of the class variables, in the same order as they were specified on the class statement. If the bit for a particular class variable is '1'B, then the record represents a particular value of the variable. If the bit for a class variable is '0'B, then the record summarizes all values of the variable.

Let's reexamine our example, __TYPE__ = '101'B. Remember our class statement was:

```
CLASS AGE ED_LEVEL CITY;
```

The first bit tells us how AGE is being used. The second bit tells us about ED_LEVEL, and the third bit about CITY. Now we apply our rule. The AGE bit is '1'B, so the record represents only one value of AGE. The ED_LEVEL bit is '0'B, so the record summarizes all values of ED__LEVEL. Finally, the CITY bit is '1'B, so our record represents only one value of CITY. Thus, there will be a record with __TYPE__ = '101'B for every age*city combination, but each one of these will include all education levels in the age*city class.

Of course, we normally do not start out with a mysterious bit pattern and try to figure out what it means. It is more likely that we would want some particular totals or subtotals from the PROC SUMMARY output, and then construct the appropriate __TYPE__.

For example, consider a dataset containing statistics of active baseball players. Each player's record includes, among other things, the team (TEAM), fielding position (POS), and number of home runs (HR). We'd like to find the total number of home runs for each team and for each fielding position. We'd also like to have available the total home runs for each combination of team and fielding position. This can be done with PROC SUMMARY as follows:

```
PROC SUMMARY;
    CLASS TEAM POS;
    VAR HR;
    OUTPUT OUT=SUMOUT
        SUM(HR) = TOT_HR;
DATA SUM_TEAM;
    SET SUMOUT;
    IF _TYPE_ = '10'B THEN OUTPUT;
DATA SUM_POS;
    SET SUMOUT;
    IF _TYPE_ = '01'B THEN OUTPUT;
DATA SUM_BOTH;
    SET SUMOUT;
    IF _TYPE_ = '11'B THEN OUTPUT;
```

The PROC SUMMARY step collects the totals by team and position, and outputs a dataset. The first DATA step picks out the subtotals for each team. Notice that the bit corresponding to TEAM is '1'B and the bit for POS is '0'B. Figure 10.21 exhibits the SUM__TEAM dataset.

The second DATA step picks out the subtotals for each fielding position. Now the TEAM bit is '0'B and the POS bit is '1'B. Figure 10.22 shows the SUM__POS dataset.

The final DATA step picks out all the details of each combination of team and fielding position. Note that both bits are '1'B. Figure 10.23 shows a portion of the SUM__BOTH dataset.

10.3.2 Using PROC SUMMARY

Although PROC SUMMARY contains numerous options, the basic syntax is fairly simple (see Figure 10.24). The PROC SUMMARY

```
┌OUTPUT════════════════════════════════════════════════════════
│Command ===>

                              SAS

     OBS    TEAM            POS    _TYPE_    _FREQ_    TOT_HR

      1     Chicago                  2         9          96
      2     Montreal                 2         9         102
      3     New York                 2         9         106
      4     Philadelphia             2         9          94
      5     Pittsburgh               2         9         135
      6     St. Louis                2         9          81
```

Figure 10.21   Baseball example—SUMMARY by team

```
┌OUTPUT════════════════════════════════════════════════════════
│Command ===>

                              SAS

     OBS    TEAM    POS    _TYPE_    _FREQ_    TOT_HR

      1             1B       1         6         109
      2             2B       1         6          34
      3             3B       1         6          88
      4             C        1         6          71
      5             CF       1         6          97
      6             LF       1         6          79
      7             P        1         6           9
      8             RF       1         6         111
      9             SS       1         6          16
```

Figure 10.22   Baseball example—SUMMARY by position

statement itself starts the step, and names the input SAS dataset. The CLASS statement, including a simple list of variables, sets up the classification levels to use in grouping observations. The VAR statement, also including a simple list of variables, tells PROC

```
┌─OUTPUT════════════════════════════════════════════════════════
│Command ===>
│
│                              SAS
│
│     OBS    TEAM      POS    _TYPE_    _FREQ_    TOT_HR
│
│      1    Chicago    1B       3         1         15
│      2    Chicago    2B       3         1         18
│      3    Chicago    3B       3         1          7
│      4    Chicago    C        3         1         17
│      5    Chicago    CF       3         1         21
│      6    Chicago    LF       3         1         18
│      7    Chicago    P        3         1          2
│      8    Chicago    RF       3         1          9
│      9    Chicago    SS       3         1          5
│     10    Montreal   1B       3         1         12
│     11    Montreal   2B       3         1          2
│     12    Montreal   3B       3         1         19
│     13    Montreal   C        3         1          8
│     14    Montreal   CF       3         1         23
│     15    Montreal   LF       3         1         22
│     16    Montreal   P        3         1          1
│     17    Montreal   RF       3         1         15
```

Figure 10.23   Baseball example—SUMMARY by both

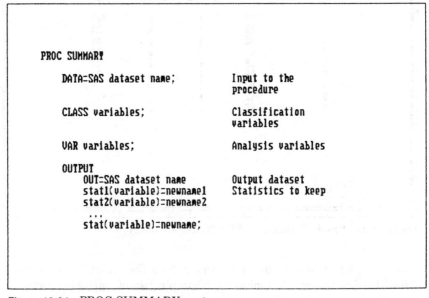

```
PROC SUMMARY

    DATA=SAS dataset name;              Input to the
                                        procedure

    CLASS variables;                    Classification
                                        variables

    VAR variables;                      Analysis variables

    OUTPUT
        OUT=SAS dataset name            Output dataset
        stat1(variable)=newname1        Statistics to keep
        stat2(variable)=newname2

        ...
        stat(variable)=newname;
```

Figure 10.24   PROC SUMMARY syntax

SUMMARY what analysis variables will be needed to collect the desired statistics.

Finally, the OUTPUT statement specifically describes the statistics to be kept. Each statistic begins with a statistic keyword, followed by the name of the analysis variable in parentheses, then an equal sign ("=") followed by a new variable name to be used for the statistic in the output dataset. You can list as many statistics as you like within the OUTPUT statement. Put a semicolon after the last one. The OUTPUT statement also includes an OUT= option, which specifies the name of the output SAS dataset.

Valid statistic keywords include the following. Other statistic keywords are also available, and you should check your SAS Systems manual for details.

N	number of observations
MEAN	arithmetic mean
STD	standard deviation
VAR	variance
MIN	minimum value for the variable
MAX	maximum value for the variable
SUM	sum of all occurrences of the variable

Keep in mind that the statistics will appear on every output record. For each record, they will include only the observations in that class. Thus, if you ask for MEAN(INCOME)=MEAN_INC, you will probably see different values for MEAN_INC on every output record, because the mean income is different for each class.

PROC SUMMARY is primarily designed to produce an output dataset which can then be used in another PROC or DATA step. The output dataset is sorted by __TYPE__, which was discussed in the previous section.

10.4 OTHER SAS STATISTICAL AND REPORTING PROCEDURES

We have selected only several SAS statistical and reporting procedures to include in this book. However, you should be aware that SAS software features many more statistical procedures which can be used by anyone with a basic understanding of statistics, as well as more special-purpose procedures. Some of these include:

PROC CORR	Calculates correlation coefficients
PROC REG	Linear regression
PROC STEPWISE	Stepwise analysis for regression
PROC ANOVA	Analysis of variance
PROC UNIVARIATE	Simple statistics in one variable
PROC TABULATE	Complex formatted summary reports

11

Constructing Reusable SAS Code

The SAS System provides several constructs for creating reusable code. These range from the simple %INCLUDE to a sophisticated macro language. This chapter introduces the various ways to create reusable SAS code.

11.1 WHAT IS REUSABLE CODE AND WHY USE IT?

Reusable code is code that you modularize so that it can be used in other programs. Reusable code can include entire programs, procedures, statements, expressions, down to character strings. There are several benefits related to the modularizing of SAS code. These include:

- standardized processing of repetitive tasks
- shortened SAS program development time
- shortened maintenance time (especially if structured techniques are used)

- improved readability of large programs

11.1.1   SAS tools that allow you to create reusable code

In Sec. 6.3.2, we described how to use the LINK statement to create modular code. The LINK allows you to isolate a section of code and perform it from anywhere within the DATA step. But you are not limited to storing modules within the same DATA step. You can code your reusable module in one library and access it from the same or other libraries, using any of these SAS tools:

- MACROs: Allow you to identify and name text, statements, and/ or programs, then access them with a simple invocation
- %INCLUDE: a SAS MACRO that lets you copy code "as is" from another library
- User-written PROCs and subroutines: Enable the advanced SAS programmer to create and store customized programs

You will be introduced to MACROs and the %INCLUDE statement in this chapter. User-written PROCs and subroutines require more specialized programming, and are outside the scope of this book.

11.1.2   Including SAS statements from other programs

Although %INCLUDE is actually a MACRO invocation, you need not know the details of its construction in order to use it effectively. The %INCLUDE acts like a COPY statement in COBOL: it lets you store code in a separate module, then access it in another program. The format is:

```
%INCLUDE (member name);
```

This statement is equivalent to copying the code identified by the name in the argument where the %INCLUDE statement is placed.

Example 11.1 Using %INCLUDE to copy program statements. Suppose you have a list of financial equations that are to be applied to several files. Instead of coding the statements every time you process a file, you could code the equations and store them in a separate file to be included each time they were needed.

We will assume that we are in a PC environment, and that these equations are stored on the file 'a:\Finance.equ':

```
Wk_Cptl = CCasset - C_liab;
C_Ratio = C_asset / C_liab;
Quick   = (Cash + MS + AR)/C_liab;
Profit_M= NI/Sales;
```

Here is the data read:

Cash	C__Asset	C__Liab	MS	AR	NI	Sales
100	13909	11090	200	750	88	1200
2335	25788	20011	1100	1594	115	1500
987	3909	1446	422	156	12	900

Here is the DATA step that performs the calculation:

```
DATA Analysis (DROP = Cash MS AR NI Sales);
SET Corpstat;
%INCLUDE  'a:\Finance.equ';
RUN;
```

And the result is shown in Fig. 11.1. Note that the equations saved in 'a:\Finance.equ' were executed just as if they had been coded directly in the program.

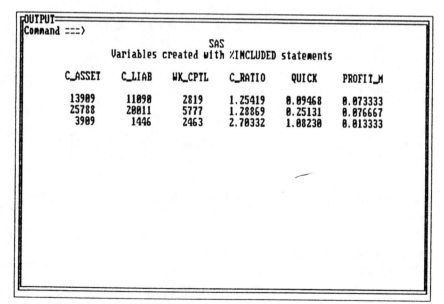

Figure 11.1   Result of %INCLUDE statements

Example 11.2 Using %INCLUDE to copy a file layout. We would like to be able to create an input record layout which can be included in any SAS program. We isolate the INPUT statement and store it in a partitioned dataset called DATA.LIBRARY, with member name LAYOUTC:.

```
Input  @1  Catlg_id        9.
       @10 Sub_grp      $CHAR5.
       @15 Order_cd        7.
       @22 Cost          PD5.2
       @27 Markup        PD3.2 ;
```

Now any program can conveniently include the full record layout:

```
DATA Readit;
INFILE CATDATA;
%INCLUDE LAYOUT(LAYOUTC);
RUN;
```

Note how the %INCLUDE includes both the DDname and member name. The JCL might look like this:

```
//CATDATA  DD DSN=CATLG.AUG88.UPDATE,DISP=SHR
//LAYOUT   DD DSN=DATA.LIBRARY,DISP=SHR
//SYSIN    DD DSN=SAS.LIBRARY,DISP=SHR
```

Alternatively, you could specify the member on the DD statement

```
//LAYOUT   DD DSN=DATA.LIBRARY(LAYOUTC),DISP=SHR
```

And your SAS program would look like this:

```
DATA Readit;
INFILE CATDATA;
%INCLUDE LAYOUT;
RUN;
```

Both would produce the same effect: a complete converting DATA step.

11.2 INTRODUCTION TO THE SAS MACRO SUBSYSTEM

The SAS macro subsystem was designed to allow you to isolate and customize coding of simple or complex blocks of SAS code. Usually the definition of these blocks of code is such that they are easily used in other SAS programs.

The macro subsystem consists of the macro definition, its invocation and processing. The elements of macro definition include macro variables, control statements, and functions. Because the macro subsystem is highly flexible and sophisticated, new users may require a bit more time understanding the underlying concepts than are required in the PROC and DATA steps.

11.2.1 Macro definition and invocation

A SAS macro is simply a designated block of text identified by a SAS name. The text block is defined as that code lying between the boundaries of the %MACRO and %MEND statements. Figure 11.2 shows the general syntax of a macro definition.

The name of the macro must conform to standard SAS naming conventions. The text block can contain just about anything that you feel needs to be named for ready access, including:

- constant text
- multiple SAS statements
- one or more SAS steps
- text containing macro variables, macro control statements, and/or macro functions

```
%MACRO name [(parameter, parameter,..)];
   ... text ...

%MEND
```

Figure 11.2 Macro definition

Example 11.3 Sample macro. Like the %INCLUDE, you can use macros to store text that is reused frequently. Macro STDRPT contains two SAS steps:

```
%MACRO STDRPT;
  PROC PRINT DATA = _LAST_ (OBS=10);
  PROC FREQ;
  TABLES Latitud Longitud Rt_Decln /MISSING;
  RUN;
%MEND;
```

You would invoke the macro after your DATA step.

```
     DATA Astronmy;
 ... DATA step statements ...
     %STDRPT
```

There are three things to be aware of:

1. You invoke the macro by coding a percent sign as a prefix to its name.
2. The invocation does not require a semicolon.
3. Placement of the RUN statement inside the MACRO indicates that the FREQ step is complete and executable as represented in the macro definition. If the RUN statement were placed outside the macro definition, you would have the flexibility of adding additional statements (such as a WEIGHT or BY statement) prior to the execution of the PROC FREQ.

11.2.2 Macros with parameters and defaults

You can make your macro definition even more flexible through the use of parameters. Parameters allow you to perform the same processing using variable names other than those coded in the macro. They also allow you to set up default processing.

SAS macros have two different types of parameters: positional parameters and keyword parameters. Macros that contain positional parameters, when invoked, match your invoked parameter list one for one against the macro definition parameter list.

Example 11.4 Macro with positional parameters. This macro will let you read in a file even if the header information length varies. The user can specify both the dataset name (DD) and the offset relative to the start of the record of detail information (OFFSET):

```
%MACRO INIT  (DD, OFFSET);
DATA Output.&DD;
INFILE &DD;
INPUT @ &Offset + 45 Mailcnt    PD5.
      @ &Offset + 5  Zip_4        9.
      @ &Offset + 60 Cume_ord    PD5.
      @ &Offset + 65 Pd_Ord      ZD9.2
;
%MEND;
```

Note the positional parameters in parentheses after the macro name. These parameters are actually "empty" macro variables, waiting to be replaced with the values you supply at invocation. The invocation:

```
%INIT  (JANPRO, 12)
```

will read the external file identified by DD name JANPRO (which identifies a dataset with a 12-byte leading header on all records) and produce an output SAS dataset named 'OUTPUT.JANPRO'.

You must use positional parameters in the same order on the %MACRO statement and on the macro invocation. You have to save a place for parameters that are not included on your macro invocation. For example,

```
%INIT (,12)
```

Within the body of the macro, you must include an ampersand (&) before the name of a parameter. You also have to include a period (.) after the name if ambiguity might result without it. These rules do not apply on the %MACRO statement itself.

In addition to positional parameters, you can define keyword parameters. Keyword parameters are especially useful for default processing. The keyword sets up a default that you can override on invocation. Unlike the positional parameter, keywords need not be listed in the same order on the %MACRO statement and on the macro invocation.

Example 11.5 Keyword parameter macro. Here is a different version of the previous example using keyword parameters to provide default values:

```
%MACRO INIT1 (DD=Promo Offset = 0);
DATA OUTPUT.&DD;
INFILE &DD;
```

```
INPUT @ &Offset + 45 Mailcnt    PD5.
      @ &Offset + 5  Zip_4         9.
      @ &Offset + 60 Cume_ord   PD5.
      @ &Offset + 65 Pd_Ord     ZD9.2
;
%MEND;
```

You can invoke the macro with this statement to create SAS code using the defaults listed on the MACRO statement:

```
%INIT1 ( )
```

To change the values, invoke the macro with new values after the keywords. You can omit any keywords for which the default values are acceptable.

```
%INIT1 (DD=Mar89 Offset = 4)
```

You can use both kinds of parameters in the same macro, but you must remember that on invocation, the positional parameters must be listed first before any keyword parameter associations. Figure 11.3 shows the error response if the order of the parameters is incorrect.

Example 11.6 Error in the definition of a combined keyword/positional parameter macro.

```
%MACRO INIT2 (DD=Promo,Offset);
 DATA OUTPUT.&DD;
 INFILE &DD;
 INPUT @ &Offset + 45 Mailcnt    PD5.
       @ &Offset + 5  Zip_4         9.
       @ &Offset + 60 Cume_ord   PD5.
       @ &Offset + 65 Pd_Ord     ZD9.2
;
%MEND;
```

The correct definition would be:

```
%MACRO INIT2 (Offset,DD=Promo);
 .....
%MEND;
```

And you could invoke it with as little as an offset value:

```
┌LOG══════════════════════════════════════════════════════════════════════╗
║Command ===>                                                               ║
║                                                                           ║
║  72                                                                       ║
║  73              %MACRO INIT2 (DD=Promo, Offset);                         ║
║ERROR: All positional parameters must precede keyword parameters.         ║
║  74              DATA OUTPUT.&DD;                                         ║
║  75              INFILE &DD;                                              ║
║  76              INPUT @ &Offset + 45 Mailcnt    PD5.                     ║
║  77                    @ &Offset + 5  Zip_4         9.                    ║
║  78                    @ &Offset + 60 Cume_ord   PD5.                     ║
║  79                    @ &Offset + 65 Pd_Ord     ZD9.2                    ║
║  80              ;                                                        ║
║  81              %MEND;                                                   ║
║  82                                                                       ║
║  83              %INIT2 (DD=Junpro, 8);                                   ║
║WARNING: Apparent invocation of macro INIT2 not resolved.                 ║
║         %INIT2 (DD=Junpro, 8);                                           ║
║         -                                                                 ║
║ERROR: Statement is not valid or it is used out of proper order.          ║
║                                                                           ║
║  84              RUN;                                                     ║
║                                                                           ║
║                                                                           ║
╚══════════════════════════════════════════════════════════════════════════╝
```

Figure 11.3 Error in macro parameters

```
%INIT2 (0);
```

11.2.3 Simple macro debugging tools

There are several ways to display macro resolution processing. These include:

- the MPRINT system option
- %PUT to write resolved references to the log

The OPTIONS statement allows you to override system options put into effect at the time of installation. IF NOMPRINT is the preferred option, your macro will not be displayed on the SAS log in expanded form. In order to see the expansion, code the OPTIONS statement prior to invocation of the macro.

The MPRINT options remains in effect for the duration of the SAS session or until you change it with a OPTIONS NOMPRINT statement.

Example 11.7 Macro diagnostics with MPRINT. MPRINT tells the supervisor to print the expanded macro on the SAS log during processing. In this example, the macro %FREQIT produces frequencies based on the values passed to the input parameter VARLIST.

```
      OPTIONS MPRINT;
   %MACRO Freqit (varlist);
      PROC FREQ;
      TABLES &varlist /MISSING;
   %MEND;
   DATA _DATA_;
   INPUT Age Hobby $ Income;
   CARDS;
22 Racing 23000
22 Music 24000
26 Art 26000
26 Jogging 25000
26 Music 24000
32 Art 30000
33 Jogging 35000
 ;
   * Macro invocation follows:
   %Freqit (Age*Hobby);
   RUN;
```

Note in Fig. 11.4 how the resolved value of VARLIST is printed.
%PUT can be used to display the value of the macro variable on the
SAS log. It is different from PUT, which writes the macro variable
value as SAS text.

```
┌LOG─────────────────────────────────────────────────────────────┐
│Command ===)                                                      │
│                                                                  │
│    1      OPTIONS MPRINT;                                        │
│    2         %MACRO Freqit (varlist);                            │
│    3            PROC FREQ;                                       │
│    4            TABLES &varlist /MISSING;                        │
│    5         %MEND;                                              │
│    6                                                             │
│    7         DATA _DATA_;                                        │
│    8         INPUT Age Hobby $ Income;                           │
│    9         CARDS;                                              │
│   17      ;                                                      │
│NOTE: The dataset WORK.DATA1 has 7 observations and 3 variables.  │
│NOTE: The DATA statement used 14.00 seconds.                      │
│   18         %Freqit (Age*Hobby); /* MPRINT WILL SHOW EXPANDED MACRO    */│
│MPRINT(FREQIT):   PROC FREQ;                                      │
│MPRINT(FREQIT):   TABLES AGE*HOBBY /MISSING;                      │
│   19         RUN;                                                │
│NOTE: The PROCEDURE FREQ used 31.00 seconds.                      │
│                                                                  │
│                                                                  │
└──────────────────────────────────────────────────────────────────┘
```

Figure 11.4   MPRINT examples

Example 11.8 Macro diagnostics with %PUT.

```
OPTIONS MPRINT;
    %MACRO Freqit (varlist);
        %PUT &varlist;
        PROC FREQ;
        TABLES &varlist /MISSING;
        TITLE "Frequencies on &varlist";
        PUT &varlist;
    %MEND;
    DATA _DATA_;
    INPUT Age Hobby $ Income;
    CARDS;
22 Racing 23000
22 Music 24000
26 Art 26000
26 Jogging 25000
26 Music 24000
32 Art 30000
33 Jogging 35000
  ;
    %Freqit (Age*Hobby);
    RUN;
```

```
┌LOG───────────────────────────────────────────────────────────────────┐
│Command ===>                                                            │
│                                                                        │
│NOTE: The dataset WORK.DATA2 has 7 observations and 3 variables.        │
│NOTE: The DATA statement used 15.00 seconds.                            │
│   43        %Freqit (Age*Hobby);                                       │
│Age*Hobby                                                               │
│MPRINT(FREQIT):    PROC FREQ;                                           │
│MPRINT(FREQIT):    TABLES AGE*HOBBY /MISSING;                           │
│MPRINT(FREQIT):    TITLE 'Frequencies on Age*Hobby ';                   │
│ERROR: Syntax error detected.                                           │
│                                                                        │
│MPRINT(FREQIT):    PUT AGE*HOBBY;                                       │
│NOTE: Expecting one of the following:                                   │
│                                                                        │
│BY FREQ TABLE TABLES WEIGHT                                             │
│                                                                        │
│   44        RUN;                                                       │
│NOTE: The SAS System stopped processing this step because of errors.   │
│NOTE: The PROCEDURE FREQ used 13.00 seconds.                           │
│                                                                        │
│                                                                        │
└───────────────────────────────────────────────────────────────────────┘
```

Figure 11.5   %PUT example

The reference created by %PUT is displayed on the log in Fig. 11.5, but the PUT reference is written out by the macro as SAS text. When SAS tries to process this statement, it detects an error because the PUT statement is not valid outside a DATA step.

11.3 PROCESSING THE MACRO

Macro processing is a bit more complicated than regular SAS compilation and execution. The macro processor must compile portions of the macro needed for the SAS read. It must manage a symbol table of macro variables and their values in the current reference environment, and it must successfully resolve macro and macro-variable references.

11.3.1 MACRO compilation and execution

When you submit your macro definition for processing, the macro compiler stores the macro name plus any default values that will be used for later execution. It compiles the MACRO, MEND, and other macro control statements and stores the rest as uncompiled text. (Uncompiled text includes macro-variable references, nested macro invocations and definitions, and most macro functions.)

When you submit for execution the job that invokes your macro you actually begin a series of processing cycles. The SAS compiler reads your code and begins processing the words (tokens) it encounters. When it finds a % or & that indicates a macro reference, it suspends regular instruction processing and gives control to the macro processor.

The macro processor uses its own instruction stack to create text that will be read by the SAS compiler. If the SAS compiler finds another macro reference it starts the cycle again.

It is important to remember that macros are resolved in two distinct phases: compilation and execution. This can help you in macro debugging and in performance considerations.

For example, if you create a macro (the "outer macro") that contains the definition of another macro (the "inner macro") within it, you'll be recompiling the inner macro every time the outer macro is invoked.

11.3.2 The current environment

An environment is defined in the SAS System by the execution of SAS code. The DATA step, for example, does not create an environment until the supervisor determines that it is complete (by reading a RUN or new DATA or PROC step) and then executes it. A MACRO, too, creates no environment until it is invoked. The entire SAS job is considered a global environment that includes one or more local environments. Macros, on the other hand, create only local environments. But these local environments can contain nested local environments (such as other macro invocations).

Example 11.9 Nested local macros. This simple illustration shows a nested macro invocation. The inner macro (CNVRT) is defined first, then the outer one. Macro READ reads in the sample cards and invokes the CNVRT macro to convert the coded entry for PANEL to PC hex format.

```
%MACRO CNVRT (Onebyt);
 Hexcharz = PUT (&Onebyt,HEX2.);
%MEND;
%MACRO READ (DD);
 DATA OUTPUT;
 INFILE &DD;
 INPUT @ 45 Book      $CHAR1.
       @ 12 Premium   $CHAR1.
       @ 51 Panel     $CHAR1.
 %CNVRT (Panel);
%MEND;
%READ (CARDS);
CARDS;
..........A...............................Y.....1.......
.. •
..........7...............................N.....B.......
..
..........0...............................N.....2.......
..
..........C...............................Y.....F.......
..
;
RUN;
```

Figure 11.6 contains the result of the conversion.

11.3.3 Permanent storage of macros

Although the SAS supervisor stores a compiled version of the macro on the temporary workfile prior to its execution, you cannot save this form of the macro in a permanent library. It is possible, in fact rec-

```
┌OUTPUT════════════════════════════════════════════════════════╗
│Command ===>                                                   ║
│                              SAS                              ║
│                    Results of Macro 'Read'                    ║
│                                                               ║
│        OBS    BOOK    PREMIUM    PANEL    HEXCHARZ             ║
│                                                               ║
│         1      Y         A         1        31                ║
│         2      N         7         B        42                ║
│         3      N         8         2        32                ║
│         4      Y         C         F        46                ║
│                                                               ║
│                                                               ║
│                                                               ║
│                                                               ║
│                                                               ║
│                                                               ║
│                                                               ║
└═══════════════════════════════════════════════════════════════╝
```

Figure 11.6   Nested macros

ommended, that you keep your original macros in a macro source library attached to your SAS session for easy access.

11.4 MACRO ELEMENTS

The macro definition can also contain macro variables, functions and control statements. Each element is similar to elements in the regular SAS language but specifically designed to handle simple and complicated macro expressions.

11.4.1 Creating and assigning macro variables

Macro variables are different from DATA step variables. Where DATA step variables are created on an initial read and associated with many values, macro variables have only one value specifically assigned in specialized macro assignment statements.

The %LET statement creates a new macro variable and assigns a value to it. It is the most frequently used macro-assignment statement:

```
%LET macro variable = text;
```

%LET can be used within a macro or within a DATA step or even between DATA steps. When it is used in a macro, the scope of the macro variable it creates is local. When it is used outside a macro, it produces a variable with global scope. Text can include:

- a null value: %LET Mvar = ;
- a string of constant text
- a string of text that contains macro and macro
- variable references

Examples of %LET statement are:

%LET DDname = FM591;

%LET Richard = Now is the winter;

%LET Third = of our discontent:

To access the value of a macro variable, simply put a "&" immediately before its name.

```
%PUT &Richard &Third;
```

results in printing "Now is the winter of our discontent" on the SAS log.

The scope (local or global) dictates the creation or resolution values for macro variables. Global macro variables are accessible to all environments. Local macro variables are available only during the duration of the local environment.

Example 11.10 Local scope of a macro variable. This example is the same as Example 11.9 but with an assignment statement accessing the macro variable ONEBYT.

```
%MACRO CNVRT (Onebyt);
 Hexcharz = PUT (&Onebyt,HEX2.);
 Cnvrtone= &Onebyt;
%MEND;
%MACRO READ (DD);
 DATA OUTPUT;
 INFILE &DD;
 INPUT @ 45 Book      $CHAR1.
       @ 12 Premium   $CHAR1.
       @ 51 Panel     $CHAR1.
       ;
 %CNVRT (Panel);
 Readone= &Onebyt;
%MEND;
```

In order for you to see which macro produced the error, use the MPRINT option described earlier. It stays in effect for the duration of your SAS session.

The log in Figure 11.7 shows the macro variable Onebyt is not resolved in macro READ. This is because it was created locally within CNVRT.

If you wanted to access Onebyt from READ (or other macros), you could have identified it as GLOBAL in the CNVRT macro.

```
%MACRO CNVRT (Onebyt);
%GLOBAL Onebyt;
    Hexcharz = PUT (&Onebyt,HEX2.);
    Cnvrtone= &Onebyt;
%MEND;
```

There is a twin to %GLOBAL that forces a local scope on a macro variable. It is the %LOCAL statement. Because the default is to always try to change the value of an existing macro variable (regardless of the environment) rather than create a new one, you should use %LOCAL to prevent inadvertent changes to global values.

This code will change the value of the global variable TOTALS:

```
%LET TOTALS = 100;
    %MACRO SUBTOT;
        %LET TOTALS = 2;
    %MEND;
```

```
┌LOG─────────────────────────────────────────────────────────────────────┐
│Command ===>                                                              │
│                                                                          │
│   38      DATA OUTPUT;                                                   │
│   39      INFILE &DD;                                                    │
│   40      INPUT @ 45  Book      $CHAR1.                                  │
│   41            @ 12  Premium   $CHAR1.                                  │
│   42            @ 51  Panel     $CHAR1.                                  │
│   43            ;                                                        │
│   44      %CNVRT (Panel);                                               │
│   45      Readone= &Onebyt;                                              │
│   46      %MEND;                                                         │
│   47                                                                     │
│   48      %READ (CARDS);                                                │
│MPRINT(READ):    DATA OUTPUT;                                             │
│MPRINT(READ):    INFILE CARDS;                                            │
│MPRINT(READ):    INPUT @ 45 BOOK $CHAR1. @ 12 PREMIUM $CHAR1. @ 51 PANEL  │
│$CHAR1. ;                                                                 │
│MPRINT(CNVRT):   HEXCHARZ = PUT (PANEL,HEX2.);                            │
│MPRINT(CNVRT):   CNVRTONE= PANEL;                                         │
│MPRINT(READ):    ;                                                        │
│WARNING: Apparent symbolic reference ONEBYT not resolved.                 │
│                                                                          │
│                              -                                           │
│                                                                          │
└──────────────────────────────────────────────────────────────────────────┘
```

Figure 11.7 Local scope symbol resolution

By using the %LOCAL statement, you avoid changing the value of the global variable:

```
%LET TOTALS = 100;
 %MACRO SUBTOT;
   %LOCAL TOTALS;
   %LET TOTALS = 2;
%MEND;
```

11.4.2 Macrovariable usage and the double quote

Putting an ampersand before your macro variable allows you to replace that text with a resolved value. But that resolved value can actually function in two distinct ways within your SAS program: as a variable name or as a quoted constant.

Example 11.11 The function of resolved macro variable values in a SAS program. A sample from the back-order file is shown so you can see the values for variables MONTH and TOTALS:

```
DATA Backord;
INFILE CARDS MISSOVER;
INPUT Month $3. Totals;
CARDS;
JAN 11012
JAN 00995
JAN 00034
FEB 33219
DEC 00090
;
```

Your program is to read the BACKORD file and report on back-order totals for the current month. You'd also like to have a flexible title that always reflects the current month.

```
%LET Current = JAN;
    %MACRO Test;
      DATA Season;
      SET Backord;
      IF Month = &Current then OUTPUT;
    %MEND;
    %TEST;
    PROC PRINT;
    TITLE "BACKORDER TOTALS FOR THE MONTH OF &Current";
    RUN;
```

Note in Fig. 11.8 how the resolved value for macro variable CUR-RENT is used. The system is looking for a variable named JAN so that it can compare the value in JAN with the value in MONTH. That's not what we wanted!

But look what happens if we put double quotes around the macro-variable reference (Fig. 11.9).

```
%MACRO Test;
   DATA Season;
   SET Backord;
   IF Month = "&Current" then OUTPUT;
%MEND;
```

Now we compare the value in MONTH with a constant: the quoted value of CURRENT. Because the DATA step processed successfully, you'll find three matches and the resolved value for CURRENT in your Title (Fig. 11.10).

The double quote is a signal to first resolve the macro-variable reference, and then treat it as if it were a constant. This is the result we wanted.

The double quote acts similarly to a single quote when there is no text to be resolved. (If you can't get double quote to work, check that

```
LOG
Command ===>

   73        %LET Current = JAN;
   74
   75             %MACRO Test;
   76                DATA Season;
   77                SET Backord;
   78                IF Month = &Current then OUTPUT;
   79             %MEND;
   80
   81             %TEST;
MPRINT(TEST):   DATA SEASON;
MPRINT(TEST):   SET BACKORD;
MPRINT(TEST):   IF MONTH = JAN THEN OUTPUT;
   82
   83             PROC PRINT;
NOTE: Variable JAN is uninitialized.
NOTE: The dataset WORK.SEASON has 0 observations and 3 variables.
NOTE: The DATA statement used 17.00 seconds.
   84             TITLE "BACKORDER TOTALS FOR THE MONTH OF &Current";
   85             RUN;
WARNING: No observations in dataset WORK.SEASON.
NOTE: The PROCEDURE PRINT used 8.00 seconds.
```

Figure 11.8 Wrong use of a macro variable

```
┌LOG════════════════════════════════════════════════════════════════╗
│Command ===>                                                        ║
│                                                                    ║
│   96                                                               ║
│   97          %LET Current = JAN;                                  ║
│   98                                                               ║
│   99             %MACRO Test;                                      ║
│  100                DATA Season;                                   ║
│  101                SET Backord;                                   ║
│  102                IF Month = '&Current' then OUTPUT;             ║
│  103             %MEND;                                            ║
│  104                                                               ║
│  105             %TEST;                                            ║
│MPRINT(TEST):   DATA SEASON;                                        ║
│MPRINT(TEST):   SET BACKORD;                                        ║
│MPRINT(TEST):   IF MONTH = 'JAN' THEN OUTPUT;                       ║
│  106                                                               ║
│  107             PROC PRINT;                                       ║
│NOTE: The dataset WORK.SEASON has 3 observations and 2 variables.   ║
│NOTE: The DATA statement used 17.00 seconds.                       ║
│  108                TITLE "BACKORDER TOTALS FOR THE MONTH OF &Current"; ║
│  109                RUN;                                           ║
│NOTE: The PROCEDURE PRINT used 12.00 seconds.                      ║
└════════════════════════════════════════════════════════════════════╝
```

Figure 11.9 Correct use of a macro variable

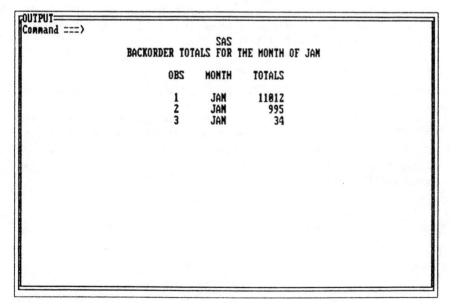

```
┌OUTPUT══════════════════════════════════════════════════════════════╗
│Command ===>                                                        ║
│                                SAS                                 ║
│                BACKORDER TOTALS FOR THE MONTH OF JAN               ║
│                                                                    ║
│                   OBS     MONTH     TOTALS                         ║
│                                                                    ║
│                    1       JAN      11012                          ║
│                    2       JAN        995                          ║
│                    3       JAN         34                          ║
│                                                                    ║
└════════════════════════════════════════════════════════════════════╝
```

Figure 11.10 Output from Figure 11.9

your installation does not have the default system option NOD-QUOTE on.)

11.4.3 Automatic macro variables

There are a few automatic macro variables that you can access for information. These macro variables are global in scope (which means they can be accessed in a regular DATA step, too).

&SYSDAY will return the day of the week. &SYSDATE will return the current date. It's an easy way to include the date in your report title:

```
TITLE " Distribution Report prepared &SYSDATE ";
```

The date is formatted for you, but don't forget to use double rather than single (or no quotes) around the title text.

The automatic variable &SYSPARM can be invoked to retrieve a parm coded on the SAS exec statement of your JCL.

11.4.4 Creating macro variables from DATA step variables

Another way to define and assign a macro variable is through the SYMPUT subroutine. In Chapter 8 you learned a way to use SYMPUT to create a variable whose value was that of a DATA step variable, and make it accessible to another DATA step. SYMPUT is actually more flexible than this. It allows you to:

- create multiple-macro variables

- create a macro-variable name from a DATA step variable's value

Example 11.12 Using one SYMPUT statement per macro variable created. File ALLTOT1 contains one observation with three variables identifying the number of accounts adding recipients (ADDRCP), the number of accounts that renewed (RENEW), and the number of accounts that canceled (CANCEL).

```
      DATA Alltot1;
   INPUT Addrcp$ Renew$ Cancel$;
   CARDS;
300  9000 30
   ;
```

File Deptot1 contains the subtotals by department.

```
DATA Deptot1;
   INPUT Addrcp$ Renew$ Cancel$ Dept $;
   CARDS;
050   1000  0
150   6000  25
100   2000  5
   ;
```

The following code creates macro variables with the constant names identified between the quotes. SYMPUT assigns the macro variable named ADDRCP the value that is found in DATA step variable ADDRCP for observation 1. It does the same for RENEW and CANCEL.

```
DATA _Null_;
SET Alltot1;
IF _N_ = 1 THEN DO;
   CALL SYMPUT ('Addrcp', Addrcp);
   CALL SYMPUT ('Renew', Renew);
   CALL SYMPUT ('Cancel', Cancel);
END; STOP;
```

This step accesses the macro variables created in the last step and their resolved values are used in the calculation. Figure 11.11 shows the output.

```
DATA Ratios;
SET Deptot1;
Pctadd = (Addrcp / &Addrcp)* 100;
Pctren = (Renew  / &Renew) * 100;
Pctcan = (Cancel / &Cancel) * 100;
RUN;
PROC PRINT; TITLE 'Contributions by Department';
SUM Pctadd Pctren Pctcan;
RUN;
```

Example 11.13 Using one SYMPUT statement to create many macro variables.
The main difference in this example is that file ALLTOT2 contains three observations with two variables each: one variable identifies the type of total; the other its amount.

```
DATA Alltot2;
INFILE CARDS MISSOVER;
INPUT Var $ Amt;
```

```
┌─OUTPUT══════════════════════════════════════════════════════════════┐
│ Command ===)                                                         │
│                              SAS                                     │
│                    Contributions by Department                      │
│                                                                      │
│    DEPT       ADDRCP    PCTADD    RENEW    PCTREN    CANCEL    PCTCAN │
│                                                                      │
│    Catalogs     850    16.667     1000    11.111       0     0.000   │
│    Cards        150    50.000     6000    66.667      25    83.333   │
│    News         100    33.333     2000    22.222       5    16.667   │
│                       ───────            ───────           ───────   │
│                       100.000            100.000           100.000   │
│                                                                      │
│                                                                      │
│                                                                      │
│                                                                      │
│                                                                      │
│                                                                      │
│                                                                      │
│                                                                      │
└──────────────────────────────────────────────────────────────────────┘
```

Figure 11.11   Output from SYMPUT Type 1

```
        CARDS;
Addrcp2 300
Renew2 9000
Cancel2 30
      ;
```

This alternate use of the SYMPUT statement allows us to create a macro variable for each observation on the ALLTOT2 dataset.

```
DATA _Null_;
SET Alltot2;
    CALL SYMPUT (Var, Amt);
```

Note that argument 1 is no longer in quotes. By not quoting VAR, you're saying that the name for the macro variable you want to create should not be VAR but should be taken from the value of VAR for that observation. (For observation 1, VAR's value is ADDRCP2; for observation 2, it is RENEW, and so on.)

Argument 2 functions the same in both forms of SYMPUT. Its function is to supply the value found for the variable named "argument 2" to the macro variable named in argument 1.

Here the DATA step accesses the macro variables your previous step created:

```
DATA Ratios2;
SET Deptot1;
Pctadd = (Addrcp / &Addrcp2)* 100;
Pctren = (Renew  / &Renew2) * 100;
Pctcan = (Cancel / &Cancel2) * 100;
RUN;
```

The results are the same (compare Fig. 11.11 to Fig. 11.12).

11.4.5 Overview of macro functions. Since macros manipulate stored text, it shouldn't surprise you that many of the character functions you learned in Chapter 8 have been copied into the macro language. These functions are not only named the same (except for the required %PREFIX), but also perform the same processing:

* %INDEX (arg1, arg2)
* %SCAN (arg,n,delimiters)
* %SUBSTR (arg,relative start position,length)

The arguments can all be macro expressions as long as they resolve to values that can be used in the functions. There is also a %EVAL function that allows you to perform integer arithmetic operations on the character data. The quoting functions allow you to per-

```
┌OUTPUT══════════════════════════════════════════════════════
│Command ===>
                            SAS
                  Contributions by Department

    DEPT       ADDRCP    PCTADD    RENEW    PCTREN    CANCEL    PCTCAN

    Catalogs    850     16.667     1000    11.111      0       0.000
    Cards       150     50.000     6000    66.667     25      83.333
    News        100     33.333     2000    22.222      5      16.667
                      ---------            --------           --------
                      100.000              100.000            100.000
```

Figure 11.12 Output from SYMPUT Type 2

form even more sophisticated manipulations of macro variables and data.

11.4.6 Macro control statements

IF . . . THEN . . . ELSE . . . DO . . . GOTO . . . are used in regular SAS code to control the flow of processing in a DATA step. Their counterparts %IF, %THEN, %ELSE, %DO, %GOTO allow you to use macro variables to structure the processing sequence of your macros. The macro control statements give you the freedom to code alternative actions or text based on conditions found in the parameters or macro variables.

Example 11.14 Multistep processing with %DO . . . %END;. This example uses the three datasets below as input.

```
      DATA IN1;
      INFILE CARDS MISSOVER;
      INPUT Code Descript $ Valid;
      CARDS ;
101   Recent 1
102   Expired .
109   Damaged 1
110   Return 1
         ;
      DATA IN2;
      INFILE CARDS MISSOVER;
      INPUT Code Descript $ Valid;
      CARDS ;
991   Drytitle .
888   Deleted 1
990   Unwanted .
999   Unknown 1
         ;
      DATA IN3;
      INFILE CARDS MISSOVER;
      INPUT Code Descript $ Valid;
      CARDS ;
456   OOS 1
678   OOP 1
789   OOD 1
         ;
```

The macro uses the parameter variable HOWMANY to tell it how many datasets to read. It creates the macro variable I to keep track of the iterations and to identify the different datasets.

```
%MACRO Check (Howmany);
%DO I = 1 %TO &Howmany;
     DATA Out&I;
     SET IN&I;
     If Valid THEN Output;
     PROC PRINT;
     VAR Code Descript;
     TITLE "These Codes from File &I are valid ";
     RUN;
%END;
%MEND;
%Check (3)
```

Figure 11.13 provides a sample of the MPRINT expansion on the log.

```
┌LOG──────────────────────────────────────────────────────────────────┐
│Command ===)                                                          │
│                                                                      │
│MPRINT(CHECK):    DATA OUT1;                                          │
│MPRINT(CHECK):    SET IN1;                                            │
│MPRINT(CHECK):    IF VALID THEN OUTPUT;                               │
│NOTE: The dataset WORK.OUT1 has 3 observations and 3 variables.       │
│NOTE: The DATA statement used 16.88 seconds.                         │
│MPRINT(CHECK):    PROC PRINT;                                         │
│MPRINT(CHECK):    VAR CODE DESCRIPT;                                  │
│MPRINT(CHECK):    TITLE 'These Codes from File 1 are valid ';        │
│MPRINT(CHECK):    RUN;                                                │
│NOTE: The PROCEDURE PRINT used 14.88 seconds.                        │
│MPRINT(CHECK):    DATA OUT2;                                          │
│MPRINT(CHECK):    SET IN2;                                            │
│MPRINT(CHECK):    IF VALID THEN OUTPUT;                               │
│NOTE: The dataset WORK.OUT2 has 2 observations and 3 variables.       │
│NOTE: The DATA statement used 15.88 seconds.                         │
│MPRINT(CHECK):    PROC PRINT;                                         │
│MPRINT(CHECK):    VAR CODE DESCRIPT;                                  │
│MPRINT(CHECK):    TITLE 'These Codes from File 2 are valid ';        │
│MPRINT(CHECK):    RUN;                                                │
│NOTE: The PROCEDURE PRINT used 16.88 seconds.                        │
│MPRINT(CHECK):    DATA OUT3;                                          │
└──────────────────────────────────────────────────────────────────────┘
```

Figure 11.13   %DO . . . %END expanded iterations

Note how the macro variable is used to create array-type dataset names simply by concatenating a prefix to it. Adding a suffix is only slightly more difficult: precede the suffix with a "." to preserve the name of the macro variable. (In our example, OUT&I.SET would resolve to OUT1SET on the first iteration, OUT2SET on the second, and so on.) See Figs. 11.14, 11.15, and 11.16.

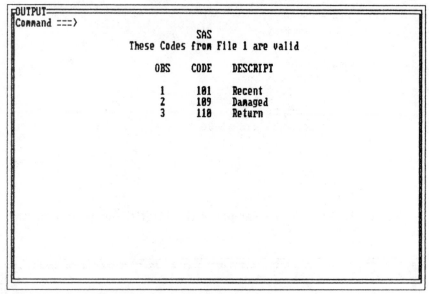

Figure 11.14   Output 1 from Figure 11.13

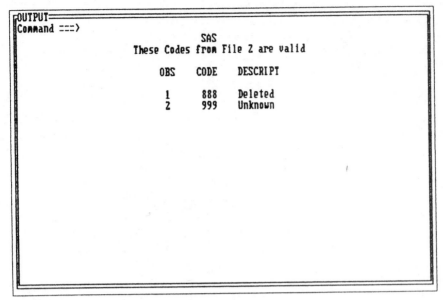

```
┌OUTPUT═══════════════════════════════════════════════════════
│Command ===>
                              SAS
                  These Codes from File 2 are valid

                    OBS     CODE     DESCRIPT

                     1      888      Deleted
                     2      999      Unknown
```

Figure 11.15 Output 2 from Figure 11.13

```
┌OUTPUT═══════════════════════════════════════════════════════
│Command ===>
                              SAS
                  These Codes from File 3 are valid

                    OBS     CODE     DESCRIPT

                     1      456      00S
                     2      678      00P
                     3      789      00D
```

Figure 11.16 Output 3 from Figure 11.13

12

Special Features for PC Users

Although the SAS language is essentially similar across all of the supported operating systems, there are some differences. We have already noted the unavoidable differences in external file references between MVS and PC-DOS systems. In this chapter, we discuss some features of the SAS System for personal computers that are specific to this implementation. These features define a flexible, window-based environment. Menus and panels are available for many standard activities; in particular, all PROC steps can be built through formatted panels.

In general, the PC extensions to SAS software represent something of a tradeoff. They sacrifice some of the universality of the language, by permitting the creation of programs that may run slightly differently on two different systems. In return, they provide a more responsible and personalized environment for SAS users.

12.1 STARTING THE SAS SESSION

SAS software is typically started from DOS by entering the SAS command when you are in the directory containing the SAS software. A typical sequence is:

```
cd      \sas
sas
```

There are several modes of SAS execution. We will discuss two of them.

The SAS Display Manager system provides for interactive creation and execution of SAS programs. It features a full-screen, window-based environment.

Batch mode permits you to execute a SAS program which has already been written, without entering the interactive display manager environment.

12.1.1 Display manager mode

The display manager provides a full development environment for creating, testing, and running SAS programs. You will probably be using display manager mode for most of your SAS work. Most of this chapter concerns aspects of the display manager. Some display manager features are:

- full-screen program editor
- multiple window environment, including separate displays for program, output, and SAS log
- color and display control commands
- formatted data entry through customized windows
- simplified program creation through formatted procedure menus
- DOS commands available

The display manager is invoked by including the -dms option when you enter the SAS command to start SAS execution:

```
cd      \sas
sas     –dms
```

However, when display manager mode is the default (it usually is), you can omit the -dms option.

12.1.2 Batch mode

You can save a SAS program and re-execute it without entering the display manager environment. This is useful when your program is to be run in sequence with programs written in other languages, or when you simply want to provide a "turnkey" function without the SAS System being visible.

To execute a stored SAS program, type:

SAS filename

For example, suppose the file 'c:\sasapps\sales2.sas' contains SAS statements which will read in a file of current sales data and compute projected sales figures for the next period. The program does not require any interaction with the PC user, and it already contains the correct fully qualified input and output file names.

To run the program, you would simply type

SAS 'c:\sasapps\sales2.sas'

You can include this form of SAS execution in any .BAT file, including AUTOEXEC.BAT. For example, if you must first run a compiled C program called "sales1" to create the current sales data, your .BAT file might look like Fig. 12.1.

12.1.3 Creating your own startup procedure

If you have a series of SAS statements you routinely execute at the start of your SAS session, you should consider using the AUTO-EXEC.SAS file. This file can contain any SAS statements, including complete DATA and PROC steps. All of the statements contained in

```
c:
cd \capps
sales1
cd \sas
sas '\sasapps\sales2.sas'




C:\>
```

Figure 12.1   Sample .BAT file including SAS step

AUTOEXEC.SAS are executed at initialization, before you can access the display manager.

Figure 12.2 shows an AUTOEXEC.SAS file that does several things:

- The TITLE1 statement sets a standard title to be used on output.
- The DM commands set window sizes and positions to your preference.
- The FILENAME commands set up some fileref associations you commonly use.
- The DATA and PROC PRINT steps display an external file which has been created since your last SAS session.

12.2 USING THE DISPLAY MANAGER

The display manager is simple to work with. Its essential components are common to all SAS environments: there is a log file, an output file, and an area for the SAS program itself. What is new is that these components are integrated into a flexible window-based environment. This means that you control which ones appear on your screen, where they appear, and which one is "active" at any given time.

The design of the display manager has also allowed the SAS Sys-

```
title1 'INFORMATION MANAGEMENT ASSOCIATES';
dm 'log;wdef 1 1 5 80';
dm 'output;wdef 6 1 5 80';
filename sales 'sales.dat';
filename sasprog 'sasprog.tmp';
data;
   infile sales;
   input @1 custid $5.
         @7 n_units 4.
         @12 dlr_amt 6.2;
   format dlr_amt dollar8.2;
proc print;




c:\>
```

Figure 12.2   Sample AUTOEXEC.SAS file

tem to add additional components in a structured way. New windows are introduced to provide a "notepad" facility, a panel-driven environment for building PROC step requests, directory displays, and more.

12.2.1 The windowing environment

Window-based systems are now common in PC environments. Each window is a miniature screen which holds a logical piece of your work. The windows are independent of the actual video monitor, so that their total display area may greatly exceed the monitor size. To accomplish this, they may appear to be "stacked up" like papers of differing sizes.

There is always one "active" window, which appears to be on top. You can request to activate another window; that is, to bring it forward and allow you to work on its contents. In the SAS System for PCs, the primary windows are the program editor window, the log window, and the output window. Various other windows are available. Every window has a command line, which appears at the top of the window following the prompt:

Command = = = >

The command line can be used for several purposes. You can:

- End the current window with the END command.
- Activate another window by entering its name (e.g. OUTPUT or LOG or OPTIONS).
- Enter window control commands for the current window; for example, to change its size or position.
- End the SAS session with the BYE or ENDSAS command.
- Execute DOS commands directly with the X command.
- Clear the contents of the current window with the CLEAR command.
- Position the display at the TOP or BOTTOM of the current file.
- Set window colors with the COLOR command.
- Perform special control commands defined for each window.

12.2.2 The primary windows: PGM, LOG, and OUTPUT

The functions of the primary windows should be familiar to you by now. The PGM window is where you write your SAS program. The

LOG window provides a runtime journal as you run your program, including error and informational messages. The OUTPUT window displays print output you request in DATA or PROC steps.

The PGM window provides a full-screen editor similar to many editors on mainframe and PC systems. If you are familiar with any common text editor, you should have no problem using the PGM window.

In the PGM window, the command line can be used for several special purposes. For instance, you can:

- Run your program using the SUBMIT command.

- Save the program using the FILE 'filename' command.

- Print the program using the FILE 'PRN:' command.

- Retrieve a saved program using the INCLUDE 'filename' command.

- Perform global find and replace functions with the FIND and CHANGE commands.

The LOG window displays all output written to the SAS log. This includes the source lines you've executed, informational and error messages, summary messages at the completion of each step, and any output not otherwise directed.

In the LOG window, the command line can be used for several special purposes. For instance, you can:

- Save the log using the FILE 'filename' command.

- Print the log using the FILE 'PRN:' command.

- Find specified text with the FIND command.

The OUTPUT window displays all output written to the standard SAS print file. This includes PROC step output as well as DATA step output directed to FILE PRINT. In the OUTPUT window, the command line can be used for several special purposes. For instance, you can:

- Save the print file using the FILE 'filename' command.

- Print the print file using the FILE 'PRN:' command.

- Find specified text with the FIND command.

12.2.3 Other windows

Many other windows are available, although they are not displayed automatically like the primary windows. To activate any of the following windows, enter its name in any window's command line.

The CATALOG, LIBNAME, DIR, and VAR windows provide a complete cross-reference of elements defined in your SAS environment. You will probably find the most use for the DIR window, which displays all SAS files in a given library, and the VAR window, which displays all variables in a SAS dataset. The DIR window is shown in Fig. 12.3, and the VAR window in Fig. 12.4.

The FOOTNOTES and TITLES windows allow you to specify page titles and footnotes to appear on all printed output from DATA and PROC steps. Figure 12.5 shows the TITLES window. The FOOTNOTES window is similar.

The HELP window is activated whenever you type HELP in a command line. It displays HELP information relevant to your current screen.

The KEYS and OPTIONS windows are used to view or specify the setting of function keys and SAS System options, respectively. The KEYS window is shown in Fig. 12.6. The OPTIONS window is shown in Fig. 12.7.

The NOTEPAD window allows you to create free-form documentation or notes which are saved from session to session. It includes a full-screen editor similar to the one in the PGM window. You may save multiple notepad entries with the SAVE command, and recall them with the COPY command.

The MENU window activates the SAS Procedure Menu System. This provides a friendly, panel-driven interface to all the SAS PROCs. We'll cover this in detail in Section 12.3.

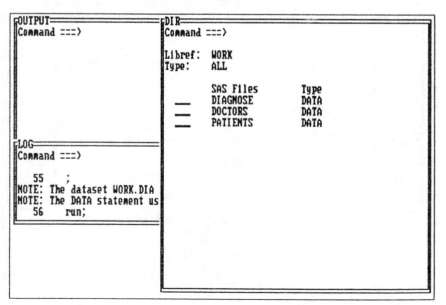

Figure 12.3 The DIR window

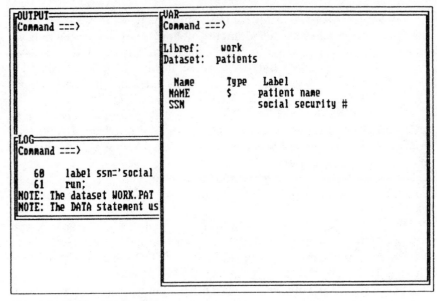

Figure 12.4 The VAR window

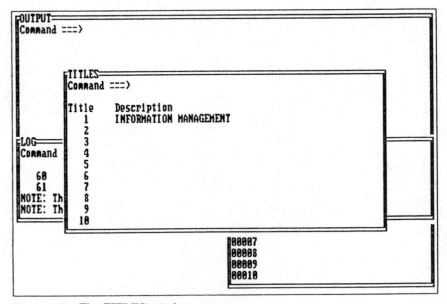

Figure 12.5 The TITLES window

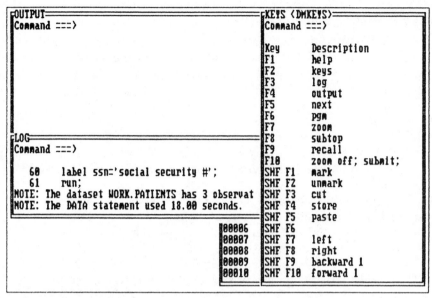

Figure 12.6   The KEYS window

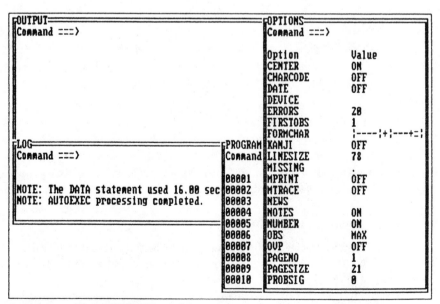

Figure 12.7   The OPTIONS window

12.2.4   Defining your own windows

The WINDOW and DISPLAY statements help you define your own windows. The WINDOW statement names the window and describes its position, size, and color. It also identifies the variables and constants to be displayed. The DISPLAY statement actually displays the window.

Both statements are used within a DATA step. The following DATA step reads an external file containing payroll information. If an hourly rate of zero is encountered, an error window is displayed. The resulting screen, including the error window, would look like Fig. 12.8.

The # and @ modifiers are used similarly to the way they are used in the PUT statement; i.e., to indicate the row and column, respectively. In the WINDOW statement, the position they define is relative to the upper-left corner of the new window.

IROW and ICOLUMN define the upper-left corner of the window. ROWS and COLUMNS specify the number of rows and columns.

```
DATA HRLYINFO;
    FILE PAYROLL;
    INPUT @18 HRLYRATE 5.2;
    WINDOW BADRATE
        COLOR=RED
        IROW=8
        ICOLUMN=11
        ROW=10
        COLUMNS=60
        #3 @3 'WARNING: An hourly rate of $0.00'
                'has been encountered.'
        #5 @3 'Press ENTER to continue'
        #6 @3 'Or enter the END command to stop.';
    IF HRLYRATE = 0.00
        THEN DISPLAY BADRATE;
```

You can also define your own windows for data entry or any other purpose. Windows can be integrated into any SAS application.

12.2.5   Changing window configuration

Figure 12.9 shows the display-manager screen as it might appear when you begin a SAS session. The LOG, PGM, and OUTPUT windows are displayed and their size and position are preset.

You can change the configuration of the display-manager screen to suit your preferences. You can change the size or position of any

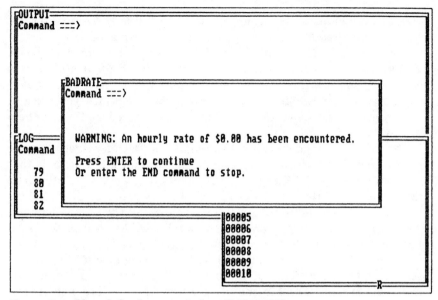

```
┌OUTPUT═══════════════════════════════════════════════════════════════╗
│Command ===>                                                          ║
│                                                                      ║
│                                                                      ║
│      ┌BADRATE══════════════════════════════════════════════╗        ║
│      │Command ===>                                          ║        ║
│      │                                                      ║        ║
│┌LOG──┤ WARNING: An hourly rate of $0.00 has been encountered.║══════╗║
││Command                                                      ║      ║║
││      │ Press ENTER to continue                              ║      ║║
││  79  │ Or enter the END command to stop.                    ║      ║║
││  80  │                                                      ║      ║║
││  81  │                                                      ║      ║║
││  82  └──────────────────────────────────────────┬─────────╝       ║
│└──────────────────────────────────────────────────┤00005│          ║
│                                                    │00006│          ║
│                                                    │00007│          ║
│                                                    │00008│          ║
│                                                    │00009│          ║
│                                                    │00010│          ║
│                                                    └─────┤R═════════╝
└──────────────────────────────────────────────────────────────────────┘
```

Figure 12.8 User-defined error window: BADRATE

```
┌OUTPUT═══════════════════════════════════════════════════════════════╗
│Command ===>                                                          ║
│                                                                      ║
│                                                                      ║
│                                                                      ║
│                                                                      ║
│                                                                      ║
│                                                                      ║
│                                                                      ║
│┌LOG══════════════════════════════════════════════════════════════════╗
││Command ===>                                                          ║
││                                                                      ║
││NOTE: The DATA statement used 16.00 seconds.                         ║
││NOTE: AUTOEXEC processing completed.                                 ║
│┌PROGRAM EDITOR═══════════════════════════════════════════════════════╗
││Command ===>                                                          ║
││                                                                      ║
││00001                                                                 ║
││00002                                                                 ║
││00003                                                                 ║
└──────────────────────────────────────────────────────────────────────┘
```

Figure 12.9 Initial window configuration

window, or temporarily "zoom" it so that it fills the entire screen. You can also request that other windows be displayed.

Any changes may be made on a temporary or permanent basis. Permanent changes will make your new window configuration active whenever you use the SAS System. Temporary changes in a window typically last for the duration of the window; i.e., until you close it. However, you can save the commands you entered and reuse them at any time.

The simplest window control command is ZOOM, which expands any window to fill the entire screen. The advantage, of course, is that you can see more data. Figure 12.10 shows a "standard" SAS screen after running PROC PRINT. Much of the output data is hidden behind the program and log window. To expand the output window, we have entered "zoom" on its command line. As soon as we press the Enter key, the display will change to that of Fig. 12.11.

In Fig. 12.11, notice that the OUTPUT window now fills the entire screen. "ZOOM" appears at the bottom of the screen to remind you that you are in ZOOM mode. The other windows are not visible. They are still present, only "behind" the ZOOMed window. To view another window, just enter its name in the control line as you would normally do. Note that the new window is ZOOMed also; ZOOM applies to all windows until you turn it off.

To get out of ZOOM mode, simply retype ZOOM in the command line. You will return to the window configuration that existed before you entered ZOOM mode (e.g., Fig. 12.10).

For more flexibility in defining your windows, you should consider the window control commands WGROW, WSHRINK, WMOVE, and WDEF. These permit you to establish window sizes and positions interactively using the arrow keys, or (in WDEF) by specifying exact screen positions. A WSAVE command allows you to save the configuration in your user profile, so that it will be active whenever you start a SAS session.

Suppose that, as in our ZOOM example, you want to expand the OUTPUT screen. Rather than take over the entire screen, though, you just want to enlarge the window by a few lines so that the PGM window is still visible. You're willing to sacrifice some of the LOG window; after all, you can always ZOOM it if necessary.

Figure 12.12 shows the display-manager screen as we enter the WGROW command in the OUTPUT window. WGROW will let us expand the window by using the arrow keys. While we are in GROW mode, pressing the "down" arrow will move the bottom border of the window down one line. The "up" arrow will move the top border up one line. Pressing the "left" and "right" arrows will move the left and right borders, respectively, one column out toward the edge of the screen.

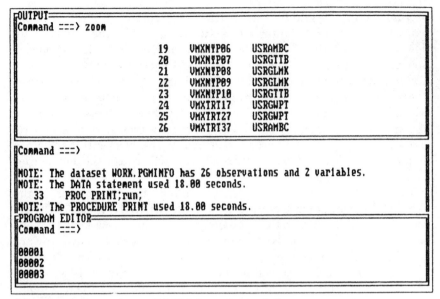

```
┌OUTPUT══════════════════════════════════════════════════════════════════╗
│Command ═══> zoom                                                         ║
│                                                                          ║
│              19   VMXNYP06    USRAMBC                                     ║
│              20   VMXNYP07    USRGTTB                                     ║
│              21   VMXNYP08    USRGLMK                                     ║
│              22   VMXNYP09    USRGLMK                                     ║
│              23   VMXNYP10    USRGTTB                                     ║
│              24   VMXTRT17    USRGWPT                                     ║
│              25   VMXTRT27    USRGWPT                                     ║
│              26   VMXTRT37    USRAMBC                                     ║
╠══════════════════════════════════════════════════════════════════════════
│Command ═══>                                                              ║
│                                                                          ║
│NOTE: The dataset WORK.PGMINFO has 26 observations and 2 variables.       ║
│NOTE: The DATA statement used 18.00 seconds.                              ║
│   33    PROC PRINT;run;                                                  ║
│NOTE: The PROCEDURE PRINT used 18.00 seconds.                             ║
│┌PROGRAM EDITOR════════════════════════════════════════════════════════════
││Command ═══>                                                             ║
││                                                                         ║
││00001                                                                    ║
││00002                                                                    ║
││00003                                                                    ║
└──────────────────────────────────────────────────────────────────────────
```

Figure 12.10   Preparing to ZOOM the output window

```
┌OUTPUT══════════════════════════════════════════════════════════════════╗
│Command ═══>                                                              ║
│                                                                          ║
│                        SAS                                     1         ║
│                                                                          ║
│              OBS    PGM        USER                                      ║
│                                                                          ║
│               1   TORCYJ01    UDMGSWR                                    ║
│               2   TORCYJ02    UDMGSWR                                    ║
│               3   TORCYJ03    UDMGMHK                                    ║
│               4   TORCYJ04    UDMGSWR                                    ║
│               5   TORCYJ09    UDMGSWR                                    ║
│               6   TORCYJ10    UDMGSWR                                    ║
│               7   TORCYJ11    UDMGMHK                                    ║
│               8   TORCYJ12    UDMGSWR                                    ║
│               9   TSRMNJ70    UDPQARJ                                    ║
│              10   TSRMNJ72    UDPQARJ                                    ║
│              11   TSRMNJ74    UDPQARJ                                    ║
│              12   TSRMNJ75    UDPQARJ                                    ║
│              13   TSRMNJ76    UDPQARJ                                    ║
│              14   VMXNYP01    USRGWJR                                    ║
│              15   VMXNYP02    USRGLMK                                    ║
│              16   VMXNYP03    USRGLMK                                    ║
│              17   VMXNYP04    USRGLMK                                    ║
│                                                        ═══ZOOM═══        ║
└──────────────────────────────────────────────────────────────────────────
```

Figure 12.11   ZOOMed output window

In Fig. 12.13, we see the result of pressing the down arrow three times while in GROW mode. The OUTPUT window is now three lines taller, hiding part of the LOG window.

Notice the word "GROW" at the bottom of the screen, reminding us that we are in GROW mode. This will remain in effect until we exit GROW mode by entering WGROW again in the output window's command line. It is wise to turn off GROW mode as soon as you are satisfied with the window size. Otherwise, every time you accidentally press an arrow key, the window will continue to grow!

Another thing to keep in mind is that there is not "backing up" while in GROW mode. If you enlarge a window by three columns to the right and you really meant to grow only two, it is almost irresistible to press the left arrow and expect the border to back up a column. This will not work! Instead, you will cause the left border to grow one column.

To shrink a window, you must enter (not surprisingly) the WSHRINK command. This places you in SHRINK mode. SHRINK mode acts similarly to GROW mode; you use the arrow keys to move the window's borders. Now, however, they always move inward toward the center of the window. You will shrink the window one line or column each time you press an arrow key. Figure 12.14 shows the screen of Fig. 12.13 after we have "shrunk" the PGM window three left columns and three right columns.

All the warnings we issued about WGROW also hold true for WSHRINK. You cannot reverse the result of a "shrink" operation while in SHRINK mode. SHRINK mode remains in effect until WSHRINK is entered again on the command line. To reverse a shrink operation, you must get out of SHRINK mode and enter GROW mode.

```
┌OUTPUT════════════════════════════════════════════════════════════════
│Command ===> wgrow
│
│
│
│
│
│
│
│Command ===>
│
│
│
│
│Command ===>
│
│00001
│00002
│00003
```

Figure 12.12   Preparing to use WGROW

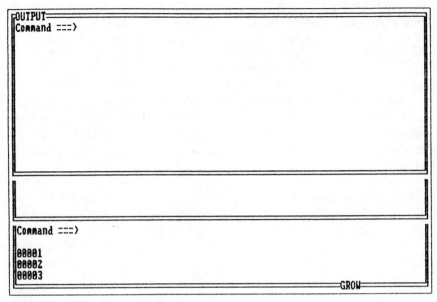

Figure 12.13 Result of WGROW

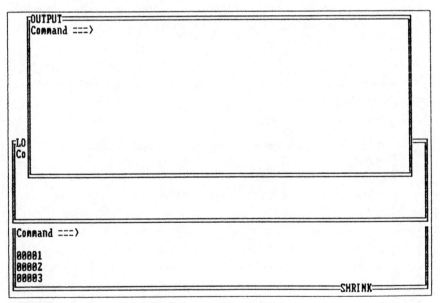

Figure 12.14 Result of WSHRINK

If the size of your window is acceptable, but you would like to position it somewhere else on the screen, you can use the WMOVE command. Like WGROW and WSHRINK, WMOVE activates a special mode in which the arrow keys are used to adjust the window configuration. WMOVE does not change the size of the window. Instead, each arrow key "drags" the window in the indicated direction. Figure 12.15 shows the screen we left in Fig. 12.14 after we have entered WMOVE followed by five down arrows and two right arrows.

Like SHRINK and GROW modes, MOVE mode remains in effect until you reissue the WMOVE command. However, our warning about not being able to undo an operation does not apply here. To reverse the effect of a move operation, simply move in the opposite direction.

Another window control command, WDEF, allows you to resize and reposition a window without using the arrow keys. With WDEF you specify four numbers, which must be entered in order:

- starting row number of the window border
- starting column number of the window border
- number of rows, not including borders
- number of columns, not including borders

For example, we could move our PGM window to start at row 3, column 1, and resize it to be eight rows high and thirty-eight columns wide by entering the following in the command line of the PGM window (the result is shown in Fig. 12.16):

    wdef 3 1 8 38

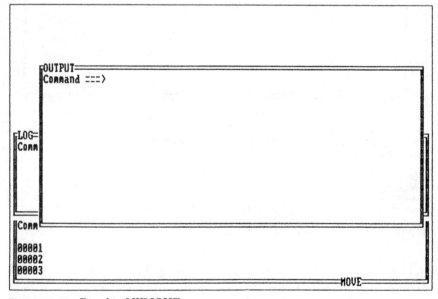

Figure 12.15   Result of WMOVE

One thing to keep in mind when moving or resizing windows is that even though you may be hiding all or part of another window, it is not lost. You can bring it "forward" by entering its name in the command line of any window. It will appear in full, in its current position. This may cause it to hide part of the original window, but of course you can bring that one forward again just as easily.

One benefit of this layering effect is that you can grow your windows to any size without worrying about losing information. In fact, you can grow all the windows to cover the entire screen, if you want! If you then enter the name of any window, it will take over the screen.

One warning, though. When things are going well, it is tempting to hide the LOG window in favor of larger OUTPUT or PGM windows. If you do this, though, you should always remember to check the log for syntax errors and other messages. Otherwise, you may find yourself trying to screen out why the system is acting so strangely, or running an "old" version of your program.

Once you find a window configuration you like, you can save it by entering the WSAVE command. WSAVE will store the window settings in your user profile. These will become the default settings whenever you start a SAS session.

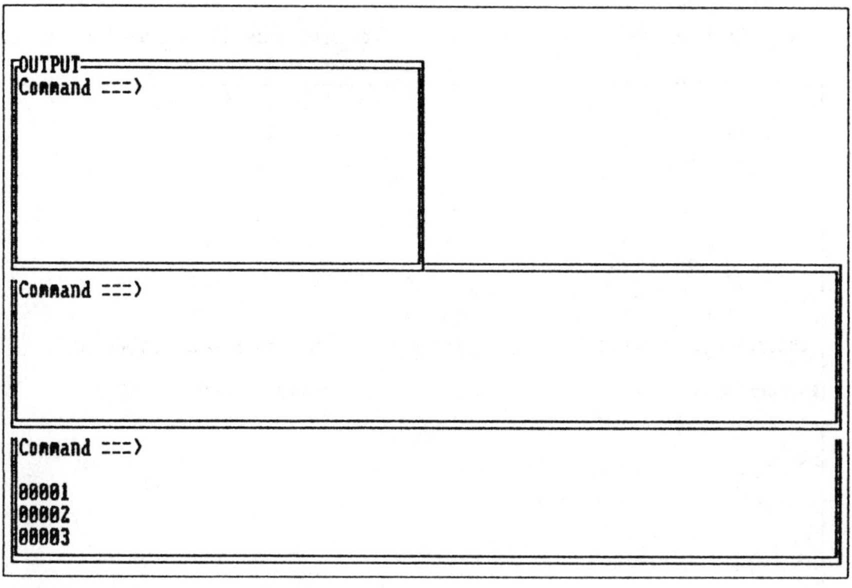

Figure 12.16   Result of WDEF

12.2.6   Saving display-manager commands

Any command which is entered on the command line can also be invoked from within a SAS program by using the DM statement. DM (which stands for display manager) is a special SAS statement designed specifically for this purpose. The syntax is shown in Fig. 12.17.

The DM (display manager) statement consists of two parts. The first is a string of one or more display-manager commands, separated by semicolons, with the whole string enclosed in single or double quotation marks. Any display-manager command can be included.

The second part of the DM statement is optional. It consists solely of the name of a window. The cursor will be left in this window after execution of the DM statement. If you omit this parameter, the cursor will be in the PGM window.

Some examples of the DM statement, based on our previous discussion, are:

```
DM 'LOG;WDEF 3 1 8 38';
DM 'OUTPUT';
DM 'PGM;WDEF 1 1 10 78;LOG;WDEF 31 1 10 78';
DM "INCLUDE 'c:\sasapps\sales1.sas' ";
```

Using the DM statement to save commands is convenient when

```
DM

'dmcommand1; dmcommand2; . . . ; dmcommand'    Display manager commands

cursorwindow;                                  Where to leave cursor
```

Figure 12.17   DM statement syntax

you have several window configurations you would like to keep available. For example, in some situations you need a large OUTPUT window to check PROC step output; at other times, you will be primarily interested in checking the LOG window.

One or more DM commands can be saved in a SAS program file. You create the SAS program in the PGM window and use the FILE command to save it. You can then execute them at any time by using the INCLUDE command to recall the SAS program. You can also include DM statements in your AUTOEXEC.SAS file. This makes them active whenever you run SAS, without altering your user profile.

12.2.7 Using function keys

Any SAS statement or combination of statements can be assigned to a function key. Function keys are assigned in the KEYS window. Type KEYS in the command line of any window to start the KEYS window. Figure 12.6 shows the KEYS window with default function key settings.

Once you are in the KEYS window, you can assign any value to any key. For example, Fig. 12.18 shows the KEYS window with Shift-F9 and Shift-F10 assigned to create two different window sizes for the LOG window.

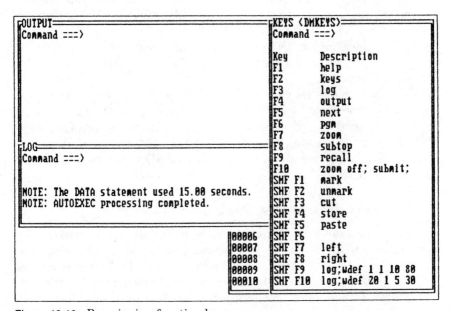

Figure 12.18 Reassigning function keys

12.3   THE PROCEDURE MENU SYSTEM

The Procedure Menu System is one of the most interesting new features in the SAS System. It frees you from having to know the syntax of the many SAS procedures. (By "SAS procedures", we mean PROC PRINT, PROC FREQ, PROC SORT, and so on.)

Each procedure is represented by a formatted data entry screen. The screen provides a short description of the various parameters and options for the procedure. You can enter all of them without knowing the particular keywords (CLASS, VAR, WEIGHT, BY, and so on) or how to place your semicolons and slashes.

Of course, as with all menu-driven systems, this has the disadvantage of slowing you down if you are familiar with the procedure in question. Fortunately, you can still enter your procedure requests by coding them as program statements in the PGM window.

12.3.1   Invoking a procedure menu

You enter the Procedure Menu System by opening the MENU window. This is like opening any other window. Enter MENU in any window's command line to open the MENU window and display the main menu.

We recommend that you use the AUTOSAVE=YES option when you open the MENU window. This option saves your input after the window is closed. You can then recall it the next time you use the menu (by using the RECALL command). Specify this option by entering MENU AUTOSAVE=YES (instead of just MENU) when you open the window. Of course, you can assign this to a function key. Currently, you can also enter the Procedure Menu System by pressing Control-A.

The main menu is shown in Fig. 12.19. From this screen, you select the Procedure Menu you are interested in by typing its name in the command line. For instance, to work with the screen for PROC SUMMARY, you would type SUMMARY in the command line.

To exit the Procedure Menu System, type END in the command line on the main menu.

12.3.2   Example: The PROC SORT menu

Figure 12.20 shows the menu for PROC SORT. It closely mirrors the syntax of PROC SORT as you would code it in a SAS program. Notice the DATA=, OUT=, and BY keywords. They are just as you would normally code them, but here they have been supplied for you.

Options of the "on/off" variety are even simpler to use. Just enter an "X" next to any option you want to turn on. To select NODUP-

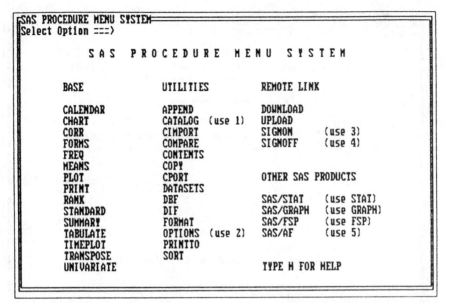

Figure 12.19 Main Procedure Menu

KEY, place an "X" next to that option. To select TAGSORT, place an "X" next to it. Of course, you may select both by placing "X" in both places. If you leave the "X" off any option, it will not be used.

You will notice that the screen contains considerable help for filling in the fields. Each field is described, and required fields are clearly marked (see BY). Sometimes usage hints are provided, as with the TAGSORT option. You can always request additional help by entering HELP in the command line.

In some cases, you can get help for a specific situation by typing a "?" in the data entry field. For example, if you type "?" in the BY field, you will see a list of variables in the SAS dataset you selected.

Once you have filled in all the information to create your procedure request, you can check it by pressing the Enter key. The SAS supervisor will inform you of any errors or inconsistencies.

To process your request, type SUBMIT in the command line. The procedure will be processed just as if you had typed it in full in the PGM window. Your output will appear in the OUTPUT window, and any log messages will be in the LOG window.

```
┌─SORT: Sorts a data set═══════════════════════════════════════════════┐
│Command ===>                                                           │
│                                                                       │
│                                                                       │
│     PROC SORT   DATA =                         Input dataset          │
│                        ------------------                             │
│                  OUT =                         Output dataset         │
│                        ------------------                             │
│                                                                       │
│     Options:                                                          │
│       NODUPKEY [ _ ]  Eliminates observations with identical keys     │
│       TAGSORT  [ _ ]  Saves disk space but it is slower               │
│                                                                       │
│                                                                       │
│     BY .......................................  ;  REQUIRED FIELD     │
│        Variables that supply sort keys                                │
│                                                                       │
│                                                                       │
│                                                                       │
│        Enter SUBMIT to run; CANCEL to quit without running            │
│                                                                       │
└───────────────────────────────────────────────────────────────────────┘
```

Figure 12.20   Procedure Menu for PROC SORT

12.4 INTERFACING WITH OTHER SOFTWARE

You can issue DOS commands from within a SAS session in two ways. You can issue the X command from the command line. You will be put in a DOS-like environment where you can issue any series of DOS commands. To return to the SAS session, type EXIT.

Use the CALL SYSTEM statement to issue DOS commands from within a SAS program. CALL SYSTEM takes one argument, enclosed in parentheses. This argument can be either a quoted character literal or a SAS character variable; in either case, it must contain a valid DOS command:

```
CALL SYSTEM ('dir c:\sas\');
CALL SYSTEM (DOS_CMD);
```

SAS datasets are stored in an internal format that cannot be read by other software. However, you can convert any SAS dataset to a format that can be read.

The most generic solution is to create a flat external dataset as described in Chapter 6. You will need to do this if SAS software does not provide a specific conversion for your needs.

SAS software does include PROC DBF, to transport data between the SAS System and dBase II and III. You can invoke PROC DBF from the Procedure Menu System. The procedure menu for PROC DBF is shown in Fig. 12.21.

PROC DIF can be used to convert SAS datasets to or from Data Interchange Format (DIF). DIF format can be used to transport data between the SAS System and Lotus 1-2-3. (Use the Translate Utility in Lotus 1-2-3.) Figure 12.22 shows the procedure menu for PROC DIF.

For interfaces to FOCUS, you may want to consider the mainframe FROMFOC and TOFOC procedures, which are available in the SUGI Supplemental Library.

12.5 THE MICRO-TO-HOST LINK

The SAS Micro-to-Host Link can be used to connect your personal computer SAS environment with SAS installed on a "host" computer. The host is typically a mainframe computer running TSO, CMS, or VMS.

The link is started from within a SAS session on the PC. It starts a SAS session on the host, and establishes a connection between the two SAS sessions. For the duration of the link, you can work in either environment, or transfer data from one to the other. You terminate the link from the PC session.

The real work of establishing the link is done by a special SAS

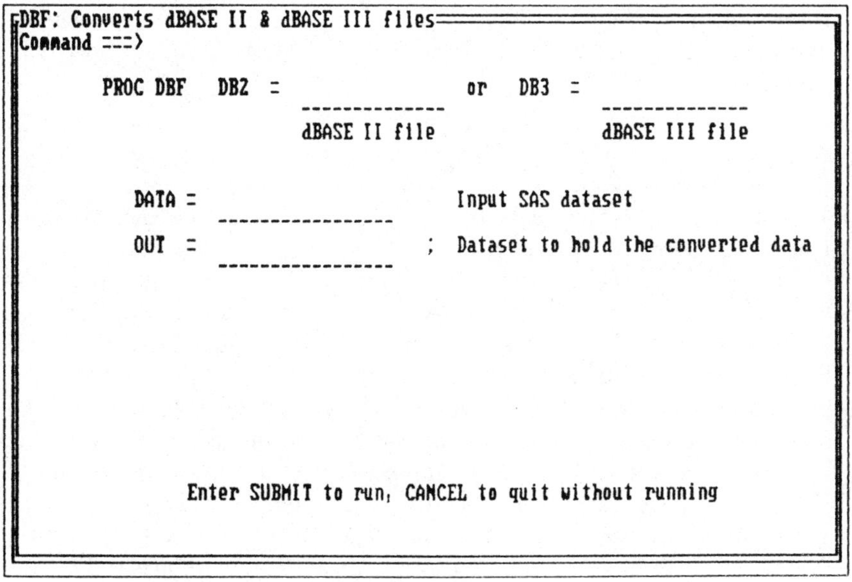

```
┌─DBF: Converts dBASE II & dBASE III files──────────────────────┐
│ Command ===>                                                  │
│                                                               │
│    PROC DBF    DB2 =                    or    DB3 =           │
│                ----------------               ----------------│
│                dBASE II file                  dBASE III file  │
│                                                               │
│                                                               │
│        DATA =                     Input SAS dataset           │
│                ------------------                             │
│        OUT  =                     ; Dataset to hold the converted data
│                ------------------                             │
│                                                               │
│                                                               │
│                                                               │
│                                                               │
│                                                               │
│            Enter SUBMIT to run; CANCEL to quit without running│
│                                                               │
└───────────────────────────────────────────────────────────────┘
```

Figure 12.21 Procedure Menu for PROC DBF

```
┌─DIF: Converts DIF files to SAS data sets───────────────────┐
│ Command ===>                                                │
│                                                             │
│    PROC DIF    DIF  =  _____    Specifies the filref of DIF file │
│                                                             │
│                                                             │
│           DATA =  _____   OR   OUT =  _____ │
│                   Input SAS dataset          Output SAS dataset │
│                                                             │
│           LABELS [ _ ]    Writes variable names as first row of DIF file │
│                                                             │
│           LCHAR [ _ ]     Uses the length of the longest character variable │
│                           in a DIF file column for the corresponding │
│                           SAS variable length │
│                                                             │
│           PREFIX = _____  Prefix to be used in constructing variable names │
│           SKIP   = ___ ;   Specifies to skip first n rows of the DIF file │
│                                                             │
│                                                             │
│           Enter SUBMIT to run; CANCEL to quit without running │
│                                                             │
└─────────────────────────────────────────────────────────────┘
```

Figure 12.22   Procedure Menu for PROC DIF

file called a script. Since you will probably be using an existing script written by SAS Institute or your installation, we will not be discussing scripts in this book.

The Micro-to-Host link provides many new possibilities for SAS users. We will cover two key features: moving SAS files between PC and host SAS Systems, and running SAS programs on the host from your PC.

12.5.1   Using the micro-to-host link

Two special commands are used to start and stop the SAS Micro-to-Host Link. They are SIGNON and SIGNOFF. In both commands, you must specify the script you'll be using. SAS Institute supplies sample scripts for TSO, CMS, and VMS hosts, but your installation may have created its own standard script. The script is a PC file; all you have to know about it is its name.

Various communication adapters are supported. We will assume that you are using an IRMA board and that the IRMA software has been made resident. Hot key to the host system and log on normally. Then, hot key back to your PC and start your SAS session.

You must identify your communication configuration by typing the following statement in the command line. (You will probably want to make this part of your AUTOEXEC.SAS file.)

```
OPTIONS      REMOVE=IRMA
```

Now enter the SIGNON command in the command line, naming the appropriate script. For example, if you are connected to a host system running TSO, your signon may be

```
SIGNON      '\sas\tso.scr'
```

This will start a SAS session on the host system and activate the link.

When you are done, enter the SIGNOFF command to deactivate the link. For instance,

```
SIGNOFF      '\sas\tso.scr'
```

12.5.2 Submitting SAS programs to run on the host

You can request that any SAS program written on your PC be executed on the host system. The program must be in your PGM window. The only difference between running the program on the host and running it on the PC is that the RSUBMIT command is used instead of SUBMIT.

Even though the SAS program runs on the host system, all the messages and output will appear on your PC. You can expect log messages to appear in your LOG window, procedure output in your OUTPUT window, and so on.

12.5.3 Transferring files between the PC and the host

To transfer files, you will use the UPLOAD and DOWNLOAD procedures. UPLOAD transfers files from the PC to the host. DOWNLOAD transfers files from the host to the PC.

Both the UPLOAD and DOWNLOAD procedures must be submitted using the RSUBMIT command rather than SUBMIT. This is because they execute on the host system rather than the PC.

To copy a SAS dataset from the PC to the host:

```
PROC UPLOAD
    DATA = dataset name on the PC
    OUT = dataset name on the host;
```

To copy a SAS dataset from the host to the PC:

```
PROC DOWNLOAD
    DATA = dataset name on the host
    OUT = dataset name on the PC;
```

To copy an external file from the PC to the host (the file must be preallocated on the host):

```
PROC UPLOAD
    INFILE = fileref (or 'filename') on the PC
    OUTFILE = ddname (or 'dsname') on the host;
```

To copy an external file from the host to the PC:

```
PROC DOWNLOAD
    INFILE = ddname (or 'dsname') on the host
    OUTFILE = fileref (or 'filename') on the PC;
```

For example, the following SAS statements will copy a SAS dataset called FEB in library SALES from the host to the PC. (We assume that a LIBNAME statement has identified the SALES library.) It will then copy an external file called 'c:\analysis\janrpt.dat' from the PC to a PDS member called 'PROD1.SALES.ANALYSIS.REPORT(JAN)' on the host.

Remember, you must submit DOWNLOAD and UPLOAD requests with RSUBMIT rather than SUBMIT.

```
PROC DOWNLOAD
    DATA=SALES.FEB
    OUT=sales.feb;
PROC UPLOAD
    INFILE='c:\analysis\janrpt.dat'
    OUTFILE='PROD1.SALES.ANALYSIS.REPORT(JAN)';
```

13

Optimizing SAS Applications

SAS applications in production status should be scrutinized for potential savings in speed or resource utilization. Even one-shot applications can be developed more painlessly with an understanding of some techniques of SAS optimization.

13.1 SYSTEM OPTIONS

SAS System options allow you to affect global defaults throughout your SAS System. Although the permanent defaults are normally set at installation time, you can override these options temporarily by using an OPTIONS statement in your SAS program.

SAS System options can be set anywhere in a SAS job by using the OPTIONS statement. They remain in effect until the end of the SAS job or until you override them with another OPTIONS statement.

On PCs, you can also enter system options in the OPTIONS window. You may also request that the new options settings be saved in your user profile by setting the PROFILE option before changing other options.

The following options may help speed up your SAS jobs or reduce resource requirements. Other options are available.

FIRSTOBS=n

Identifies the first observation to be read from SAS datasets. Allows you to skip observations you know you don't need.

GEN=n

Allows you to specify how many generations of history information are stored with SAS datasets. This may help reduce storage requirements.

OBS=n

Specifies the last observation to be read from SAS datasets. Allows you to skip observations you know you don't need. Use OBS=0 with NOREPLACE to check a SAS program for syntax without executing it.

REPLACE|NOREPLACE

Causes deletion of SAS datasets whenever a new dataset of the same name is created. NOREPLACE suppresses this automatic deletion. Use NOREPLACE with OBS=0 to check a SAS program for syntax without executing it.

SORT=n

Specifies the size, in cylinders, of sort work space on disk. See the discussion later in this chapter.

13.2 OPTIMIZING THROUGH PROGRAM DESIGN

Good design can often improve the performance or resource requirements of a SAS application. Of course, general principles of good program design are as applicable to SAS programs as they are to any programming language. This section focuses instead on some techniques useful specifically in SAS applications.

13.2.1 Optimizing storage of SAS datasets

For large SAS datasets, the size of the dataset is roughly equal to (number of observations * sum of all variable lengths). If most of your variables are character variables, increase your estimate by half. In general, there are three ways to reduce the size of a SAS dataset:

1. Reduce the number of variables.
2. Reduce some or all of the variable lengths.
3. Reduce the number of observations.

13.2.2 Reducing the number of variables

You can reduce the number of variables by using DROP and KEEP. These were introduced in Chapter 5. The DROP statement names certain variables which will not be included in the output dataset. KEEP names variables to be kept, implying that all other variables should be dropped.

In some cases, you may not know what variables are in the dataset. In these cases, you may find it helpful to run PROC CONTENTS on the input dataset. This will tell you all the variables it contains.

When a DATA step creates several SAS datasets, you may specify different DROP or KEEP options on each. For example,

```
DATA DOMESTIC (DROP=COUNTRY FGN_PSTG)
     FOREIGN (DROP=DOM_PSTG);
```

13.2.3 Reducing variable lengths

Reducing some or all of the variable lengths is the function of the LENGTH statement. The LENGTH statement has a simple format, but must be used carefully. For numeric variables, you code:

```
LENGTH variablename n;
```

For character variables, code:

```
LENGTH variablename $ n;
```

The rule for character variables is straightforward; n should be the maximum length of any character value you want to store. For a name field, n might be 20; for a state code, n would be 2. n can be anywhere from 1 to 200, inclusive.

For numeric variables, things get trickier. First, determine the largest possible value, then use the table in Fig. 13.1.

The cutoffs listed in Fig. 13.1 are conservative. For example, in the SAS System for PCs, the number 8192 will fit in a variable with length 3; however, 8193 requires a length of 4. We have accordingly listed 4 as the required length for numbers up to 9999.

Remember that decimal digits must be counted in determining the length of a number. That is, 81.93 requires the same precision as 8193.

If you look closely at the first few rows of Fig. 13.1, you will see something interesting. The required length for small numeric variables is actually larger than the number of digits. If your dataset contains one- or two-digit numerics, you may want to consider treating them as character variables.

Numeric values which are used only as codes can safely be read

LARGEST POSSIBLE VALUE	REQUIRED LENGTH VALUE	
	PC	MAINFRAME
9	3	2
99	3	2
999	3	3
9,999	4	3
99,999	4	4
999,999	4	4
9,999,999	5	4
99,999,999	5	5
999,999,999	6	5
9,999,999,999	6	6
99,999,999,999	6	6
999,999,999,999	7	6
9,999,999,999,999	7	7
99,999,999,999,999	8	7
999,999,999,999,999	8	8
9,999,999,999,999,999	8 *	8
99,999,999,999,999,999	-	8 *

* The highest value stored on PCs is 9,007,199,254,740,992.
  The highest value stored on mainframes is 72,057,594,037,927,935.

Figure 13.1   Largest possible values for different LENGTHS

in and stored as character variables. For example, a two-digit transaction code can be read as

    TRANCODE $2.

just as well as

    TRANCODE 2.

Actually, if a numeric variable is not used in arithmetic calculations, you should consider storing it in character form whenever
space permits. This saves the work of converting it to and from the
internal numeric format. However, numeric values which are used
in arithmetic calculations should not be in character variables. A
two-digit variable representing number of children should be read as
a numeric variable because it may be used in a sum or some other
calculation.

13.2.4 Reducing the number of observations

Reducing the number of observations can be accomplished in several
ways. All involve using a DATA step to read the original dataset
and create a new one. Note that if you give the new dataset a dif-

ferent name, or the NOREPLACE system option is in effect, the original dataset will still exist. It is up to you to delete it using PROC DATASETS.

The most obvious method of deleting unneeded observations is to use IF..THEN DELETE (or ELSE DELETE). The IF condition identifies records which can safely be deleted.

When reading an external file, you can achieve further savings by first reading only the variables needed to evaluate the IF, including a "trailing @" to hold the input record. If you decide to keep the record, then you can read the remaining variables:

```
DATA BOOMERS;
    INPUT @412 AGE 2.  @;
    IF AGE < 30 OR AGE > 40 THEN DELETE;
    INPUT remaining variables;
```

A more efficient way to accomplish the same thing uses the WHERE statement. WHERE works only on SAS datasets; you cannot use it when reading an external file. The syntax of WHERE is generally similar to IF (without the THEN and ELSE). One advantage to WHERE is that it screens out the unwanted observations before they are read into the DATA step. Another advantage is that WHERE can be used on PROC steps which do not allow IF. For example,

```
PROC SORT;
    BY IDNUM;
    WHERE SICKDAYS > 5;
```

If you simply want to pick a small number of observations for testing, you can specify the FIRSTOBS= and OBS= options on the dataset statement. FIRSTOBS identifies the first record to be read, and OBS identifies the last record. (Note that OBS is not the number of records to be read.) The following code will read records 21 through 30 of the SAS dataset JOBCODES:

```
DATA;
    SET JOBCODES(FIRSTOBS=21 OBS=30);
```

While FIRSTOBS and OBS will provide you with a limited sample, the sample is not random. If the dataset is sorted, you will be completely ignoring certain ranges.

For a somewhat more random sample, you can choose every nth record. This method selects observations evenly spaced across the entire dataset. Although not preferred for statistical analysis, it provides a rough-and-ready subset for program testing. A disadvantage is that you will still have to read through the entire large file, though just once. The following code selects every 100th record:

```
DATA NTH;
    SET BIGDATA;
    RETAIN I 1;
    IF I = 100
        THEN DO;
            OUTPUT;
            I = 1;
            END;
        ELSE I + 1;
```

A more correct random sample is possible using the RANUNI function. For example, you can use the following DATA step to select a 25% sample:

```
DATA RAN;
    SET BIGDATA;
    IF RANUNI(0) <= .25 THEN OUTPUT;
```

Finally, the most radical way of reducing the number of observations is by not creating any at all. You should always use DATA __NULL__ when the output dataset is not needed. This situation arises, for example, when a DATA step is used solely to create an external file or report.

13.2.5 Handling sorts

When tuning a SAS System, you should pay special attention to sorts and merges. Like sorts everywhere, SAS sorts are CPU-intensive, and may temporarily consume large quantities of disk space. Very often, you can rethink a program design in order to accomplish one of your three primary objectives:

1. Cut down on the number of records sorted.
   OR
2. Cut down on the size of each record.
   OR
3. Avoid the sort altogether.

Ask yourself any one of the seven questions that follow if sorts seem to be a problem in your application:

1. Do I need the detail information? If you are sorting the dataset only to collect summary totals, the rule is: don't.

Either PROC FREQ or PROC SUMMARY will produce output datasets containing all the totals you need, without any need to pre-sort the input dataset. Moreover, these summary datasets can be used as inputs to any other procedures for reporting or further analysis, without referring to the original dataset at all.

Remember, though, that FREQ and SUMMARY will only keep the variables you explicitly mention in your PROC step request. Other variables will not be available in the output dataset.

Another warning about this method: it may require additional memory resources.

2. Do I need *all* the detail information? The input dataset may contain many variables, some of which will not be necessary for your application. If many of them can be dropped, consider one of the subsetting or storage optimization techniques described earlier in this chapter.

3. Can I combine sorts for efficiency? If your application is doing several sorts, consider whether you can combine two or more of them. In the simplest case, you may already have the combined sort without realizing it. For example, consider the following BY statement:

```
BY DIVISION DEPT GROUP EMPLOYEE;
```

The dataset produced by PROC SORT using this BY statement will also satisfy the following BY statements. So if you are using several of these "nested" sorts, do the most detailed one right away and skip the rest. The one output dataset can be used for all purposes.

```
BY DIVISION DEPT GROUP;
BY DIVISION DEPT;
BY DIVISION;
```

4. How much information can I get now? You should generally try to collect as much information as possible from the dataset in its current sequence. This may avoid the need to re-sort it later, or may allow you to "spin off" several smaller datasets which do not have to be sorted. Remember that a DATA step can create multiple SAS datasets.

5. Is there an alternative to sort/merge? Very often, sorts are performed on two or more datasets solely to set up a match-merge oper-

ation. When one of the datasets is very small relative to the other, it may be more efficient to load the small dataset into an array.

6. Can I do the sort elsewhere? If your input is a large external file, and you need only one sort, you may want to consider a system sort on the external file before it is read into a SAS dataset.

7. Can I cut down on system resources? On mainframes, the SORT=n system option can be used to control the amount of sort work space (in cylinders) allocated to your job. There is a tendency to ignore this until some job exceeds the allocation, then raise it to some arbitrary large number and leave it there. If your installation is complaining about excessive space requests, check to see that you are not routinely requesting SORT=50 or some other unnecessary number.

The amount of sort work space required for sorting a dataset with n observations and v variables, using 3380 drives, is roughly

$$(n*v)/164000$$

On PCs, you must have enough room on your hard disk to hold two additional copies of the input dataset; i.e., room for three copies in all.

13.2.6 Error exits

Sometimes, you can improve the "performance" of an application simply by cutting down on the number of unnecessary reruns. Often, a long job is allowed to run to completion, only to be discarded because of incorrect data or programming.

The SAS System permits you to identify error conditions early in a job and take appropriate action. The __ERROR__ automatic variable can be used to signal an error condition. The ABORT statement ends the SAS job, optionally setting a return code. The STOP statement ends a DATA step, but allows following steps to proceed normally.

The __ERROR__ automatic variable is set to 1 by the SAS supervisor whenever invalid numeric data is encountered. You can also set __ERROR__ yourself to identify any error condition. (See Chapter 8 for a discussion of __ERROR__.) A common use for this is to decide whether to issue the ABORT or STOP statements.

The STOP statement stops execution of the current DATA step whenever it is encountered. It has no effect on other DATA or PROC steps, and thus can be used to "shut out" only one component of a program. You may want to stop the current DATA step if any error has occurred:

```
IF _ERROR_ = 1
   THEN STOP;
```

STOP can also be used to stop a DATA step when you know that it has accomplished its purpose. This may permit you to avoid processing many irrelevant observations. For example, if you know that there is one "bad" record somewhere in a SAS dataset containing a negative salary and you want to print it, you can use the following code:

```
DATA BADREC;
   IF SALARY < 0
      THEN DO;
           PUT _ALL_;
           STOP;
           END;
```

To completely stop execution of a SAS job, you can use the ABORT statement. ABORT stops the current step and prevents execution of all subsequent steps. You have two options on the ABORT statement. Use the ABEND option to choose abnormal termination of the SAS step. Use the RETURN option to specify normal termination.

You may specify a completion code with either RETURN or ABORT. If you do not, ABORT defaults to a user abend code of U0999, while RETURN defaults to a condition code of 12.

On PCs, ABORT and RETURN are synonymous. Both simply cause immediate termination of the SAS job, and make the return code available in the DOS error level.

Examples of ABORT:

```
ABORT ABEND 301;
ABORT RETURN 16;
```

13.2.7   When to create permanent datasets

If you find yourself repeatedly using the same external file, you should consider creating a permanent SAS dataset. This can be done by using a two-level name on the DATA statement (for example, GRADES.FALL93). The first level specifies a permanent SAS library that you have identified in a DD statement or SAS LIBNAME statement.

Using a permanent SAS dataset means that you no longer have to access the original external files. You also save the overhead of reading the external data and formatting it into SAS datasets. In addition, other SAS users may benefit from referencing the permanent dataset; they do not need to know the external format or code the INPUT statements.

Another practical advantage is that your SAS dataset is saved, regardless of what happens to the original file. This is helpful if the external file may be deleted, or when your application requires a "constant" snapshot of a file that may be updated. It is also useful when the SAS analysis application is run on a long-term cycle relative to the source application.

Your applications may require the latest version of an external dataset which is updated on a regular schedule. In that case, consider adding a SAS job to the schedule, containing the DATA step necessary to create the new SAS dataset. Be sure to use the REPLACE option if it is not the default.

Of course, the disadvantage to using permanent SAS datasets is that they require space on tape or disk. You will have to consider whether your application justifies the additional resource requirements.

13.2.8 Storing compiled formats

In general, the SAS System does not provide the ability to save compiled code. An exception is that formats created with PROC FORMAT can be saved. If your application makes heavy use of formats, you can create a permanent format library.

The permanent format library is a PDS containing output of PROC FORMAT. To add formats to the library, specify the DDNAME= option when you run PROC FORMAT. To use the formats, allocate this library to SASLIB.

Even if your application does not require complex formatting, you should always specify formats for any variable to be printed. This will save time at execution involved in determining the "best" format.

13.3 DATABASE DESIGN

We have dealt primarily in this book with simple SAS datasets. All of the principles of dealing with SAS datasets can be extended to the design of SAS databases consisting of multiple datasets. SAS databases are organized within one or more permanent SAS libraries.

When developing your SAS database, keep in mind that SAS datasets are tables. They are well-suited to the type of normalized design emphasized in discussions of relational database structures.

SAS databases should be divided into logical tables. Each table is a SAS dataset. Each observation within a dataset should have at least one variable which provides a unique identifier. While SAS software does not explicitly provide for key fields, you can use any SAS variable to join two tables by using the MERGE statement.

A classic example involves the database of STUDENTS, CLASSES, and TEACHERS. Each student, teacher, and class has a unique identifier, so we can safely store them as three separate SAS datasets. If necessary, we can MERGE two datasets using the identifier variables. We can also read each dataset independently.

Try to avoid variable length structures, or structures that mimic the COBOL OCCURS..DEPENDING ON clause. In the CLASSES dataset, it is tempting to include a variable array of student IDs for each class. However, this makes it difficult to join directly on the student ID. It also wastes space, since the system will allow the maximum size for every observation. Instead of the variable array, each student should be represented by an observation containing both the class ID and the student ID. You will have more observations, but the dataset will be more compact.

Needless to say, if you can predict the sequence in which a dataset will usually be used, sort it into that sequence when it is first created. Then you will not have to use PROC SORT before you MERGE it.

If several sequences are used often, and the file is fairly small, you might want to consider creating several datasets, each one sorted in a different sequence. Of course, this is not a good option for datasets which will be updated.

Never be afraid to split a complex external file into multiple SAS datasets. Keep in mind that a single DATA step can output all the SAS datasets in one pass. By taking advantage of the tabular organization of SAS datasets, and using MERGE as needed, you can achieve a simple and flexible database.

Index

ABORT statement, 314–315
ARRAY statement, 157–165
Attached files, 16–17
Automatic variables, 167–183
  ALL, 168, 181–182
  CHARACTER, 181
  DATA, 167, 175–176, 181, 312
  ERROR, 167, 172–175, 181,
    314–315
  _I_, 167–169
  INFILE, 168, 178–180
  LAST, 167, 175–176, 181
  _N_, 167, 169–172, 178, 181
  NULL, 167, 177–180
  NUMERIC, 181–183

BASE= option, 194
Batch mode, 282–283
BY group, 209–215
Bypass processing, 103–107
BY statement, 10, 61–65, 100, 197,
  203–204, 258, 313
By variable, 100–102, 203–204, 235

CALL SYSTEM statement, 302
CARDS statement, 25, 32, 42, 47
Character formats, 70, 78
Character functions, 184–186
Character variables, 29–30
Chi-square test, 239–243
CLASS statement, 245, 249–250
Compiled format storage, 316
Concatenation, 115–117
Conditional processing, 103–105
Control breaks, 62–64

Creation of:
  custom reports, 129–140
  datasets, 94–97
  external files, 121–129
Custom formats, 76–86, 130–140

Dataset options:
  DATA=, 54, 59–61, 64–66, 92,
    101, 175, 181, 194–195
  DROP=, 94, 96–98, 111–113
  FIRSTOBS=, 103–104, 311
  KEEP=, 95, 98, 111–113
  OBS=, 59–61, 64, 94–95, 103–104,
    311
  RENAME=, 95, 111–113
DATA statement, 9, 15, 21–22, 29,
  94–96, 108–109, 124, 133
DATA step, 5–16, 20–29
  conversion, 13–16
  instream, 47
  regular, 13–16
Date formats, 27–128
DDname statement, 23–25, 30, 83,
  94, 97, 122, 130, 256, 259, 316
DELETE statement, 43, 104–106,
  311
DISCRETE option, 223–224
Display manager system, 282, 284–
  285, 298–299
DO OVER statement, 161–164
DO statement, 142, 150–153, 156–
  157, 160–161
DO UNTIL statement, 155–157
DO WHILE statement, 155–157
DROP statement, 112–113, 308–309
Duplicates, removal of, 100–102

End of file processing, 19, 40–42
  END= option, 40–42, 96–97
  EOF= option, 42
  FINISH= option, 41–42
END statement, 141–142
Error exits, 314–315
Error messages, 31–34, 37
  LOSTCARD, 32, 40
  non-numeric value, 32
External files, 121–125

FILE statement, 122–124, 131–134
FILENAME statement, 122–123, 139
FOOTNOTE statement, 87–89
FORMAT statement, 70–71, 74–79, 84–86, 127

GOTO statement, 104—106, 146–147, 153–154

Headings, 7–8, 12, 131–134

ID statement, 57–60, 63–65
IF statement, 10, 15, 96–100, 104, 140, 150–151
  ELSE . . . , 96, 99–100, 104, 140
  THEN . . . , 96–97, 99, 104, 140
IN= option, 205, 207, 214
%INCLUDE statement, 254–256
INFILE statement, 9, 15, 21–22, 24–25, 29–30, 34, 36–37, 47, 94, 122, 180
INPUT statement, 9, 13–15, 21–22, 25, 27, 29, 32–34, 36, 40, 42–48, 94, 107, 125, 221–223, 256
  Trailing @ or @@ signs, 43–46
Interfacing, system, 302–304
I/O observation, 41, 97–99

JCL language, 13, 16, 23, 25, 122–123, 138, 256

KEEP statement, 112–114, 308–309
Keywords, 18, 81, 84, 149–154, 159–160

LABEL statement, 90–92,
LENGTH statement, 115, 193–194, 309–310
%LET statement, 266–271
LEVELS option, 223–224
LIBRARY= option, 82–84
LINK statement, 143–146, 154, 254
List input, 47–50
%LOCAL statement, 268–269
Loops, 44, 149–156, 159–160, 163–165

Macro subsystem, 254, 256–279
MERGE statement, 199–216, 317
MIDPOINTS option, 223–225
MISSING keyword, 68–69, 84, 86
MISSOVER option, 36–40, 106
MPRINT option, 261–263, 268, 277
Multiple datasets, 107–111

Nonexecutable statements, 112, 114
Numeric formats, 70–71, 78, 84–85
Numeric variables:
  BETA, 29–30
  DELTA, 29–30

Observation reduction, 310–312
Operators:
  $ sign, 18, 48–49, 70, 79
  % sign, 18, 258, 264
  + sign, 18, 117, 126
  − sign, 18, 78
  * sign, 18, 97
  / sign, 18, 125, 234
  = sign, 18, 79, 90, 114, 117, 251
  # sign, 125–126
  @ sign, 125–126
  & sign, 259, 264, 267
  ? sign, 301

OPTIONS NOMPRINT statement, 261
OPTIONS statement, 261, 307–308
OS systems, 130, 138
OTHERWISE statement, 141–143
OUT= option, 61, 101–102, 181, 251
Output datasets, 22, 94, 96, 124
  temporary, 22–24
  permanent, 22–24
OUTPUT statement, 96–100, 102, 108–111, 124–125, 205, 207–208, 214, 246, 251

Page breaks:
  LINESLEFT option, 136
  PAGE variable, 134–135
  PAGESIZE option, 134–135
Period, 70, 78–79
Permanent dataset creation, 325–326
PICTURE clause, 78, 82, 85–86
PRINT files, 130–131, 138–139
PROC ANOVA, 251
PROC APPEND, 194–198
PROC CHART, 4, 220–228
PROC CONTENTS, 50–51, 309
PROC CORR, 251
PROC DBF, 302–303
PROC DIF, 303–304
PROC FORMAT, 53, 70–72, 78–84, 128–129, 236, 243, 316
PROC FREQ, 20, 33–35, 53, 65–69, 79, 87, 100, 105, 139, 181–182, 231–244, 258, 313
PROC PRINT statement, 4, 6, 10–11, 17, 20, 29–30, 50, 53–66, 71–77, 84–87, 89–92, 103, 107, 131–132, 181, 196–197, 208–209
PROC PRINTO, 138–140
PROC PLOT, 220–231
PROC REG, 251
PROC SORT, 4, 6, 10, 53–54, 60–65, 100–101, 300–302, 313
PROC steps, 5–10, 53–54, 69, 74–75, 85, 88, 90, 93, 158
PROC STEPWISE, 251
PROC SUMMARY statement, 68, 100, 243–251, 300, 313
PROC TABULATE, 251

PROC UNIVARIATE, 251
Procedure Menu System, 300–303
%PUT option, 251–254
PUT statement, 122–127, 131–134, 137, 264

Quotes, use of, 79, 90, 272, 298

RANUNI function, 312
RENAME statement, 112–113
RETAIN statement, 119–120
RETURN statement, 42–44, 98–99, 105, 133, 144–146, 315
Reusable SAS code, 253–256
RUN statement, 9–10, 17, 30, 88–90, 258

SAS code, 19, 264
SAS functions, 115, 182–188
  SUBSTR, 115–116
  SYMGET, 186–187
  SYMPUT, 186–187
SAS/GRAPH software, 2, 220
SAS log, 16–18, 29–31, 37–38, 139
SAS Micro-to-Host Link, 303–306
SAS output formats, 127–128
SAS/STAT software, 2
SAS supervisor, 2, 16–18, 25, 29, 40–41, 88, 100, 117, 133, 158, 301
SAS System for PCs, 2, 121, 281–306
SELECT statement, 140–143, 208
Semicolon, 18–19, 25, 42, 64, 70, 79, 96–97, 126, 142, 150, 251, 258, 298
SET statement, 14–15, 94–97, 100–101, 103, 189–190, 197, 200
Sort handling, 312–314
SPLIT option, 91–92
STOP statement, 314–315
STOPOVER option, 36–40
Storage optimization, 308
SUM statement, 58–60, 63–65
Summarizing information, 100–103

SYMGET function, 186–187
SYMPUT function, 186–187, 272–275

Tables, 149, 156–165
TABLES statement, 66–69, 234–242
Temporary worklife, 16
TITLE statement, 87–90, 131, 132
TSO Allocations, 25, 83, 122–123, 138

UPDATE statement, 215–218

VALUE clause, 78–85
Values, accumulation of, 117–120
VAR statement, 30, 57–59, 64–65, 245–246, 249–250, 274
Variable reduction, 308–310
Variables, 25–29, 32–33, 36–38, 41, 43, 46–48, 111–120
VSAM file, 25

WEIGHT statement, 236–237, 243, 258
WHEN statement, 141–143
WHERE statement, 311
Window-based systems, 285–299
DIR window, 287
FOOTNOTES window, 287
GROW mode, 292–296
HELP window, 287–301
KEYS window, 287, 289, 299
LOG window, 285–286, 290, 292–293, 297, 299, 301, 305
MENU window, 287, 300
MOVE mode, 295–296
NOTEPAD window, 287
OPTIONS window, 287, 289, 307
OUTPUT window, 285–286, 290, 292–293, 297, 299, 301
PGM window, 285–286, 290, 292, 297–298, 305
SHRINK mode, 294–296
TITLES window, 131, 287, 288
VAR window, 287–288
WDEF mode, 296–297
ZOOM mode, 292–293

ABOUT THE AUTHORS

Monte Aronson is a technical consultant with Automated Concepts, Inc. He has over ten years' experience in the design and development of on-line customer information systems for financial, publishing, and business applications.

Alvera L. Aronson is an analyst with the Quantitative Analysis Department at Reader's Digest Associations, Inc., and has an extensive background in the design and development of large-scale marketing and promotion analysis systems.